SPEAKING
OF SLAVERY

COLOR, ETHNICITY,

AND HUMAN BONDAGE

IN ITALY

SPEAKING
OF SLAVERY

STEVEN A. EPSTEIN

Cornell University Press

Ithaca and London

First published 2001 by Cornell University Press

Printed in the United States of America

Library of Congress Cataloging-in-Publication Data

Epstein, Steven, 1952–
    Speaking of slavery : color, ethnicity, and human bondage in Italy /
Steven A. Epstein.
        p. cm. — (Conjunctions of religion and power in the medieval
past)
    Includes bibliographical references and index.
    ISBN 0-8014-3848-9 (alk. paper)
    1. Slavery—Italy—History.   2. Ethnicity—Italy—History.   I. Title.
II. Series.
    HT1191 .E67 2001
    306.3'62'0945—dc21
                                                    00-010868

Cornell University Press strives to use environmentally responsible suppliers and mate-rials to the fullest extent possible in the publishing of its books. Such materials include vegetable-based, low-VOC inks and acid-free papers that are recycled, totally chlorine-free, or partly composed of nonwood fibers. Books that bear the logo of the FSC (For-est Stewardship Council) use paper taken from forests that have been inspected and cer-tified as meeting the highest standards for environmental and social responsibility. For further information, visit our website at www.cornellpress.cornell.edu.

Cloth printing   10 9 8 7 6 5 4 3 2 1

For Jean

Both life itself and the good life are impossible without the essentials. . . . So a possession is also a tool for the purpose of living, and property is an assemblage of tools; a slave is a sort of living possession, and every assistant is like a superior tool among tools. For if each tool could perform its own task either at our bidding or anticipating it, and if . . . shuttles shuttled to and fro of their own accord, and pluckers played lyres, then master-craftsmen would have no need of assistants nor masters any need of slaves.

ARISTOTLE, *Politics*, Book I

Man cannot so far know the connexion of causes and events, as that he may venture to do wrong in order to do right.

SAMUEL JOHNSON, *Rasselas*

The pride of man makes him want to domineer, and nothing mortifies him so much as to be obliged to condescend to persuade his inferiors. Wherever the law allows it, and the nature of the work can afford it, therefore, he will generally prefer the services of slaves to that of free men.

ADAM SMITH, *The Wealth of Nations*

CONTENTS

PROLOGUE

C iao! This familiar greeting and salutation derives from the expression "(vostro) schiavo," "(your) slave." Probably first used in Venice, the word recalls the elaborate courtesies of past centuries, when refined people spoke as though they were slaves or servants, without irony or comradely solidarity with their inferiors. And yet, why a slave? Why would a free person want to be a slave in any context? The meaning of this type of reversal is hard to recover, but a small problem of etymology in Italian prompts larger questions about slavery.

How the language of Italian slavery began and endured is the subject of this book. Since the book is not a narrative or chronological study of Italian slavery, the reader might benefit from some general remarks about the basic story, before and after the medieval experience of slavery in Italy, the main subject here. When Italy was the center of the Roman Empire, a high percentage of the peninsula's population consisted of slaves. The Roman state was a genuine slave culture, and bequeathed to posterity a sophisticated legal tradition on slavery as well as habits of expression in Latin that eventually shaped the Italian dialects. In the early Middle Ages the Roman slave culture collapsed, even in the Byzantine-held areas of southern Italy, and was replaced by other cultures that owned some slaves—the Lombard states in the north and center of the peninsula, and Sicily under Muslim rule. Why the Roman slave culture gave way to a culture with slaves is a complex issue, but the answer must depend on the state's power to maintain slavery, and the market's ability to supply slaves. Slavery always rested on violence, and the Roman Empire was simply more effective than its successors in Italy in providing an experienced mix of force and incentives to sustain an economic system with many slaves. The habit of owning slaves continued in the early Middle Ages, and the old legal and moral arguments for the legitimacy of slavery remained convincing at least to the owners. Early medieval Italy attracted merchants who brought people from the Balkans, Sardinia, and across the Alps who replenished the stock of slaves. Rural slaves gradually became peasants, more efficiently exploitable and likely to produce more peasants, at no capital expense to the masters. A continuous if low-level slavery continued in Italy up to the first documents around the year 1000 that illuminate medieval slavery.

In the central Middle Ages, 1000–1350, slaves became more common as possessions and items of commerce in the northern maritime states of Venice and Genoa, and also appeared in the territories the Normans took from the Byzantines, Lombards, and Muslims in the south. This revived slavery probably resulted from increased military and commercial interactions with the Muslim world, which brought Italians more wealth and new sources of and markets for slaves. Slaves were still rare in some parts of Italy, like Rome itself or the Po valley. They seem to have been more numerous in the ports having external sources of supply, and in the newly conquered Muslim and Byzantine lands, where some of the local population was already enslaved. Estimates of population are educated guesses in these centuries, but slaves probably comprised no more than a percent or two of the population in the northern ports in the thirteenth century, and a little higher percentage in Sicily. Yet these small numbers should not obscure the startling fact that slavery had revived and found a place in Italian society and law, just as it was disappearing for good in much of Europe. The chronology of slavery reveals the choices Italians made about whether or not to practice slavery. Why is there slavery? Why is there not slavery? These are important questions to ask in every phase of slavery's history.

After the devastating plague of 1348, slaves became more expensive but also more useful in a world of labor shortages. In the fifteenth century Genoese slaves were perhaps 4 to 5 percent of the population, a figure matched by some areas of the south. In Renaissance Florence there were only a few hundred expensive slaves, all women working in domestic service. The increasing prices of slaves explain why they were more numerous at the points where they entered Italy, the ports and the Mezzogiorno, and rarer in the interior. As slavery became increasingly a luxury in the north, the slave population consisted increasingly of women from distant lands in eastern Europe and Africa. Slavery began to wane in Italy in the sixteenth century except on the galleys, where male slavery experienced a second wind as slaves, mostly captured North Africans and convicts, replaced the free men who were no longer as willing to row for their cities against the formidable Ottoman Empire. These slaves were mostly destined to be quickly exterminated by the exhausting work of rowing or by the diseases rife on the galleys. Free servants working for low wages largely replaced expensive slave women in the houses of the wealthy, and international supplies of slaves flowed toward the New World. Plantation-style agriculture never established itself in Italy, and slavery could not be made to pay in farming or even in the galleys. By the late eighteenth century slavery had virtually disappeared in Italy, and the few relics of it were swept away in the disorders and reforms of the revolutionary era. The gradual withering away of slavery must be attributed to either the high prices of slaves or an aversion to purchasing the kinds of slaves available in the early modern, increasingly global economy.

By 1871 Italy was a unified country, and soon its belated search for colonies took Italians to Libya, Eritrea, and Benadir (Somalia), where they found traditional slave regimes as yet unaffected by western European attitudes against slavery, and so Italians resolved to impose enlightened practices on their colonial peoples. The Antislavery Society of Italy formed to combat slavery in the world and in Italy's own colonies. During World War II many thousands of Italians eventually found themselves as forced laborers, de facto slaves of the Reich, and thousands of Italian Jews became slaves exterminated through labor. All these subsequent episodes of slavery bear the traces of the medieval Italian experiences with the institution.

Although Italy has been a fully realized country for only a little more than a century, the Italian sense of cultural identity has existed since Roman times. In this book I write about Italians where appropriate, and the Genoese, Pisans, Florentines, Sicilians, and all the rest of the strong local identities where necessary. Since this book focuses on the language of slavery—mainly Italian, but also Latin and the dialects—I have tried to be careful about not using "Italian" anachronistically. I do believe the seas and mountains have given the peninsula and islands a cultural, legal, and social unity or experience, even as rivalries and bitter wars frequently overwhelmed the sense of common identity.

Let me conclude this prologue with a quotation that helps to explain why the history of Italian slavery repays an extended study. In 1498 Cristoforo Colombo wrote back to his patrons in Spain, Ferdinando and Isabella. He described the island of Hispaniola as capable of exporting four thousand slaves a year.[1] I have always been puzzled by this unusual skill Columbus possessed—how and where did he learn to size up an island so that he could estimate the number of slaves it could yield in a year? Centuries of Genoese experience with the realities of the slave trade could produce this kind of expertise. But Columbus knew more than island demographics. He went on to observe that even if these slaves died in the crossing to Europe, it would not always be this way. For the blacks and Canary Islanders also died at first, and he implies that once the routine of the transit was established, the

---

1. *Cristóbal Colon: Textos y documentos completos*, ed. Consuela Varela and Juan Gil (Madrid, 1992), pp. 407–8.

death rate of what would become the Middle Passage would fall. It is intriguing to see Columbus contemplate the use of these slaves in Europe, and already in his time thousands of African slaves were working in Portugal itself. At one level this book is an extended effort to understand the broadest possible context that created Columbus and his way of seeing and describing the people of Hispaniola.

A study of Italian slavery accomplishes two important tasks. The European background to New World slavery matters, and the story of Columbus reveals that there is a vital Italian component to that heritage. The practice of slavery in Italy, from the Roman slave culture down to the late medieval Genoa that formed the sensibilities of Columbus, shaped habits of mind and language that reverberated through the centuries and live on in the ways Italians use language today.

SPEAKING
OF SLAVERY

INTRODUCTION

This book concerns the language of Italian slavery and how its changes over time reveal larger shifts in how Italians thought about people, property, ethnicity, and work. The theme is twofold. The history of slavery in Italy, largely a medieval story, provides a rich context for exploring the connections between a social institution and the language so necessary to perpetuate it. Second, historians need to remember that they study words, language in a context. "La schiavitù" in Italian exists in a historical setting only slightly influenced by the English language and experience. The meaning of the Italian experience with slavery can provide important fresh perspectives on this fundamental, global human institution.

Medieval and modern Italian slavery is the subject of this book, but I want to introduce this study by exploring why this slavery was and is important to the Italian understanding of race, and how it still matters to Italians today, even though they do not always think so. The connections in Italy between slavery and attitudes toward ethnicity and race are complex. We need to put aside modern ideas on race and look instead at skin colors and ethnic labels as two signifiers about a person. Can one be black and Italian, white and African? For our people, the answers are Yes. But ethnic hostility is not quite the same as racism, though the two certainly at times overlap. Genoese attitudes in the Middle Ages about Lombards reflect ethnic tensions; their opinions of black Africans reveal a deeper aversion based on ideas about color that we will explore in more detail in Chapter 1. One of this book's purposes is to explain how slavery and racism changed over time. To make sense of how the story unfolds, we need to understand too that slavery and racism are not the same things and can easily exist apart. Of course they may also reinforce one another. Slavery became an entrenched way of life in parts of Italy before, but not long before, the first solid evidence for racism appears. Hostile attitudes toward people viewed as "others," on the grounds of color, religion, or ethnicity, also became entrenched ways of thinking among Italians and fostered the practice of slavery. When slavery began to wane, the racism remained and caught its second wind, as we will shortly see, when some nineteenth-century historians and social scientists modernized racism at the same time as they rediscovered their own traditions of slavery. Just as slavery and racism affected the ways Italians used language, the endurance of racism shows another of slavery's legacies to Italian culture. Slavery is rightly understood primarily as a system of labor, and its main ideology might simply be efficiency or necessity. Racism became another powerful means to justify slavery in the Middle Ages precisely because it helped to excuse practices that occasionally raised ethical worries in the most calloused souls.

My other purpose in writing this book is to use medieval history in a new way. The fact is that medieval history appears increasingly distant and remote from contemporary concerns, and in many historical issues people's eyes glaze over when they begin to hear about the medieval origins of anything. What I propose to do here is show that the language used centuries ago to sustain a relatively unknown system of slavery still has profound effects on the ways Italians use language and think about race today. So I'm going to accept the challenge medievalists must face and make diachronic, even polychronic connections between what I study and what is happening today, and not simply leave it to other specialists to fill in the gaps. I am not a medievalist depreciating my field of study, and I do think that a medieval perspective on contemporary issues like labor and race can yield useful results.

I have one other aim, which I hope will be congenial to a wider audience. It may seem that a history of Italian slavery that depends on a close study of the Italian language would best be undertaken by an Italian scholar raised in the language and culture. And yet the perspective of an outsider may yield some new insights the Italians have not yet observed. For far too long Americans have studied their own slavery as if it were the only one ever to have existed, as if it were the archetype of all others. This is a typical argument for American exceptionalism, and I think a wider view of slaveries across the globe will help place the American variant in its proper context, as well as provide ample grounds for exploring the neglected field of slavery in Italy. The Italian audience for this book may find that the outsider's perspective provides a broader context for this sad part of their own history. The wider audience may find that the pivotal role Italy played in Western history in so many fields needs to be extended to yet another: the story of slavery.

I need to begin by making a preliminary case that the broader context provided by medieval history helps us to make sense of the long and complicated story of slavery in Italy. This point struck me with particular force when I was in Genoa in the autumn of 1998 and read in the local newspaper *Il secolo XIX* a story about Nigerian prostitutes being sold in Genoa. The newspaper reported on 30 October that the local police had discovered a market in black slaves. Young girls arrived in Europe at Paris and then came to Genoa to be sold like animals. These "African Venuses," *as the paper described them*, were auctioned off at prices between eighteen and fifty million lire (between ten and thirty thousand dollars), depending on their age and beauty. Their new owners then put them to work as prostitutes in northern Italy, and kept them in line through beatings and black magic. By 30 October the police had managed to arrest only the Nigerian members of the ring.

And beyond the drama of this slavery episode, there is a gray zone in which actual slavery merges into more ambiguous styles of exploitation. Anyone who flies to Italy off season is likely to see that a large number of the fellow passengers will consist of Peruvians or Filipinos or others being brought into Italy to work as domestic servants and in other labor-intensive capacities. Italy is by no means alone in this type of exploitation of or provision of economic opportunity (depending on your point of view) for the less wealthy peoples of the world. A very low birth rate (actually below replacement) creates eery parallels to the situation in plague-stricken fifteenth-century Italy. Slavery is of course now illegal, but labor shortages are not. The latest style of colonization conveniently ignores Africans, and no longer goes out and conquers land somewhere out there, but instead brings the currently most valuable resource, the humans, back home and leaves the troubles of ruling places like Peru or the Philippines to someone else. Slavery may be mostly gone, but the habit of privileging some ethnic groups over others, forged during slavery, endures. And how these latest in a long series of newcomers are to be absorbed or not into the Italian people is anyone's guess. But other innocent people in modern Italy also have experienced the condition of slavery, and their stories also reflect deep roots in language and culture.

One of the most famous and articulate of these innocents was of course Primo Levi (1919–1987), who certainly knew what it meant to be a slave, admittedly in a system the Italians neither invented nor adopted in their own country. At the beginning of his time in Auschwitz, a fellow prisoner offered Levi some advice, which he did not completely accept. But part of the advice must have seemed true: "that we are slaves, deprived of every right, exposed to every offense, destined to a death more or less certain, but there is a power that remains to us, and we ought to defend it with all vigor because it is the last: the power of refusing our consent."[1] At the start of the

---

1. Primo Levi, *Se questo è un uomo*, in *Opere I* (Turin, 1987), p. 35. Here and throughout the book, the translations from Italian and other languages are my own unless otherwise noted.

next section of his memoirs, slavery remained on Levi's mind, for he saw to the heart of slavery: "slaves and masters, the masters themselves slaves; fear moves the one and hatred the other, all other powers silent. All are enemies or rivals to each other."[2] Levi knew that he was a slave at the Buna synthetic rubber works because of the lucky accident that he was trained as a chemist. His useful skill helped to spare him the fate of the majority of prisoners being quickly worked to death. Many years later, in 1986, when Levi published *The Drowned and the Saved*, his last reflections on his life, he was still convinced that the work in the camps, besides its murderous purposes, was pure and simple slavery. Haunted in his last years by the fear of new holocausts and the possibility that the world of the camps might return, he asked, "how much of the world of the concentration camps is dead and will not return again, like slavery and the code of duels?"[3] Many thousands of Italians—Jews and gentiles—experienced deportations, forced labor, and worse during World War II. For Levi of course the distinguishing feature of his experience as a slave was that it was intended to kill him and yet he survived. Unlike Levi, most slaves in previous centuries could believe that their value to the masters would preserve them, but for a time in Europe in the 1940s human life was so cheap that this assumption ceased to apply.

What did Levi mean when he feared the return of the camps yet also thought that slavery itself was as dead as the duel? Perhaps he considered the buying or selling or renting of slaves, a feature of the Third Reich (which did rent its slaves to German industry) to be now inconceivable, but that the ethnic and religious hatreds making the extermination of the "other" a plausible policy remained a threat in modern Europe. Certainly the ethnic cleansing in Bosnia in the 1990s proves that Levi was right to be afraid of the world of the camps returning, but the buying and selling of human beings remains illegal in Italy and the rest of Europe, though as we have seen, it is still occurring. Levi was typical of people in Italy and elsewhere who feel that truly the last nail has been hammered into slavery's coffin and it is gone for good. Maybe Levi believed that too, but we should take a little of his fear, and our own perspective, and ask whether this is the last, or one of a series of the deaths of slavery? We must respect Levi's perspective on his own enslavement, and use it to explore the vicissitudes of slavery. Also, it must serve as a warning that the privileging of one group over another always carries with it the possibility of forced labor without compensation. Whether this is slavery or not is in some ways a technicality.

2. Ibid., pp. 37, 42.
3. Primo Levi, *I sommersi e i salviati*, p. 661.

The best way to demonstrate the validity of a polychronic approach to the ways Italians have spoken about slavery is to start with some other recent contexts. Encouraged by the spirit of reform in the papacy of Leo XIII, some Italians established in 1888 an organization, like similar ones in England and France, to combat the by now stereotypical evils of slavery. The Italian Antislavery Society held its first national congress in Rome on 22–24 April 1903.[4] On the first day of the conference, as is so often the case with these events, the organizers had planned a local excursion they thought was relevant to the theme of their meeting. The conferees went on a tour of the catacombs, certainly one of Rome's many impressive places to see, but not one that is obviously tied to antislavery activities. But in the catacombs the official record stated that they saw evidence "recording the abolition of slavery, accomplished by the brotherhood and charity of Christians, from the very beginnings of the new society, in which free and slave were all considered as sons of the same Heavenly Father."[5] There was of course no such evidence, and even though the society later put up an inscription praising Constantine the Great as an opponent of slavery, some members must have understood that in fact slavery continued on in late antiquity under the Christian emperors pretty much as it had before. This point of historical accuracy is not the issue here. What is important to observe is that these good people—and I think they were mainly that—in 1903 were inspired by the idea that they were carrying on the traditions of the early church, as they understood the language of history. As erroneous as they may have been on these matters, these words encouraged them to do good works. Or, they found it necessary to clothe their antislavery activities in a suitable historical framework, and they did not find, or perhaps even look for, significant assaults on slavery in Italy between their own time and Constantine's. We will see the same myth-making at work, with good and bad consequences, in the ways medieval people, by using language, tried to understand and shape what we call the economy. But for the Antislavery Society of Italy there was an immense gulf of historical amnesia between the kindly acts of Constantine and the origins of their own antislavery work, encouraged by the eloquent, formal condemnation of slavery by Pope Leo XIII in his bull *In plurimis* of 1888.

4. My source for this meeting is the *Bolletino della Società Antischiavista d'Italia*, 16 (1903) which I found in Archivio Segreto Vaticano, Segreteria di Stato, Anno 1903, Rubrica 204, where there are also many other documents concerning the antislavery work of the Catholic Church around the world.

5. Ibid., p. 12.

Let us consider another recent context in which the polychronic context of slavery and language is even more explicit, and where an archeological approach to language use will enable us to see how the Italian understanding of slavery changed over time. Salvatore Bongi published an article in 1866 revealing that thousands of Mongol or Tartar slaves had been imported into Italy in the fourteenth and fifteenth centuries. According to Bongi, Italians had largely forgotten this historical fact, and his survey of the documents reveals genuine surprise at his discovery. Bongi believed that this slavery was important for understanding the history of Italian customs, yet it remained buried up to recent times in "the dust of old contracts, unobserved in statutes and in the more neglected volumes of canonists and jurists."[6] Bongi thought that slavery had never been formally abolished in the republics of Genoa, Venice, and Lucca, and in his view it was perhaps better that it had disappeared through changes in customs and manners rather than legal decrees. He concluded his essay by observing that at least Italian slavery had never reached the proportions of the American variety, which produced a "mournful pilgrimage of the black race (*gente nera*) to America, an occasion for much weeping by the unfortunate race (*stirpe*) and much misfortune to their owners"—recently defeated, as Bongi knew, in civil war.[7] The significance of Bongi's research was that he rediscovered a slavery that had been forgotten.

A contemporary Italian scholar was also turning his attention to ethnicity in Italy. Cesare Lombroso (1836–1909) was not so much interested in slavery as in his favorite subjects: crime, anthropology, race, the law, and punishment. Lombroso was rethinking racism for Italians just as scholars were looking for new ways to write about slavery. It is worth our time to visit the intellectual world in which slavery was rediscovered. The human face was for Lombroso the key for understanding modern ideas of race. The science of physiognomy had deep roots in a culture whose people were accustomed to believe that the face was indeed the mirror of the soul, and much more. Stephen Jay Gould points out that Lombroso needed crime to be a natural, inherited trait, though he was not without humanity and he eventually considered criminality to be a mental illness that needed to be treated.[8] But Lombroso's search for the biological origins of crime was so

6. Salvatore Bongi, "Le schiave orientali in Italia," in *Nuova antologia di scienze, lettere ed arti* 2 (1866): 215–46; quote from p. 215.

7. Ibid., p. 246.

8. Stephen J. Gould, *The Mismeasure of Man* (New York, 1981), pp. 134–40; quote from p. 140. As Gould notes, groups as diverse as gypsies, epileptics, and Down's syndrome patients suffered because of Lombroso's bogus science.

intense that it took him deep into the animal and plant kingdoms, where he found murderous plants and thieving insects enough to prove to his satisfaction that crime was a universal, natural phenomenon. For Italians, Lombroso found that the criminal face had a larger and longer nose, bigger lips, more cavities, predominantly black hair, and a slight or nonexistent beard.[9] The zany research that produced these results is not our concern here, though it did allow Lombroso to make connections like this one: "The greater frequency of homicides in Calabria, Sicily, and Sardinia is fundamentally owed to the African and eastern elements in the population."[10] Here we see that Lombroso was well aware of the medieval slaves who carried this blood into Italy. This type of research also fostered northern Italian feelings of superiority over their southern neighbors, and provided simple answers to complex questions. And of course, what could be done about the African blood down there in Calabria? Nothing at all.

In another work Lombroso expressed himself more forcefully on race—in his *The White Man and the Man of Color*, published in 1871. Here are two revealing quotations from the master.

> It's a question of knowing if we whites, who haughtily tower over the summit of civilization, ought one day to bow down before the prognathous muzzle of the black, and the yellow, and to the frightful face of the Mongol; if, in the end, we owe our primacy to our biological organism or to the accidents of chance. And it would be a good twist to decide it, if we can, without fear, without shameless audacity, by being concerned more than with tradition, but with the sole authority of our time—Science."[11]

All this within twelve years of Darwin's *Origin of Species*. Lombroso is asking if the dominance of the white race results from chance or the struggle for the survival of the fittest. For if it were by chance, the Mongols would have their day. Two hundred pages later he offers this startling conclusion.

> Only we whites have achieved the most perfect symmetry in the forms of the body. Only we whites, with alphabetical writing and inflected languages, furnishing thought with a more ample and comfortable garb, are able to spread and eternalize thought in monuments, in books, and in the press. Only we whites possess a true musical art. Only we whites, through the mouth of Christ and Buddha, have proclaimed the freedom of the slave, the right of

9. Cesare Lombroso, *L'uomo delinquente* (Rome, 1971), p. 77.
10. Ibid., p. 361.
11. Cesare Lombroso, *L'uomo bianco e l'uomo di colore* (Padua, 1871), p. 10.

man to life, respect for the aged, for women, and for the sick, and the for-
giveness of enemies. Only we whites, with Washington, Franklin, and
Mirabeau, have proclaimed and put into effect the true concept of nationality. Only we whites, in the end, with Luther, Galileo, Epicurus, Spinoza, Lu-
cretius, and Voltaire, have procured the liberty of thought, of which you,
gentle hearers, offer an example, helping, without disgust, to develop some
themes so unorthodox!"[12]

A bravura ending, and heady advice to an Italian people on the verge of
assuming their share of the "white man's burden" in Africa.

Lombroso was interested in race long before he latched onto criminality.
From his perch at the University of Pavia, he quickly absorbed and repack-
aged the latest scientific thought for his fellow Italians, so recently themselves discovering in their new country the true spirit of nationality. Lombroso was a good liberal reformer who intended to use all the fruits of
modern science to benefit society. And examine his construction of white
identity for an Italian audience as he assembles an incongruous group with
Buddha, Spinoza, Mirabeau, and only one Italian, Galileo, to engross all of
humanity's accomplishments for "we whites"—and shows his grasp of the
latest Aryan thinking by getting ahold of Buddha for his "we." The real
tragic irony of this is that Lombroso was constructing a white racial identity
for an ethnic group of Europeans whose own traditions were more tolerant
and less xenophobic than most others. And yet to be modern and scientific,
Italians had to join up with the rest of the whites. Italians wanted to be just
as white as their northern neighbors. This new interest in color, with deep
roots in the Middle Ages, would soon be joined to the study of slavery.

12. Ibid., pp. 222–23. It is sometimes necessary in this study to offer the reader
the original Italian. This is one of those times. "Noi soli Bianchi abbiamo toccato la
più perfetta simmetria nelle forme del corpo. Noi soli, con la scrittura alfabetica e
con le lingue a flessioni, fornendo il pensiero di una più ampia e commoda veste,
potemmo difonderlo ed eternarlo nei monumenti, nei libri e nella stampa. Noi soli
possediamo una vera arte musicale. Noi soli abbiamo, per bocca di Cristo e di
Budda, proclamata la libertà dello schiavo, il diritto dell'uomo alla vita, il rispetto al
vecchio, alla donna, ed al debole, il perdono del nemico. Noi soli abbiamo con Was-
inghton [sic], con Franklin, con Mirabeau, proclamato ed attuato il concetto vero
della nazionalità. Noi soli, infine, con Lutero e Galileo, Epicuro e Spinoza, Lu-
crezio e Voltaire, abbiamo procacciata la libertà del pensiero, di cui, voi, gentili
uditrici, offrite un esempio, assistendo, senza ribrezzo, allo svolgersi di temi si poco
ortodossi." In the second edition published in 1892, Lombroso repeated this conclusion word for word. *L'uomo bianco e l'uomo di colore* (Turin, 1892), pp. 222–23.

Ridolfo Livi (1856–1920) was an anthropologist active in establishing the new social sciences in Italy.[13] In the *Italian Review of Sociology*, Livi published in 1907 an article on medieval slavery and its influence on the anthropological character of Italians. Livi's interest in medieval slavery was secondary to his study of modern Italians, but he knew Latin well and went back to old sources. As a good anthropologist, Livi was bound to ask: what happened to these medieval slaves? Livi was concerned about what made an Italian, and he knew that the slaves had disappeared. Yet as an informed student of history and race, he knew that successive invasions of foreign elements (Greeks, Lombards, and Normans, among others) had formed the modern Italian people. So he believed that it was not improbable that modern Italians preserved traces of a notable infusion of Mongol blood.[14] Most of Livi's article presented the sources for late medieval slavery in places like Genoa, Venice, and Florence, and he soon discovered that the slaves he was studying were overwhelmingly women. He understood that it was infinitely more likely that the Mongols in Italy would mix with their enslavers, the Italians, than was the case for blacks in the United States. Writing during the fiercest period of lynching and Jim Crow segregation, Livi sensed that this difference did not result from purely anthropological differences (whatever they might have been) but also from the profound separation and aversion that American laws and customs maintained between the two races. So again, Italians might favorably contrast their experience with the American, because no laws in Italy (yet) prohibited relations among the races.

Then Livi set about the business of collecting from the late medieval sources Mongol racial characteristics, and he stressed the shape of the nose (snubbed or flat), the eyes (inset), and the color of the skin (olive or yellow). Was it possible to find traces of these features among modern Italians? Well, Livi thought so. He said that it was not rare to see on the streets "today" (1907) a set of features, especially among women, close to the Mongol type—brownish color, short stature, large nose, prominent cheek bones, short face, slanted eyes.[15] Although these traits were not always found together in one person, there was enough similarity to spot the type, almost exclusively in what Livi delicately calls the "less prosperous" social classes. To support these observations, he cited a recent work by Alfredo Niceforo

13. Ridolfo Livi, "La schiavitù medioevale e la sua influenza sui caratteri antropologici degli italiani," *Rivista italiana di sociologia* 11 (1907): 557–81.

14. For a more accurate definition of the Mongol/Tartar peoples, see Chapter 3.

15. R. Livi, "La schiavitù medioevale," p. 577.

(1876–1960) in which that author contended that among the poor Italians, because of prenatal malnutrition, these faces appeared and accumulated the stigmata of poverty.

Niceforo's book, *Force and Wealth: Studies on the Physical and Economic Life of the Social Classes*, was published in 1906.[16] His understanding of human development, largely based on differing soil conditions, stressed the roles of nutrition as well as heredity in shaping the differences between the poor and rich. Niceforo's search for what we would call the biological and environmental origins of poverty naturally led him to explore issues of color, but he curiously avoided the skin (in this work) and emphasized instead hair and eye color, and stature. He had a theory, based on statistics and observation, that since blond hair characterized a smaller percentage of the population as it aged, blondness itself represented a primitive stage of development.[17] In other words, as a body matured and increased in size, the evolution of pigmentation, as he called it, tended toward a general but not universal darkening of hair. In the poor, malnutrition impeded this natural order, and so blond hair was more frequent among the poor than the rich. Other research confirmed this surprising result; in Savoy the illiteracy rate was higher among blonds, and cretinism and albinism had been shown to correlate. But at the other extreme of the color spectrum, racist thinking about the colored races, as Niceforo called them, permeated his thought and he tended to group together the poor, the insane, the degenerate, and the colored races as equally victimized by ill health, bad nutrition, and to a lesser extent heredity. Niceforo in effect placed most Italians in a kind of middle place, in between the degenerate blonds and the colored races. As late as 1952 Niceforo was still arguing that a rough physiognomy derived from various pre- and postnatal environmental factors as well as hereditary, physical ones, thus moving beyond his earlier soil-centered theories. He still believed, based on the work of Rodolfo [*sic*] Livi, that "Negroid and Mongoloid types were more frequent in the lower classes."[18] Thus the an-

16. Alfredo Niceforo, *Forza e richezza: Studi della vita fisica ed economica delle classi sociali* (Turin, 1906).

17. For this and what follows, ibid., pp. 120–25. the key passage on p. 120 is worth quoting in the original: "La colorazione dei capelli, dunque, o pigmentazione, segue un'evoluzione che va dalle tinte più chiare a quelle più scure: le condizioni di vita che arrestano lo sviluppo della statura arrestano anche lo sviluppo completo della colorazione, e la miseria fisiologica che impedisce all'organismo di evolversi completamente, mantenendolo in forme povere e stentate, impedisce anche l'evoluzione completa della pigmentazione."

18. Alfredo Niceforo, *La fisionomia nell'arte e nella scienza* (Florence, 1952),

cient and medieval science of physiognomy staggered on into the twentieth century and helped to shape the context for the Italian understanding of race and slavery.

Niceforo helped to provide Livi with an anthropological and modern explanation for why some Italian poor looked like blonds, but this did not really advance his argument on Mongols or blacks. When Livi's authorities studied the face and saw stigmata—signs or symbols that needed to be deciphered by modern scientists, much as Champollion had brought Egyptian writing to life—we are again in the presence of Cesare Lombroso. Livi duly cites the master, from the fifth edition of his famous *L'uomo delinquente* (*The Criminal Man*) published in 1896. Lombroso had placed among the typical features of the born criminal the Mongol face, or Mongolism—Down's syndrome.[19] There is no point to repeating Lombroso here, especially the repellent mixing of a genetic condition (the syndrome) with racism (Mongolism) to project criminal tendencies on the innocent and disturbingly non-Mongol sufferers. In Livi's world Lombroso was still a respected, scientific thinker. So Livi had to go against his own preferred explanation for the Tartar features, the medieval slaves, and instead bow to the master Lombroso and concede that there certainly was a connection between crime, the lower classes, and a kind of racial atavism (and bad nutrition!) that produced these features in the poor. The theory of atavism proposed that the subgroups of humanity were not equal but constituted a progression from inferior, darker peoples to superior, lighter ones. Hence criminality reflected a lower, and darker stage of human development, and criminals were throwbacks. But Livi was not yet prepared to abandon his surviving Mongol traits and his discovery that they resulted from the blood of medieval slaves.

Livi's intellectual inheritance shaped his efforts to test his hypothesis on Mongol blood in modern Italians circa 1907. By then social scientists knew that they needed large runs of statistical information, and Livi made his academic reputation in his statistical studies of the vast surveys of Italian army recruits. Livi focused his attention on the Veneto, the region that his secondary sources told him had concentrated the largest number of Tartar slaves.[20] He selected as Mongol traits a big face, prominent cheek bones, low forehead, a snub nose, and a short stature. The first test failed him; 14.4 percent of the soldiers from the Veneto and 14.3 percent from Venice

---

pp. 74–75; key sentence p. 75: "la presenza di caratteri negroidi e mongoloidi più frequenti negli strati inferiori . . ."

19. See C. Lombroso, *L'uomo delinquente*, and S. Gould, *The Mismeasure of Man*.

20. For this and what follows, see R. Livi, "La schavitù medioevale," pp. 578–81.

proper had snub noses, whereas for the entire kingdom the figure was 18.7 percent—the reverse of what he wanted. Being an indefatigable and ostensibly honest researcher, Livi observed that the Veneto also had the tallest population in Italy—no support for his thesis here, since the Tartars were short. However, since "morphological laws" required that the nose was under the influence of height, his results from the Veneto needed some refinements. So he divided up his sample by height and the results changed—for the shortest soldiers the snub-nosed totals were 21.9 percent for the kingdom, 18.2 percent for the Veneto, and 22.8 percent from Venice. Still, Livi's mathematical acrobatics had only produced a .9 percent lead for Venice over the kingdom, but he wasn't through. Using improper statistical methods, he subtracted the percentage of the tallest soldiers who had snub noses from the percentage of the shortest and came up with an 8 percent difference for the kingdom, and a 12.9 percent difference for Venice, "proving" at last that there was a "Tartar element" in the population.

What Livi had done is really ironic. He proved to his satisfaction that facial characteristics had survived from a "race ("*razza*") violently and with inhuman pride" imported into Italy, where after a few generations they completely blended with the majority. He was no apologist for slavery. In a book published in 1928 after his death (by his brother), Ridolfo's last thoughts on slavery came before the public. Livi recalled his work of twenty years ago, and reprinted his old conclusions and tables without additional comment, since in his mind they still proved the survival of Mongol traits in the Veneto's population.[21] Livi also drew attention to the work of a colleague who on the basis of two African skull types he found among the modern Sicilian population, constructed a similar argument for the survival of African traits in Sicily. Livi was on very thin ice here, and he immediately denied that he was implying that Sicilians were somehow degenerate. On the contrary, just because the Tiber is muddy, does the Tyrrhenian cease being blue? Only in the waters near its mouth can one see any real difference in color.[22] Livi's point baffles, and cannot have calmed the Sicilians. If he was thinking in time, then he was saying that only centuries ago would we have seen any differences in Sicily, but if in space, well, that was the muddy spot where the races mingled.

But this is not Livi's conclusion. Instead, he congratulates the Latin people for their ability to assimilate rapidly people from other, inferior races (!) According to Livi, Nordic people lack this skill. So, the blacks in the United

21. Ridolfo Livi, *La schiavitù domestica nei tempi di mezzo e nei moderni* (Padua, 1928), p. 136.
22. Ibid., pp. 137–38.

States, probably imported from the same countries as the black Sicilians, have lived for centuries with whites, but without mixing. (He was wrong, but we know what he means.) Livi, searching again in his collection of bizarre metaphors, comes up with this. Comparing the slave populations of America to an ink spot on a piece of paper, he sees the boundaries between the black and the white as clear and always fixed. But in Italy, the Tartar, Saracen, and black slaves were more like a drop of oil on the paper, which slowly and slowly absorbed the oil until in the end the boundaries were indeterminate and in fact the oil spread evenly across the page, leaving only a very slight change in its overall color. Once again, a comparison to America allows an Italian scholar to feel superior because the genius of the Italian race is that it absorbs new ethnic or racial groups and nevertheless remains Italian, even if the odd snub nose or homicide in the population shows traces of its oleaginous past.

Antislavery became the accepted, liberal position in the newly united Italy. Campaigns against slavery produced, as we have seen, the Antislavery Society of Italy, founded in 1888 and still active into the 1920s. At its fourth national congress in 1926, the vice–director general of the Ministry of Colonies, commenting on the empire—Eritrea, Somalia, and Libya—believed that the facts showed that the work of colonization was in effect a campaign against slavery, since Italy was ending slavery where it had flourished before. The society proudly sponsored villages in Ethiopia for freed slaves, and the first one was called Villagio Benito Mussolini, after another noted humanist and opponent of slavery.[23] Soon enough, a renewed effort to conquer Ethiopia, and the passing of racial laws in Italy that went so far as to drop Jewish surnames from the phone books, signified that racial thinking in the academy, when transformed into an activist ideology, which was Fascism, an ideology on the move, had powerful and disastrous consequences—not for the academic careers of its original proponents, but for innocents everywhere. By the Fascist period the rediscovery of medieval slavery and the development of modern thinking about race, antislavery, and the colonies formed the milieu in which Italians conceived slavery's past. Race became an even more slippery category as the Italian ethnic sense of identity came to exclude, for many Italians—the nation's own Jews—and as the empire absorbed more Africans.

This archeological approach to how Italian scholars "rediscovered" medieval slavery shows how important it is for historians (and others) to be clear about how they use language. Since this book depends on careful at-

---

23. For all this see *Atti del quarto congresso nazionale della Società Antischiavista d'Italia (Decembre 1926)* (Rome, 1927), pp. 168, 231.

tention to language, modern theories of language can help to interpret the language of slavery. The relatively new discipline of pragmatics, defined as "the science of language seen in relation to its users," or "the study of the conditions of human language uses as these are determined by the context of society," or most simply "the meaningful function of language," provides new tools for interpreting the language of slavery and some of the theoretical assumptions underpinning this book.[24] This approach to language seeks the meaning of communication as it is used in a rich cultural and social context. So, for example, in legal contracts such as those for the sale of a slave, there are many bits of legal jargon and assumptions that make no sense as acts of language unless we know the conventions surrounding the contract's creation. Meaning becomes attached to phrases and words through use, but what now appear dry-as-dust legal formulae once had a lively context which we must try to resurrect. When so much of slavery's realities went unrecorded and the slaves themselves left no records, perhaps the surviving documents contain clues about their missing context—the mold, now vanished, that once shaped the words we still have. Pragmatics, by insisting on studying language in its broadest possible context, makes language behavior social as well.[25] If we go beyond the text of a contract to ask—what is the behavior of buying and selling slaves?—we can use the language to explore that behavior. In order to understand fully the activity of being or owning a slave, we must find the hidden conditions that only language preserves.

Jef Verschueren's recent and authoritative primer on pragmatics emphasizes that meaning is what someone intends to convey by using language as the carrier.[26] This approach to language, growing out of semiotics, also rests on the work John Austin did on speech acts, the things we do with words. Implicit meanings may be discovered through pragmatics by understanding context and background. The choices people make in using language reveal their use of various speech genres and their shifting membership in different speech communities. Choices about language are also variable, negotiable, and adaptable—certainly valuable reminders when unpacking the rich layers of hypocrisy and meanness surrounding slavery. The adaptability of the Latin and Italian languages creates a dynamic in which words used in markets or to describe behavior also affected the context in

24. The first two quotations are from Jacob L. Mey, *Pragmatics: An Introduction* (Oxford, 1993), pp. 5, 42; the final one is from Jef Verschueren, *Understanding Pragmatics* (London, 1999), p. 8.

25. J. Mey, *Pragmatics*, p. 185.

26. J. Verschueren, *Understanding Pragmatics*, pp. 8–10 (on meaning), pp. 22–25 (on Austin and speech acts), pp. 58–65 (on adaptability).

which people sold slaves or controlled their acts. This dynamic, at the heart of pragmatics, challenges historians to remember that they too study words in context and must become more aware of the implicit and explicit choices people make in using language. Finally, pragmatics provides historians with an alternative to the toxic wasteland that defines the prose style and content of some contemporary theory in the humanities and especially literary criticism. It may be, as George Steiner has suggested, that "[i]n humane letters 'theory' is nothing but intuition grown impatient."[27] So then this study of Italian slavery should provide a test case for at least a more precise and patient attention to language use in context.

The plan of this book is straightforward. In the first chapter I will look more closely at issues concerning language, and in the following chapters I take up the law, behavior, and the economy as fruitful ways to explore the context of slavery's language.

27. George Steiner, *Errata* (New York, 1997), p. 5.

CHAPTER ONE
THE LANGUAGE OF SLAVERY

Even the stupidest and most ignorant folk were following the whole
thread of his argument. Now if you went and asked them to repeat the
words he used . . .

ALESSANDRO MANZONI, *I promessi sposi*

In late 1926 the fourth national congress of the Antislavery Society of Italy met in Rome. Egilberto Martire, a journalist and
deputy in parliament, addressed the group on the subject of
San Benedetto of Palermo, a Franciscan saint and patron of the Italian antislavery movement. Benedetto, also known as "il Moro" (the Moor) was, as
Martire somewhat inexactly described him, "a black, an Italian, a freed
slave, and a Franciscan monk."[1] A constant theme of Martire's speech was
that it was possible to be both black and Italian, and while there were timely
reasons for this, especially Italy's colonial ambitions in East Africa, what was
really at stake were the definitions of what it meant to be black, and to be
Italian. Martire observed that Benedetto was a black born in Sicily to Christian "Ethiopian" slaves of a Christian master. (Martire took from his
sources the identifier "Ethiopian," which in the sixteenth century applied to
all of sub-Saharan Africa.) According to Martire, even though the blazing
sun of his native island preserved intact the "shining blackness" (*lucida
nerezza*) of his skin, Benedetto was a black of Italy, from a race that had suffered from and been proved by the horrors of slavery. Martire was ardently
antislavery, so his use of Benedetto as a saintly symbol of the society's crusade for Christian liberty was sincere, even if he was now compromised by
membership in a fascist parliament—after all, the Antislavery Society itself
patriotically displayed a congratulatory telegram from Mussolini at the beginning of its minutes. Italians could also be proud of the fact that the
Spanish had taken San Benedetto's cult to the New World, where he was

1. *Atti del quarto congresso nazionale della Società Antischiavista d'Italia (Dicembre
1926)* (Rome, 1927), p. 109, inexact because Benedetto was probably born free,
though his mother and father had been slaves. Also, he was Sicilian.

honored in Mexico, Bahia, Peru, Cincinnati, and Kansas City.[2] This meeting did not dwell on the slavery in Italy's own past, and some smugness also intruded; the vice president of the society said "that American slavery had been the coarsest economic exploitation."[3] But there was considerable pride that Italy had produced a black saint whose cult was strong among ex-slaves and their descendants.

We will take a closer look at San Benedetto of Palermo later, for he is an interesting character in the history of Italian slavery. Martire's speech launches us into the deep waters of just what it meant to be an Italian, to be a slave, to be black—questions as relevant in the Middle Ages as they were in the 1920s. Italy was barely fifty years old in 1926, and the idea of being an Italian in the centuries before unification had engaged writers from Machiavelli to Mazzini. Even when a nationalistic or cultural loyalty to the peninsula and its people was dim and a sense of common identity nonexistent, the Other—the slave, the black, the Tartar, Muslim, or Jew—helped define local loyalties. Was it possible to be a Genoese, a Venetian, a Palermitan, and also a black? In the 1930s fascism began to exclude Jews from the ranks of regular Italians, so questions of identity existed in every age, embedded in the common rhetoric of people and political leadership.

Many institutions over the centuries—the Church, the Franciscan order, the Spanish crown, Mussolini's government—were eager to co-opt San Benedetto il Moro for their purposes. But just on the level of language, deciding what to call Benedetto and his parents, describing them by color, ethnic origin, or religion, helped the Italians to define themselves and what they were doing to other people. The approach to linguistics called pragmatics, which emphasizes looking at the meaningful use of language in its broadest context, encourages us to begin looking at Italian slavery by closely examining the words used to define, operate, and justify the various systems of slavery the Italians invented or borrowed, from the Romans to the slave labor camps of World War II. These cycles in the history of exploitation show how Italian society moved away from oppression toward a freer system of labor—though that journey is not yet over. Historians have been closely analyzing language for a long time and were among the first to chart changes in language over time and the use of words to demean and oppress people.

Here in the Italian experience we have the chance to look at a long historical dialogue with slavery—one of the most durable in world history—and to see how language defined some people as appropriate subjects for ex-

2. Ibid., pp. 116–17.
3. Ibid., p. 105.

ploitation. Filippo Zamboni, who prefaced his late nineteenth- century account of slavery in the age of Dante with an autobiographical sketch, observed that when he was a boy his mother told him not to use the word "schiavo" because slavery "was a cruel and haughty thing."[4] Going back into the Italian past and searching for the meanings of words will help explain how color and slavery moved from facts of life to sources of shame, ever so slowly. Yet even by Zamboni's youth (1850s), when the Italian translation of *Uncle Tom's Cabin* was making a tremendous impression on liberal, reform-minded Italy, the language of Italian slavery had become permeated with other words and cultural discourses, be they the Latin of Roman slavery or the English of the American South. The broader context of Italian slavery must include those global and historical influences that affected the ways Italians understood what it meant to be a slave. Our contemporary perspective on Italian slavery must encompass recent events that permanently altered the ways Italians think about and describe slavery. Equally, the study of medieval and early modern slavery must reach forward to connect with modern slavery, or else we are left with fragmentary scholarship that means nothing.

WORDS

Our search for the language of Italian slavery must begin with individual words. The Italian word for "slave," *schiavo*, is clearly related to *esclavo* in Spanish, *esclave* in French, *Sklave* in German, and *slave* in English, among other vernacular languages in Europe. The best analysis of the possible common origins of these words points to the Balkans, the home of the southern Slavs, who in the early Middle Ages provided slaves to Carolingian Europe, the Byzantine state, and via intermediaries to the Muslim East—hence also the Arabic *sakaliba* for "slave."[5]

By a curious process, nearly everywhere the Latin for "slave," *servus*, began to transfer its meaning to the medieval serf. This change was perhaps slowest in Italy, where into the thirteenth century the most common word for "slave" remained *servus*.[6] As late as the Angevin kingdom of Naples, administrative documents referred to Saracens in the colony at Lucera as

---

4. Filippo Zamboni, *Gli Ezzelini, Dante e gli schiavi* (Rome, 1906), p. xxiv.

5. Henry and Renée Kahane, "Notes on the Linguistic History of *Sclavus*," in *Studi in onore di Ettore Lo Gatto e Giovanni Maver* (Florence, 1962), pp. 345–60.

6. Charles Verlinden, "L'origine de *sclavus* = *esclave*," *Bulletin Du Cange* 17 (1943): 97–128; pp. 104–13 for Italy. The Kahanes offer a more succinct and reliable analysis of the etymology.

"servi" of the royal household.[7] These "serfs" belonged to the monarch as surely as any slaves, as they learned when the colony was destroyed in 1300–1301 and most of the surviving population was sold as "schiavi." But as early as the eleventh century, *sclavus* appeared in southern Italy as a word for "slave."[8] Even as Greeks, Arabs, and German-speaking peoples borrowed the root *sklav-/slav-* to refer to slaves and for the Arabs particularly to light-skinned ones, southern Italians adopted the word later and probably were the ones to share it with their northern Italian neighbors through commerce in people. One of the earliest uses of the word *sclava*, from Bari in 1088, suggests that the Adriatic slave trade brought the people and the words first to southern Italy.[9] By the fourteenth and fifteenth centuries the Latin *sclavus* and the dialect forms of *schiavo* were in common use throughout the Italian peninsula.

Dictionaries are the humble but essential source for finding both words and their common meanings. In both subtle and blatant ways dictionaries also convey a broader context needed for using the words and understanding their meanings. The first dictionaries of the Italian Middle Ages were of course in Latin, still the unifying language for the peninsula's educated elite. Hence the dictionaries carried a lot of the cultural inheritance of ancient Rome to the later period, and the literate knew that old Rome was a slave society. Our worries about words must include a cautious approach to medieval Latin in Italy, which may contain and perpetuate anachronistic features of ancient Latin. The classic problem concerns the word *servus*— the ancient slave, but so often in medieval documents of practice the serf. This is not the place to become confused about serfs, whose status admittedly came at times perilously close to slavery.[10] The law, and the words, tell us that serfs lived in the shadowy world of the semifree. The dictionaries, however, emerge in a period that found earlier medieval concepts like being "half free" to be unsatisfactory, so our sources seek clarity, another purpose of the dictionary.

Dictionaries supply important evidence on both the definition of slavery and the ways in which ideas about color and humanity shaped attitudes to-

7. Pietro Egidi, *Codice diplomatico dei saraceni di Lucera* (Naples, 1917), p. 37, doc. 112, refers to all the Saracens as "servi." Another document of 1289 refers to a *miles* (knight) as a *servus* (p. 9).

8. H. and R. Kahane, "Notes," pp. 352–53.

9. *Codice diplomatico barese, Le pergamene di S. Nicola di Bari*, ed. Francesco Nitti di Vito, vol. 4 (Bari, 1900), p. 18.

10. For some thoughts on the distinction between "serf" and "slave," see Paul Freedman, *Images of the Medieval Peasant* (Stanford, Calif., 1999), pp. 79–84.

ward people. The oldest Latin dictionary from the central Middle Ages in Italy was completed by Papias in 1053.[11] Papias defined slaves in the classical Western tradition as people taken in wars, born into slavery, or acquired from enemies. He simply defined *famulus* and *manceps* as *servus* (slave), and noted that *ancilla* (female slave) derived from the Greek for "prop" or "support." This simple use of synonyms from the norms of classical Latin probably derived from Isidore of Seville. Papias defined *albus* (white) as *candidus*, which in turn meant without stain, and referred back to white. *Niger* (black) was not bright or fair but *fuscus* (dark), and again the meaning of *fuscus* simply pointed the reader back to *niger* and the classical *aquilus* (dark). "Black" and "white" contain almost no value judgments in this dictionary. In defining color Papias invoked the heat of the sun and what comes from fire as the causes of color in nature, but he did not extend this to explaining the different colors of people. To Papias *populus* is just a common humanity, and *gens* a group with a common origin, like the Jews. His dictionary gave a barebones definition of slavery and did not suggest that it might depend on ethnicity or color.

The great Latin dictionary of the Middle Ages, the *Catholicon*, was completed in 1286 by the Genoese Dominican monk Giovanni Balbi. Important changes in ideas about slavery and color enter into it. This dictionary is a good place to find the basic language of slavery, Latin.[12] Balbi explained that *servus* (slave) came from the verb *servo*, and denoted a person saved, a captive not killed but put to work. *Servus* was also related to *famulus*, a slave member of the family, and *mancipius*, a person "seized by the hand" in battle or in a pillaging expedition—here Balbi sticks close to Papias. *Famulus* hence invoked the standard definition of the ancient family as including all the members of the household, slave and free. Also, a *manceps* might be a son not yet emancipated from paternal authority. At times the head of the family seemed to have the same power of life and death over his children and slaves. Balbi also distinguished a purchased slave from one born in the household. He clearly drew on Roman tradition by highlighting the original violence of slavery—losers taken in hand and turned into property. In his definition of *servitus* (slavery) Balbi noted that sin introduced slavery into the world, citing no less an authority than the sixth-century pope and saint Gregory the Great. Balbi stressed that nature brought forth all people

11. Papias Vocabulista, *Elementarium doctrine rudimentum* (Venice, 1496) (words in alphabetical order).

12. Johannes Balbus (Giovanni Balbi), *Catholicon* (Mainz, 1460), cited by alphabetical entry, pages not numbered.

as equal, but their sinful conditions placed them wherever they ended up in society, slave or free.[13] This new comment on slavery encapsulates a great deal of medieval thought on sin, nature, and slavery. Balbi was not saying that slavery itself was a shameful and cruel practice, but that the slaves were getting what they deserved because of sin, that great medieval universal explanation.

The word for a female slave, *ancilla*, according to Balbi came from *cilleo* (to move), for a slave moved around to support and serve the master. The female slave was also curved or shaped for the service, bed, or support of the master. (Balbi goes far beyond Papias here!) Balbi only envisioned male masters of female slaves, and he resisted any mention of the word *servus* as he defined *ancilla*, for he knew they were not equal. No one wrote about male slaves as sexual partners to masters of either sex. Even in a dictionary, it was possible to learn that the female slave body was a special object for exploiting as the owner wished, and even Balbi may have been hard pressed to explain how original sin decreed a lifetime of rape for some women.

The races of humanity, as currently understood, are modern concepts, yet medieval people thought of blood, nationality, and above all, color, as ways of defining strangers. The medieval Italians inherited from the Romans a word rich in meaning for identifying "the people"—*popolo*, from the Latin *populus*, which Balbi defined as an association formed by the consent and agreement of the community. This meaning of "the people," understood in medieval communes as excluding the nobles and warriors, emphasized the voluntary and spontaneous coming together of persons to foster their collective self-interest. Balbi knew that in other contexts "the people" might include the noble as well as the common, or ignoble people. The new politicized people of the medieval Italian cities never thought of themselves as belonging to one ethnicity. Balbi did note at the end of his definition of *populus* the idea of a people tree, a collection of *gentes* (peoples) constituting humanity, so he proposed a natural as well as self-defined meaning to the notion of "people." *Gens* denoted a multitude, or a nation, uniting generations of families who shared a point of common origin. So Greece or Asia might be peopled with families all related by some distant kinship. *Gens* was also the word for an extended family—everyone with the same name. Finally Balbi noted the derivative *gentiles*, meaning for the Jews, those not circumcised, and for the Christians, those not baptized. But none of this brings us any closer to an *ethnic* understanding of peoples. Balbi (like Papias) discussed "blood" only as a fluid, and he had little to say about the

13. Ibid., "omnes homines natura equales genuit."

meaning of "tribe." He defined *natio* by using the example of the Greeks, Italians, and Franks, peoples who might have a state, or sometimes no state at all. Balbi's ethnography, if that is the right word for his terminology, grouped people by political, civic associations, or kinship, sometimes rooted to a place, other times not. He did not conceive of a humanity divided into races. A closer look at his people tree might reveal a hierarchy of peoples, but alas, he was not any more specific about what he meant.

The one group that Balbi saw as standing apart from the rest of society was of course the Jews. By coincidence we can look at a contemporary of Balbi's, the Genoese merchant Inghetto Contardo, who publicly disputed with Jews on the island of Majorca in 1286. In his diatribe Inghetto told the Jews, among other things, that they were cursed, lived in servitude and disgrace, and that all nations vilified them and held them as captives.[14] More specifically, he noted that the Jews were in perpetual slavery to all nations, in this context the Christians, Saracens, and Tartars.[15] The Jews became captives and slaves because of their transgressions, whether it was the sale of Joseph, for which they served in Egypt for 450 years, or their current predicament, caused by their treatment of Jesus.[16] By the late thirteenth century it was a commonplace that Jews deserved to be slaves, whether they remained for the moment free or not. Needless to say, Inghetto's account records no Jewish response, and deprives us of possible antislavery views. The only hint of a reply is that Inghetto concedes that the main Jewish disputant had claimed to be of the same *parentela* (lineage) as Mary and the sons of Solomon, but this gained him nothing in Inghetto's eyes.[17] Inghetto Contardo provides important insights on the language of slavery, and what we call ethnicity. The medieval Jews, a people without a land, and hence not really a nation, were seen as condemned to servitude as a just punishment for sin. In this Genoese text the Jews have become a prototype for a people meriting enslavement. There will be other peoples.

Balbi's ideas about color reveal a key stage in the development of attitudes about colored people. The first thing Balbi wrote about *albus* (white) is that it was related to *album*, the register or album which recorded the names of saints. He also cited a line from Juvenal about white wool, sym-

---

14. Ora Limor, *Die Disputationen zu Ceuta (1179) und Mallorca (1286)*, in MGH, Quellen zur Geistesgeschichte des Mittelalters, vol. 15 (Munich, 1994), p. 176. This text is about twenty thousand words in length.

15. Ibid., p. 214.

16. Ibid.: Egypt, p. 267; Jesus, p. 217.

17. Ibid., p. 222.

bolic of fineness and purity. Mentioning his predecessor Papias, Balbi stated that things were *albus* (white) by nature and *candidus* (pure white) by skill, but he conceived of the two as different types of quality—the first natural, the second artificial in its old sense as the product of skill. The parallels to the definition of *niger* (black) are striking. Huguccio of Pisa, author of a late twelfth-century *Derivationes*, derived *niger* from *nubes* (cloud, cloudy, *nubilus*), and he mentioned other words related to it.[18] But he simply listed the words without comment. Balbi too derived *niger* from *nubes*, something not clear or serene, and he closely followed Huguccio's work. Balbi also cited a line from Horace, in effect warning people to be on their guard about anything black, and this was his own contribution to the growing negative context surrounding "black." Balbi derived from *niger* the interesting adjective *subniger* (somewhat black), the verb *denigro* (to belittle or disparage) and the rare *enigro* (to remove the black from something). Given Balbi's way of associating black with bad things, there is no doubt that removing the black meant improving whatever it was that became less black. Related to the idea of blackness was the verb *fusco* (to darken) and the adjective *fuscus* (dark). In addition to all the other negative qualities of anything dark, here Balbi also conjured up *obfusco* (to obfuscate or to bewilder) and *fuscator* (a concealer or deceiver).

In his excellent study on the origins of American racism under slavery, Winthrop Jordan, also considering the words *black* and *white*, suggested that "in England perhaps more than in southern Europe, the concept of blackness was loaded with intense meaning."[19] Preoccupied as Jordan was with the vast subject of early modern English racism, there was no reason for him to suspect that Italy's long-standing connections to the rest of the world had already, for centuries, been shaping attitudes toward human color. Medieval Italians were conscious of color and associated bad traits and things with darker people. In this way language by Balbi's time, if not earlier, was oppressing people with derogatory labels and justifying their

18. Huguccio of Pisa, "Derivationes," Bayerische Staatsbibliotek, Munich, no. 14056. This manuscript is organized by derivations, so *niger* is under *nubes* at the end of "N." This text greatly influenced Balbi. Wolfgang Müller has persuasively argued that this lexicographer is a different person from the canonist Huguccio of Pisa, bishop of Ferrara; see his *Huguccio: The Life, Works, and Thought of a Twelfth-Century Jurist* (Washington, D.C., 1994).

19. Winthrop Jordan, *The White Man's Burden* (Oxford, 1974), p. 5. For another approach to English attitudes on color, see Kim F. Hall, *Things of Darkness: Economies of Race and Gender in Early Modern England* (Ithaca, 1995), esp. pp. 1–15.

enslavement. But color was not the only label attached to the slave, and the most elementary use of language in slavery, well before the dictionary, was to give the slave a name.

As Abigail reminded David, "for as his name is, so is he."[20] Adam got to name all the creatures in the world. The power to name a thing, as Scripture proclaimed, conferred dominion over it. The same principle applied to people, and there was much discussion of naming in the Middle Ages. Thomas Aquinas spoke for many when he observed that "the names of individual people are always imposed out of some property of the person to whom the name is given."[21] In the case of slaves, masters imposed a name upon birth or purchase. The name of a slave might even disappear from the historical record if the people who controlled language refused or neglected to record it. The Florentine diarist Giovanni Morelli noted that his uncle Bartolomeo had illegitimate children by both a free woman and a slave, the latter a beautiful enough woman whom he later married. But Giovanni would not write the name of his aunt, "because the marriage was not an honest thing, because she was of a different race, even if good-hearted, as they are."[22] He did not name his cousins either, even though they were presumably not slaves, so embarrassed was he by the different blood mixed with that of the old noble family of the Morelli.

In order to provide security of ownership and to aid in the pursuit of runaways, the Florentine commune in 1366 finally began to keep a record of slave sales.[23] To accomplish these goals, the Florentines collected exact physical descriptions of the approximately 357 slaves sold in the years 1366–97.[24] These descriptions, wonderful sources for understanding what some late medieval people looked like, will be examined in a later chapter. The Florentine bureaucracy also collected the slaves' names, revealing the

20. I Samuel 25:25.

21. Cited in David Herlihy, "Tuscan Names, 1200–1530," *Renaissance Quarterly* 41 (1988): pp. 561–82; here p. 56, citing *Summa Theologica* 3.37.2.

22. Giovanni di Pagolo Morelli, *Ricordi*, ed. Vittore Branca (Florence, 1969), pp. 162–63, "non gli vo' nominare, perché non è onesto, sì fatta ischiatta, come ch'e' sieno di buona condizione assai, secondo loro essere." My sense of what this means.

23. Printed in Ridolfo Livi, *La schiavitù domestica nei tempi di mezzo e nei moderni* (Padua, 1928), pp. 141–217.

24. Approximate because of the repeated sale of some slaves, and on account of multiple sales.

complex problems surrounding something so apparently simple. The Florentines wanted exact information, so in about one hundred cases more than one name for a slave was recorded, almost invariably for female Tartar slaves imported from the Black Sea. The owners knew, and almost all the slaves knew, that they had once had other names, even if, as in the case of a little nine-year-old girl now called Lucia, no one remembered what her original name was.[25] In some instances the owners simply noted that the slave had an alias. Caterina, a baptized Tartar, was also called Chutias, and at sixteen, she was the one to tell the master what was perhaps, in her mind, her real name.[26] Besides referring to the Tartar names as aliases, at times the records make clear that the name was a former one, and that people once called Cetehe and Cafisa had become Margarita and Caterina, names more familiar to Tuscan speakers. The slave and probably the owner figured that for identifying the slave, the older name was a fact worth recording. A Tartar slave originally called Ersamabi, was once named Lucia before settling down as Caterina, and all this by the age of twenty.[27] Her owner may have preferred for her to have a new name to avoid duplication of names, or perhaps as a way to forge a new, dependent identity for the slave. Even as the Tartar slaves became Christians and acquired proper baptismal names, a rich collection of Tartar names diminished to a boring set of narrow choices, with Caterina, Lucia, and Margherita leading the way, for reasons we will consider. Almost none of the Eastern names survived, perhaps as a sign that speaking Tartar was also unacceptable.

The most common setting for naming a slave was probably baptism, naturally another sign of taking up a new life, in this case as a Christian slave. This is clear in the cartulary (1392–99) of the Venetian notary Bernardo de Rodulfis, whose sale contracts frequently note an original name, and what the slave should be called upon baptism. Here are some examples—all women.[28]

Bulgarian slave called Stanna	upon baptism Baxilia
Tartar slave called Maria	upon baptism Bartolomea
Bosnian slave called Radoslava	upon baptism (blank)
Tartar slave (no name)	upon baptism Caterina
Russian slave called Malgarita	upon baptism Cita

25. Ibid., p. 172 n. 130.
26. Ibid., p. 106 n. 167.
27. Ibid., p. 197 n. 260.
28. *Bernardo de Rodolfis: Notaio in Venezia (1392–1399)*, ed. Giorgio Tamba (Venice, 1974), nos. 25, 100, 122, 128, 220.

In Palermo a century previously, where there seemed to be less emphasis on baptizing Muslim slaves and some relish in owning ones named Muhammed, Ali, and Fatima, names could change without baptism. An emancipation from 1299 freed a slave named Fatima, who was once called Chadiga.[29] Masters had power over names and could change a slave's name whenever they wished, especially when the slave did not have a baptismal name. Only very rarely, and late, do the records show that slaves had some choice in their names. The vast majority of the notices of slave names mentioned only the first name because slaves did not have a family name. Upon emancipation, a slave might acquire a last name, but it is hard to find evidence for this. A rare instance occurred in 1381, when Antonio Vayrolo da Camogli freed his slave Niccolo, who in the next notarial act called himself "Niccolo Vayrolo da Camogli once the slave of Antonio Vayrolo da Camogli."[30] Niccolo presumably chose his name, for he was now free, but he commemorated his ex-master for unfathomable reasons. This taking up of family names from the masters had a long sequel in the history of slavery. The notice of the baptism of Giovanna Maria on 7 August 1509 in Siena clearly states that she chose the name, but such liberty was the exception.[31] Even rarer was the opportunity for a runaway to change names and claim a new identity. A slave named Dobbra ran away from her Florentine owner in 1423, and turned up in Siena, where she called herself, ironically, Caterina, a common slave name. Since Caterina denied she was Dobbra, her owner had to send his son down to Siena to identify his property.[32]

Most of the known slave names come from contracts or tax records. The biggest collection of names comes from fifteenth century Genoa, and Table 1 supplies an ethnic breakdown by the six most common names for women slaves. Just these six names—Caterina, Lucia, Maddalena, Margherita, Maria, and Marta—account for about 80 percent of the names in this sample of over a thousand slaves. The table shows that "Lucia" and "Maddalena" occurred across all ethnic groups in similar percentages, but that "Caterina" especially prevailed among Moorish and Turkish women,

29. Pietro Gulotta, *Le imbreviature del notaio Adamo de Citella a Palermo (2 registro 1298–1299)* (Rome, 1982), p. 282, n. 363.

30. Archivio di Stato di Genova, Cartoli notarili Cart. N. 294, 92r-v, Benvenuto Bracelli notary (hereafter abbreviated as ASG, CN).

31. Giulio Prunai, "Notizie e documenti sulla servitù domestica nel territorio senese (secc. VIII–XVI)," *Bulletino senese di storia patria* 7 (1936): 435.

32. Ibid., pp. 287–89, outcome of story not known.

Table 1. Women's Slave Names by Ethnicity in Genoa

	Number of names	%[a]	Tartar	%	Russian	%	Circassian	%	Abkhazian	%	Moorish	%	Turkish	%
Caterina	191	17.4	17	9.8	43	14.3	67	21.8	14	9.8	39	28.9	11	28.2
Lucia	143	13.0	26	15.0	30	10.0	49	15.9	23	16.1	8	5.9	7	18.0
Maddalena	137	12.5	21	12.1	43	14.3	39	12.7	17	11.9	13	9.6	4	10.0
Margherita	168	15.3	25	14.4	49	16.3	45	14.6	35	25.2	9	6.7	5	12.8
Maria	145	13.2	19	11.0	52	17.3	26	8.5	17	11.9	26	19.3	5	12.8
Marta	78	7.1	25	14.4	19	6.3	19	6.2	9	6.3	5	3.7	1	2.6
Top six names	862	78.4												
All names	1099		173		301		308		143		135		39	

Source: Domenico Gioffrè, Il mercato degli schiavi a Genova nel secolo XV (Genoa, 1971), register in appendix.

[a]Throughout the table, percentages are of all names.

as "Margherita" did among Abkhazians and "Marta" among Tartars. It is important to understand the context of these names because someone picked the name for a reason, and the small number of names suggests some common thinking. A nearly contemporary source, Jacopo da Voragine's late thirteenth-century *Golden Legend*, the most famous medieval collection of saints' lives, illuminates what these names represented in Italian society. Voragine has the additional advantage of having been archbishop of Genoa, so his writings emerge from the milieu that yields the most slave names.

Santa Caterina, a late Roman martyr in Alexandria, is the origin of the Caterina's popularity, even though St. Catherine of Siena (d. 1380) had recently added some spiritual weight to the name. Caterina was an intelligent, beautiful, well-educated young Christian woman, the daughter of a king.[33] She chastely resisted all suitors, and converted pagan philosophers through wise arguments. Naming one's slave after a noblewoman from the eastern Mediterranean—proverbially chaste, the object of a very popular cult in Italy—expressed hopeful intentions for the slave's future conduct. Perhaps some qualities of the original model would attach themselves to the slave, or perhaps the slave would grow to emulate her namesake. Likewise, when guards came to abduct Santa Lucia, from a noble family in Sicily, the Holy Spirit "fixed her in place so firmly that they could not move her."[34] No one could move Lucia, not even a thousand oxen, so her tormentors burned her on the spot and stabbed her in the throat. Since Lucia's most distinctive quality was stability, perhaps a slave named after her was less likely to run away. Santa Margarita of Antioch, another popular medieval saint of noble stock, was also cruelly beaten and tortured. During her martyrdom she prayed that she be allowed to alleviate the pains of childbirth for those women invoking her aid.[35] Margarita the pearl—pure, lucky—was a good name to have around a household where women were having children, and evoked both good behavior and freedom from pain. Yet all these women had suffered at the hands of evil people, a lesson the masters cannot have intended to fortify the slaves against themselves.

The next three holy women, together accounting for about a third of all slave names, present some complex problems. Maria and Marta were subjects of a rich interpretive tradition by exegetes and scholars, most of which

33. Jacobus de Voragine, *The Golden Legend: Readings on the Saints*, trans. William Granger Ryan, 2 vols. (Princeton, N.J., 1993), 2:334–41.

34. Ibid., 1:27–29; quotation, p. 27.

35. Ibid., 1:368–70.

probably did not make much of an impression on popular opinion.[36] Maria Maddalena, or just Maddalena, is one of the several New Testament Marys, but Voragine tells her standard story thus: Maddalena, the rich sister of Lazarus, was a sinner in the flesh.[37] Jesus himself transformed Maddalena, and allowed her to wash his feet and anoint him, so that Maddalena became a humble and holy woman. In this version of events she and her siblings ended up in the West, first preaching the new faith in Marseilles. In a subsidiary tale Maddalena becomes the faithful handmaid, the exemplary servant. Maddalena ended her days in retreat near Aix-en-Provence, not too far from Genoa. So Maddalena presents an interesting context—an immoral woman who reforms and learns through humble service like washing feet how to be a good servant—a small step from a slave.

Her sister Martha has a different story.[38] The prudent sister who managed the wealth of Maddalena and Lazarus, Martha also came west and formed a tie to the city of Tarascon. Voragine associated Martha with the woman Jesus cured of the issue of blood, so she became a saint protecting the health of women. A good steward, faithful, self-effacing, Martha too had lessons to teach a slave. And then there is Mary. Can it really be the Blessed Virgin Mary, the Mother of God, the object of intense spiritual devotion, who gives her name to one of every eight women slaves in Genoa? Perhaps we are really dealing with someone like Saint Mary of Egypt, known as the Sinner, the reformed prostitute who became a holy woman in the desert.[39] Or even Maria Maddalena. It's easy to see that bridled female sexuality may have been on the minds of slave owners. Yet Maria's most common association will not have been with these two women, but with *the* Virgin Mary, and it is a puzzle why anyone would call a slave by the name of the mother of the Savior. There are aspects of Mary's life that were exemplary, and Mary certainly followed orders, but Voragine focused all his attention on the vexed question of the Virgin's own birth and lineage.[40] Additional evidence will help fill out the context necessary for understanding this anomaly; but for the moment let us stipulate that there were no slaves in Genoa named Gesu or Giuseppe (and apparently no free people either).

36. For the scholarly tradition, see Giles Constable, "The Interpretation of Mary and Martha," in his *Three Studies in Medieval Religious and Social Thought* (Cambridge, 1995), pp. 1–141.

37. J. de Voragine, *The Golden Legend*, 1:374–83.

38. Ibid., 2:23–26.

39. Ibid., 1:227–29.

40. Ibid., 2:149–58.

The argument for interpreting slave names requires a check on the free population to see whether slave names simply mimic the larger pool of all names. Unfortunately, there is no contemporary set of data from Genoa, but David Herlihy did examine the first names of Florentine women in the fifteenth century.[41] The top seventeen names in this large sample of 6,810 include four of our names—Caterina, the most popular name at 8.1 percent, Margarita (5.1 percent), Lucia (2.2 percent), and Maddalena at (1.5 percent). It's not surprising that these names also occur as names for free women, though at greatly reduced percentages, for the virtues of service, chastity, and stability also found favor among parents as well as slave owners. Many names of free Florentines, like Antonia, Giovanna, Francesca, and Piera, were female forms of male names; these were very rare for slaves, for whom distinctive female names were the rule in the fifteenth century. Herlihy's Florentine data, in which the top seventeen names account for only about half of the women, contrasts sharply with the six names that belonged to 80 percent of slave women. Slave names are primarily choices that reflect the values of the masters. The small pool of common names for slaves may show the generic nature of the preference, if people did not give much thought to these names. Yet the religious prominence of these names suggests that the masters chose them, over qualities like "speedy" or colors like "white" or "black," for some reason.

Male slave names pose a problem because by the fifteenth century male slaves were becoming rare in northern Italy, at less than 3 percent of the slave population in Genoa in 1458.[42] Only four names figure significantly among the Russian, Circassian, Tartar, and Moorish men (186 in total) who were slaves—Giorgio (45), Martino (16), Jacobino (14), and Giovanni (10).[43] These small numbers will not sustain any broad conclusions, but the prominence of "Giorgio" merits a comment, since it was given to about a quarter of all male slaves. San Giorgio, the military saint who killed the dragon, rescued the princess, and was himself martyred, was a popular saint across Europe and a special favorite in Italy. San Giorgio was a noble from the East who used his sword to protect people, and then loyally faced incredible tortures while witnessing to his faith.[44] Since Giorgio was the name given to only 2.5 percent of free males in Genoa in 1396, this name

41. D. Herlihy, "Tuscan Names" for the following percentages calculated from the data on p. 574.

42. Domenico Gioffrè, *Il mercato degli schiavi a Genova nel secolo XV* (Genoa, 1971), p. 79.

43. Ibid., appendix.

44. J. de Voragine, *The Golden Legend*, 1:238–42.

must have seemed an apt one for a slave, who would above all be loyal and protect his owners from the many dangers of life.[45] The other male slave names, less common among them than in the free population, were too infrequently used to yield results here. (Their female forms were also rare for women slaves.) So the male names, as is to be expected, do not tell us much.

Individual and rare names reveal some features of slave life. Some names indicated the slave's ethnic origin; thus there is the occasional Circassa or Zico to show that the female or male slave was originally Circassian. But toponymic names were rare for slaves, as they were for first names in general. Foreign names did occur among the slaves; a fair number (10) of Anastasias hailed from Russia, as did one Ivano. But we would not expect to see the one Moorish woman named Anastasia, and her example warns us that names could cross over from one ethnic group to another. Some slaves embodied the hopes of owners: there were several slaves named Divizia (riches) and even more called Melica (musical) and Cito/Cita (speedy). These encouraging or auspicious names were not very common; the saints' names met the need for names with a lesson. And yet women seemed more likely than men to be named after qualities or things. In contrast to earlier centuries when the Muslim names Muhammed, Ali, and Fatima were very common among Genoese slaves, by the fifteenth century they had virtually disappeared there. Of the 135 Moorish women slaves, only one, Macorri, had a recognizable Arabic name; as Table 1 shows, Maria and Caterina really dominated in Genoa—a sign that these slaves had been assigned new names under Christian ownership. Perhaps the desire to teach a lesson about obedience to new converts explains the wide popularity of names like Mary.

Turkish slaves were a small minority in Genoa; the Turks were winning battles against the Italians and others, and most of the eastern Mediterranean would soon be theirs. The Turks, and the Mamluks in Egypt, were in fact great purchasers of slaves. Only thirty-nine Turkish women and eleven men appeared in the Genoese sample. Among this small group was the only Fatima in the entire sample, as well as men named Cali, Macomer, and Mustafa. The Moorish men (41) supplied some original names—Abderacoman, Ali, Alonsiho, Ioham, Calem, Hamet, and Aspertino. By the end of the fifteenth century Muslim names had become rare, but they remained the most numerous type of non-Genoese names for slaves.

Trapani in Sicily was home to a small but ethnically diverse population

---

45. Male names from Benjamin Z. Kedar, *Merchants in Crisis: Genoese and Venetian Men of Affairs and the Fourteenth-Century Depression* (New Haven, Conn., 1976), p. 99; "Giovanni" was the most common at 8.7 percent.

of slaves whose names had a stronger Arabic component than the Genoese. The small number (30) of slaves known from sales contracts included ten with Arabic names, and one Jewish slave was called Musudi.[46] Good tax records from 1593/94 noted 323 slaves—120 men, 199 women, and 4 not specified—as well as some emancipated slaves living in town.[47] Caterina (16), Maddalena (12), and Marta (12) were the most common names for the women, and for men Francesco (12), Giuseppe (6), and Pietro (5). Less than 10 percent (28) of the names were Arabic, with Fatima (6), Hassan (4), Muhammed (4), and Ali (3) leading the way.[48] Even in Sicily the use of Arabic names for slaves was waning now. By the late sixteenth century the effects of Renaissance humanism had reached Trapani, and there were some slaves named for the classical Lavinia, Portia, and Pompey—a style of naming that the American South would imitate. Some augurative names like Speranza (hope) also appeared, but it took a lot of nerve or insight to name a slave Hope. By 1714 only one slave remained in Trapani, and her name was Maria Giuseppina, Mary Josephine—an ironic way to commemorate the Holy Family or to control a slave through language.[49]

This search for the voices of masters led us to names, which, like the slaves, were under the control of the masters. By the fifteenth and sixteenth centuries slaves in southern and northern Italy bore names encouraging them to lives of hard work, loyalty, stability, and chastity. Even if the Muslim slaves resisted baptism, few held on to their original names. Was the point of having slaves named after the Prophet and his family to flatter the power of the owners or to humiliate the slaves, or both? Children born into Christian slavery in Italy did not carry forward names betraying their ethnic or religious roots; instead, they bore well-known saints' names in greater percentages than the free population. Caterina and Lucia were still familiar names for both groups. Not all owners were familiar enough with the lives of the saints to understand the aptness of their name choices. One of the advantages of controlling people through language is that after a while the habits of language do their own work without those in power consciously manipulating the choices of words or even being aware of their meaning in context. For example, Jacopo was a durable favorite among men's names, yet how many Italian speakers thought of it as a classic Jewish

46. Giovanni Marrone, *La schiavitù nella società siciliana dell'età moderna* (Caltanissetta, 1972), pp. 16–24.

47. Ibid., pp. 56–57.

48. This sample was calculated from the lists in ibid., pp. 64–142.

49. Ibid., p. 186.

name? It must on some level have crossed the mind of Francesco Rossi of Trapani when in 1635 (!) he bought a Jewish slave from Palermo named Jacob di Abraham.[50] Certainly this Jacopo knew what his name really meant, and this part of his culture may have sustained him through a life of slavery. But of course we do not know anything about Jacopo's state of mind or how he interacted with his owner. Given the nature of the sources and the attitudes of the culture producing them, his own words were not likely to survive.

The masters control the record. For example, on 6 December 1450 Alessandra Strozzi of Florence wrote a letter to her exiled son in Naples. Among much news and gossip she complained bitterly about the conduct of the family slave Cateruccia (Santa Caterina's influence not strong here!), purchased a while ago.[51] Alessandra suffered a lot in this relationship, was not able to bring herself to punish the slave, and was in fact frightened of her. Alessandra wrote bitterly that sometimes it was as if Cateruccia was the mistress and she was the slave. Alessandra just wanted some peace in her household, but there was no man around to punish the slave. The only specific problem mentioned was Cateruccia's "mala lingua," her bad tongue. This was a slave in cultural resistance who had figured out how to use language to drive her owner to despair and fear, though her mistress's words are the only evidence we have. Such was the possible codependence of the relationship that fourteen years later Alessandra was still complaining about Cateruccia.[52] It is a shame that Cateruccia's words are lost, but perhaps we can recover something of their tone by examining the language of some special Italian slaves.

WORDS OF SLAVES

Slaves spoke for themselves when bureaucracies came to record their petitions and declarations, sometimes when they were still slaves, and in other instances when as freed slaves they needed to note something about the past. (The words placed in the mouths of slaves in literary sources, which are more problematic, will be considered in the next section.) In 1352 the Genoese were at war with the Byzantine Empire. During the hostilities Admiral Paganino Doria captured and enslaved some Greeks and then sold

50. Ibid., p. 154.
51. Alessandra Macinghi Strozzi, *Lettere di una gentildonna fiorentina del secolo XV ai figliuoli esuli* (Florence, 1877), pp. 103–5.
52. Ibid., p. 347.

some of them to two Genoese merchants.[53] That these combatants were all Christians did not prevent what happened. An eventual peace treaty between the states provided for returning captives, but excepted those who had already been sold. All this became relevant again around 1365, when in Genoa a slave woman named Lucia, one of the captives, became the subject of an investigation. The merchants had taken Lucia to the Ottoman Turkish city of Teologo, where in the bazaar Jacopo the brother of Violante de Golterio purchased the slave, whom Violante subsequently inherited. The issue now was the legality of Lucia's continued enslavement.

The surviving record of these events takes the form of a deposition in which Lucia testified about how she became a slave. Asked whether she was captured at Eraclea by Paganino Doria during the war, Lucia responded that she did not know who captured her since she had been about thirteen at the time. Here are the first words of the slave, a memory of a childhood trauma. Asked whether many Greek men and women had been taken, she agreed but she did not know anything about her own sale, nor did she recognize the names of her buyers or remember how she got to Teologo. Alas, at this point the record breaks off. All we know for sure is that in 1406, some forty years later, another notary copied out this record, presumably because it mattered as evidence in some legal case. By then Lucia would have been nearly seventy, if she were still living, but it makes sense that she must have become a free woman, or else there would have been no point to dredging up this old business again. Slave testimony was allowed in narrow circumstances in Genoa, and with regard to this matter—the means by which one had become a slave—the slave's information was relevant. But here a woman in her midtwenties just did not remember the details of how she came to be sold in a Muslim land by one Genoese to another. Vague memories left few words, but this kind of source, the notarial documents, will at least preserve whatever words survive.

In 1460 Giorgio da Caffa di Levante, Giorgio from the Genoese colony of Caffa in the Crimea, a sixteen-year-old "slave," petitioned the government of Siena for his freedom.[54] He said that about ten years earlier in Caffa, he and at least one other child had been secretly taken into a Genoese ship in the port. Giorgio ended up in the Genoese stronghold on the Aegean island of Chios, and was then sold to Lorenzo Ricasoli of Florence, with whom he stayed for about four years, until his master fled his credi-

53. For this and what follows see Gian Giacomo Musso, *Navigazione e commercio genovese con il Levante nei documenti dell'Archivio di stato di Genova (secc. xiv–xv)* (Rome, 1975), pp. 230–32.

54. G. Prunai, "Notizie e documenti," pp. 415–16.

tors. Then Giorgio stayed with a certain Genoese for a few years. Skipping over a lot of important details, Giorgio said he next took a ship to Ancona, where by chance he found Ricasoli, who had no need of him. What plainly happened is that Giorgio ran away, and whether he found his old master or not, he was claiming to be abandoned property and effectively free. Without saying just how he managed it, Giorgio ended up in Siena where he was training as a shoemaker. Ricasoli appeared in Siena and claimed Giorgio as his slave. Giorgio denied this, and asked Siena to make sure he remained free, because a Christian could not be seized and made a slave in Sienese territory. Instead, Giorgio asked to be sent to Talamone, the nearest Sienese port, and be put on a galley; it seems he volunteered to take the first ship out of Siena's state. What the truth was behind all this we may never know; nor does the story have an end. But we have many words, in Italian, in a clever petition designed to keep Giorgio a step ahead of his sometime owner. Raised by Italian masters, Giorgio acquired at least verbal skill in their tongue, and the fortitude somehow to make his way across the Mediterranean from Chios to Ancona to Siena, and in the meantime to learn a trade. He asked for nothing more than safe passage. Maybe the Sienese, who had little love for Florence, let him go.

We can wonder just how much Giorgio understood and told of his life. His memories of the original kidnapping in Caffa were certainly vivid. Ricasoli abandoned him when he was about ten years old, but even then Giorgio no longer felt like a slave. The Genoese he subsequently "stayed with" was probably a creditor who got this piece of Ricasoli's property, but in this case, as before, Giorgio never said he was a slave. He talked his way off Chios, which was no easy thing to do, for Genoa had terrible penalties for anyone helping a slave escape the island by sea. Giorgio was wise to pick Siena, a city with few slaves, as a refuge, and he was certainly well advised to steer clear of the Genoese and Florentine states. Finally, Giorgio claimed to be a Christian. He knew that in Siena no Christian could become a slave. So, thinking himself to be a free man, he was trying to help the Sienese to see him not as a wily runaway who deserved to be caught and turned over to his rightful owner, but as a free person being unjustly enslaved in an honorable city, or at least someone deserving a head start. Giorgio comes to life in these words, which reveal how he understood the world in which he moved. His suggested ending is a bit puzzling; he did not seem confident that he would be able to resist Ricasoli's claims. So Giorgio asked to be allowed to run away again—to find his safety in flight, the slave's best recourse.

In Pisan territory in the small town of Piombino, an ex-slave told her story in 1400 to a local notary who put it all down in proper Latin, far removed from the original words and flavor of the tale.[55] Margherita was now the wife of Pietro, but she had once been the slave of Donna Margarita the widow of Simone de San Cassiano, citizen of Pisa. In the notary's presence Margherita declared that she had become pregnant and given birth to a son named Biagio, who was now two years and six months old. Before this pregnancy, and presumably while she was a slave, she had had sex on numerous occasions with Andreotto Galletti, a citizen of Pisa, and only him, so she swore he was Biagio's father. Surely she was not explaining for the first time to her current husband that Biagio was not his. More likely, her former owner, who was probably her lover as well, had got her out of Pisa and obscurely married on Piombino as a free woman to cover up a typical scandal involving a pregnant slave. Now free to do as she liked, Margherita wanted a legal record to establish Biagio's paternity and perhaps some claim to his father's goods and estate. Probably no one expected to hear from her again, but Margherita used words that could easily change the future of her little boy.

The actual words of slaves, so hard to find, also survive in an unusual type of source, letters written by Italian slaves in captivity, usually in North African ports. These letters, from the sixteenth to the eighteenth centuries, were pleas for help mostly from common people, in a period when Muslim corsairs captured ships or occasionally raided the coasts, seized captives, and encouraged their slaves to find a way to be ransomed. This furnished a lucrative business for Barbary pirates. The Christians who were now slaves articulated their condition in pitiful letters intended to rouse their relatives, patrons, and friends to raise a ransom. The ever-practical Genoese in 1597 established a Magistracy for the Ransom of Slaves, an agency which required proofs of baptism, poverty, and enslavement before it would act on someone's behalf. It interviewed returned slaves to find out the truth about others remaining in captivity as well as general news from North Africa.[56] Slaves there, who counted among their number the Spanish author and prisoner of war Miguel Cervantes (1575–80), were overwhelmingly male and likely to be used as galley rowers if fit.[57] They had more reason to hope they would eventually obtain their freedom than the Muslim slaves who

55. Document in Amerigo D'Amia, *Schiavitù romana e servitù medievale* (Milan, 1931), pp. 260–61.

56. See in general the valuable study by Enrica Lucchini, *La merce umana: Schiavitù e riscatto dei liguri nel Seicento* (Rome, 1990).

57. For more on Spanish captives, see Ellen G. Friedman, *Spanish Captives in North Africa in the Early Modern Age* (Madison, Wis., 1983), pp. 55–76.

were kept in places like Genoa. Of course many captives died as slaves and conditions were especially hard on those who could not raise the money. Some Italian churches display to this day the chains of slaves whom local people ransomed as acts of piety.

Michel de Montaigne, while taking the waters near Lucca in 1581, came across an engaging Italian ex-slave named Giuseppe.[58] This fellow had been captured by the Turks at sea, converted to Islam in order to escape slavery, and then joined up with the Barbary pirates. As irony would have it, he ended up pillaging the territory of Lucca, and his own people captured him. Promptly returning to Christianity, Giuseppe resumed his old life after being away for ten or twelve years. What is remarkable about this vignette is that, according to Montaigne, no one trusted the sincerity of his reconversion because Giuseppe liked to slip off to Venice now and then to mix with Turks, for he remained one at heart. This curious story struck Montaigne because it revealed permeable boundaries where society saw only the absolute dichotomies Turk/Christian, slave/free. The chance that Italians might be enslaved raised questions about the firmness of these distinctions.

A collection of forty-nine letters by Sicilian slaves in North Africa in the late sixteenth century gives us some sense of how Italians experienced slavery. Their words are a proxy for the missing words of slaves held in Italy.[59] These letters, written in the language of ordinary Italians of the Cinquecento, illustrate contemporary attitudes toward slavery. To what extent they reveal the timeless miseries of slavery is hard to know, but here the emphasis must be on language in its context, not in all contexts. Many of these slaves feared being abandoned by their relatives, and of course in most cases they were probably presumed dead anyway. Just getting news of survival back to Palermo or Genoa was an accomplishment, even if Muslim owners encouraged letter campaigns for ransoms. Slaves felt that they were in Hell, in the hands of the devil, or at best in a kind of Purgatory or Limbo, and some expressed the fear that their ordeal would never end.[60] Santo Costa wrote to his sister from Tunis in 1597 that he felt lost in a labyrinth, an apt

58. Michel de Montaigne, *Travel Journal*, trans. Donald Frame (San Francisco, 1983), pp. 123–24; see Mario Lenci, *Lucchesi nel Maghreb: Storie di schiavi, mercanti e missionari*, (Lucca, 1994) for general background; for comment on this episode, see p. 34.

59. Giuseppe Bonaffini, *La Sicilia e i Barbareschi: Incursioni corsare e riscatto degli schiavi (1570–1606)* (Palermo, 1983).

60. Ibid., notices in letters: pp. 134, 140 (Inferno); p. 146; (Purgatory); p. 148 (Limbo).

metaphor for slavery.[61] A few slaves thought that their own sins had caused their enslavement, so internalized by now was the old Augustinian notion that slavery itself was a punishment from God.[62] Other slaves conceived of what happened to them as a calamity or simply a cruel fate.[63]

The Sicilian slaves, with more grounds for hope than those in Italy, expressed a need for patience, but it was hard advice to follow. Vincenzo Mancuso wrote in angry terms from Biserta to his sister, because he had written before without reply or help; he reminded her that they were born from the same mother, and not a stone.[64] But how could he be sure she had even received his first letter? Perhaps the most moving letter came from Silvestra Mula, who wrote to a noblewoman pleading for help.[65] She found herself a slave in Biserta, experiencing hard work and bad treatment, going barefoot without eating and enduring beatings without end. Silvestra belonged to a cruel man whose brother was a slave in Sicily, and she wanted help in getting him freed so that by an exchange she could avoid dying in slavery. Angelo La Galia ended his letter to his mother with a little poem or song about mothers who had sons in captivity in Barbaria—the mothers mourned and wept, the sons died of whippings and beatings.[66] All these words, mostly from unlucky ordinary Sicilians, describe a hellish slavery, probably not so different from the one experienced by the men in the galleys of Genoa and Venice. At least some Italians knew from first-hand experience how bad slavery was, and the efforts of Church and state to raise money for captives, as well as the letters and stories of Italian slaves, may have contributed to a growing distaste for the institution. In the summer of 1637 a great Algerian raid on the Ligurian coast at Ceriale and Borgheto yielded about 337 captives—men, women, and children—many of whom soon died or were never ransomed. Maybe if the Algerians had been able to raid the English or Dutch coasts as successfully, the northern zest for the slave trade might have been reduced.

A Fleming from Dunkirk, Emanuel D'Aranda, was captured off Brittany by Turks from Algiers and lived to tell the tale. While in captivity he knew a Genoese priest and Discalced Carmelite, Father Angeli, who had been captured by pirates and reduced to slavery for some time before 1641, when

61. Ibid., p. 169.
62. Ibid., p. 133 "per disgratia o pecati mei"; also p. 138.
63. Ibid., e.g., p. 146.
64. Ibid., p. 183.
65. Ibid., pp. 177–78: "per mia sorte mi ritrovo scava in biserta con tanti travagli et mal patimento con andare scalza senza mangiare et con bastonate senza fine."
66. Ibid., p. 182.

D'Aranda met him.[67] Father Angeli ministered to Christian slaves in Algiers, and he was loved even by the Protestants. Having license (in this perhaps embellished account) to freely address his master, who wondered if the devil would have his soul, Angeli told his owner, "you are a person of no Religion, and all your thoughts are bent on the robbing and ruining of Christians." Ruled by avarice, the pirate and slave owner was incapable of mercy. Perhaps Father Angeli would have addressed the same words to Genoese slaveowners.

D'Aranda also knew the story of the noble Genoese merchant Marco Antonio Falconi, who had been attacked by pirates of the coast of Valencia, and, having seen his daughter captured, gave himself up as a prisoner and slave.[68] This selfless conduct astonished his captors, who wondered why "he would of his own accord come into slavery, which makes the most confident to tremble." Falconi, claiming to be a prisoner already in his affection for his daughter, offered to pay ransom for both; "I will pay if I can, if not, the satisfaction of having done what I ought for my daughter, will make me the more easily support the difficulties and inconveniences of slavery." His captor, D'Aranda's owner, set the ransom at the immense sum of six thousand pieces of eight, which Falconi with alacrity agreed to pay. In the pirate's galley was another Genoese slave, who volunteered the information that Falconi was so rich he could easily afford to pay four times that amount. But the pirate said, in Italian, "my word is my word," and stuck to the original sum.

These final words on the language of slavery, where tragedy becomes a bit farcical, remind us that slavery was a species of kidnapping. Most of the time there was no chance of ransom by family and friends, but just a sale in a foreign market. The experiences of Italian slaves in North Africa, the closest that some Italians would get to knowing what had been inflicted on slaves in Italy for six centuries, remind us that the largely hidden conditions of this slavery, sometimes hinted at in conventional language, must be re-created by the words we have, no matter how deceitful or ironic they may be.

LITERARY WORDS ABOUT SLAVES

The study of the language of Italian slavery must include all the words free people wrote about slaves. Of course the notary drawing up a sale contract involving a slave was engaged in an enterprise similar to what Carlo

67. D'Aranda, *The History of Algiers and it's Slavery with Many Remarkable Particulars of Africk* (London, 1666), pp. 159–62, for this and what follows; quotation from p. 161.

68. Ibid., pp. 165–68.

Goldoni was doing when he cast some slaves in a comedy set in Persia: they were both free people writing about slaves. But we accept (and hope) that there is something different between works of the imagination and legal contracts. Whether or not the adjective "literary" captures these differences, there is a huge body of writing that mentions slavery in passing, and a surprisingly large amount of material in which slaves are important to the argument or story being told. These writings were *about* slaves; I have as yet found no medieval or early modern slaves or ex-slaves who themselves contributed to Italian literature.

It must be stressed at the onset that this survey is highly selective; a massive study would not begin to do justice to the complex roles slaves play in the last seven centuries of Italian poetry, prose, plays, fairy tales, sermons, moral tracts, journalism, and all the other genres we might consider here. There is, for example, a poem in which the author makes fun of how slaves mangle Tuscan, a congenial theme for poets.[69] There are also a few signs that slaves got away with some clever insults in their apparent slips of the tongue. I found troves of material almost everywhere I looked, once I began to ask the right questions. Besides writing about their own slavery, Italian authors were increasingly aware of both the Roman past and the global varieties of slavery, so there is, in the literary sources alone, an impossibly large number of sources to consider. In these circumstances selection is necessary; some prominent authors need to be explored no matter how little they offer on the subject, while some relatively neglected writers provide an abundance of material. Even more material becomes available as we approach modern times. For example, the Italians witnessed and may have even practiced slavery in their new African colonies. An immense amount of new writing on slavery appeared in the late nineteenth and early twentieth centuries, and this writing treated contemporary problems as well as asked new questions about the past.

The principles of selection here must reflect how reading and education have affected the ways subsequent Italians studied or ignored the existence of slavery. Whatever the medieval big three, Dante, Petrarch, and Boccaccio, had to say about slavery, it is worth considering both as a window to illuminate the limited Florentine experience of slavery, and more importantly, as part of the cultural heritage later Italians used to form their own

69. Considered in a short article by Mario Ferrara, "Linguaggio di schiave del quattrocento," *Studi di filologia italiana* 8 (1950): 320–28. The slave is named Marta, probably a Tartar, and she appears in a poem by Alessandro Braccesi (1445–1503)—considered a Florentine poet by Ferrara, but his name is Genoese, as may be his experience with Tartar pronunciation.

ideas. Later writers, like Matteo Bandello and Giambattista Basile, supply a useful view of slavery in its last major phase in the sixteenth and seventeenth centuries. Curiously, in the supposed afterlife of slavery from the eighteenth century forward—or the end of it which seems always just around the corner—there is more and more talk about slavery and liberty. And in the twentieth century slavery in the colonies, in the German camps, and elsewhere has prompted continuous reflection on the present and the past.

With all this material threatening to overwhelm and baffle synthesis, the best path is to provide enough examples to illustrate the main arguments in this section. First, slavery remained a vivid issue in the Italian consciousness, through the periods when there was a fair amount of slavery in Italy down to when there was hardly any. Second, the language of Italian slavery never existed in a vacuum, and especially in the literary sources we see a growing awareness of the rest of the world. For example, what the Italian missionaries saw in the Congo in the seventeenth century and then published in Italy reflects the broader context in which contemporary Italians understood slavery. Third, this long view of Italian history answers the paradoxical modern question: Why is there not slavery? And the answer partly is: because there is a broad spectrum of exploitation. When one form of exploitation wanes, another style of forced labor may replace it. As Dennis Romano has already suggested, complex relations existed between servants and slaves in the periods where they sometimes worked side by side, but it becomes even more complex when the slaves virtually disappeared and yet servants felt as though they were slaves, or masters treated them as if they were.[70] The status of some domestics in the early modern period or Sicilian peasants in the eighteenth century approaches slavery or accomplishes the same purpose. Also, there is not slavery because some Italians began to speak against it, or else how could Zamboni have told us that it had become by the ottocento a shameful thing? Examining slavery over time shows how some authors bracketed this extreme form of exploitation with other forms, and these connections, themselves choices, are signs of the enduring power of slavery's language.

We can begin with a remarkable piece of history by Jacopo da Varagine, a well educated Dominican friar, prolific writer, and archbishop of Genoa from 1292 to 1297. Jacopo wrote a work in Latin that was partly a history of Genoa, its church, and its bishops from ancient times to his own day. He was also one of the parents of social history because he devoted a section of

70. Dennis Romano, *Housecraft and Statecraft: Domestic Service in Renaissance Venice, 1400–1600* (Baltimore, 1996).

his book to domestic matters—the family and household.[71] The last part of this section concerns the relationship between the head of the household and his slaves and servants. Slaves, Jacopo says, came in four categories: (1) some were born to a slave mother; (2) other slaves were taken in war; (3) slaves can be rented for an annual fee; (4) slaves are purchased in markets. With his excellent eye for detail, Jacopo knew that slaves came in all varieties; some were filled with good sense, others were lazy and evil. Good slaves should be loved, and lazy slaves should be put to continuous labor—the standard medieval antidote to idleness, the devil's playground. To support this view Jacopo cites these remarkable lines from Ecclesiasticus 33:24–29, which by his time had become part of the broader context of Christian teaching on slavery.

> Fodder and sticks and burdens for the donkey;
> bread, and discipline, and work for the slave.
> Make your slave work, if you want rest for yourself;
> if you leave him idle, he will be looking for his liberty.
> The ox is tamed by yoke and harness,
> the bad slave by racks and tortures.
> Put him to work to keep him from being idle,
> for idleness is a great teacher of mischief.
> Set him to work, for that is what he is for,
> and if he disobeys you, load him with fetters.[72]

These biblical injunctions constitute a philosophy of slavery which Jacopo ratifies but then immediately softens by pointing out five ways in which masters and slaves are equal, an amazing gloss on this text and a disconcerting lesson to a slaveholding city like Genoa.[73] First, slaves and free people were alike born from the earth and first appear naked and crying. Second, slaves and free people possess the same world, air, and earth. Third, slaves and free people all rot and are reduced to ashes. Jacopo reinforces this point with an apt quotation from St. Cyprian, who reminded slaves and masters that they share the same destiny, death, and by the same

71. *Iacopo da Varagine e la sua cronaca di Genova*, ed. Giovanni Monleone, 3 vols. (Rome, 1941). The section discussed here is in 3:212–15. There is a new Latin text and Italian translation in *Iacopo da Varagine, Cronaca della città di Genova dalle origini al 1297*, ed. Stefania Bertini Guidetti (Genoa, 1995).

72. *The New English Bible with the Apocrypha* (New York, 1971), p. 164 in Apocrypha section.

73. G. Monleone, *Iacopo da Varagine*, pp. 213–14ff. where the archbishop relies on the Book of Wisdom and St. Cyprian of Carthage.

laws enter and leave the world. Fourth, slaves and free people have the same God, though Jacopo does not pursue this point to the troubling conclusion reached by St. Gregory of Nyssa, that they were both made in God's image, and that it is probably morally wrong to own anything made in the likeness and image of God.[74] Nor does he note the point in Isaiah 40:6 that all flesh is grass, another subtle claim for equality. In his fifth point Jacopo admits that slaves and free people both experience the same Last Judgment. These five claims to equality do not make an argument that slavery is wrong, and Jacopo does not say that it is. Even though the announced subject of this chapter is servants and slaves, Jacopo does not write one word on servants, ubiquitous enough in Italian cities. Jacopo walks a fine line; he makes no criticisms of slave owners, but he is strongly arguing for a common humanity between masters and slaves.

In the work of literature probably best known to future generations of Italians, Dante mentions slaves only once. In *Purgatorio* 20, when searching for a simile to describe the way Charles II of Naples haggled over his daughter's marriage, Dante thought of pirates bargaining over the prices of slave girls.[75] This is just an ordinary thing—what pirates do—but in Dante's time there were hardly any slaves in Florence, so slavery was not really within his mental horizon. Nor does Boccaccio have much to say about slavery. Having lived for a while in Naples, he put a few slave women in a story set in Palermo.[76] These slaves give a touch of plausibility to domestic life in the city, where a lady might have four slaves.

Petrarch has a lot more to say about *servi*, but his evidence is complex. Picking up on epistolary conventions dear to his ancient models, Petrarch pointed out how people suffered from injuries and outrages by slaves, whom he conflated with his "servants," his bitterest enemies—plotters, assassins, and domestic thieves.[77] The old Latin proverb, "totidem hostes esse quot servos," "so many slaves, just as many enemies" meant a lot to Petrarch, who claimed never to have seen a good servant. All these comments conform to classical models wherein the wealthy, leisured classes complain about the help, for them principally slaves. For Petrarch, who never owned a slave, the elegant Latin of his letters, as well as his ambition to emulate the ancients in everything, dictated that he use the word for slaves, *servi*, to describe his free servants. His readers of course knew the difference, but for

74. Peter Garnsey, *Ideas of Slavery from Aristotle to Augustine* (Cambridge, 1996), pp. 80–83.

75. Line 81: "come fanno i corsar de l'altre schiave."

76. *Decameron* 8.10.

77. The two classic notices are in Petrarch's letters, 10.3.30–35 and 20.12.6–10.

Petrarch, classical models like Cicero's or Seneca's comments on his slaves were the right parallel for the difficulties he experienced with his servants. This strengthens the argument that only a fine line separated slaves and servants in trecento Italy and highlights that by then Petrarch had a diachronic view of slavery.

The possibility remains that slavery declined (eventually) precisely because there were enough servants (and slaves were too dear). But collectively Dante, Petrarch, and Boccaccio have only a little to say about slavery, and we must go forward in time to find writers who have more.

Matteo Bandello (1485–1561) was an interesting and well-educated Dominican friar from Castelnuovo Scrivia near Alessandria between Genoa and Milan. Bandello became a court writer and for years enjoyed the patronage of Cesare Fregoso, a Genoese exile. Bandello is best known for his collection of stories, the *Novelle*. These stories, which Bandello dedicated to various people he wanted to flatter, provide insight on the language Italians used to describe slavery, and in this case the words are put into a slave's mouth. Story 21 from part three of the collection took place on Majorca not long before, when Rinieri Ervizzano owned some slaves, one of whom, a Moor, was tired of being beaten and was looking for revenge.[78] This nameless slave locked up the owner's wife and three children in a tower, raped and tortured the wife, and tormented the owner by destroying his family before his eyes. The slave required his master to cut off his own nose to get his children back, and then reneged on the deal after his owner disfigured himself in a fruitless effort to save his family. The slave taunted Rinieri by saying that this is what he deserved for his beatings and cruelty toward his slaves. The slave, finally able to be happy in his vengeance, then jumped from the tower and killed himself. Bandello declared that the lesson here was not to be served by slaves like this because they were seldom faithful, they were full of subversion, sex-crazed like goats, and of course cruel. This story, safely set on distant Majorca, was every slave owner's nightmare.

In his dedicatory letter, Bandello wrote that the point of the story was discipline, which required beating children, servants, and of course slaves. Though the story begins with a slave responding to excessive punishment, Bandello has no sympathy with slaves and seems to argue that even more beating might have prevented this tragedy. Bandello believed that the worst slaves were Moors from North Africa. He had a story from Milan to prove it, about a Moor belonging to Monsignore di Negri, abbot of San Simpliciano. After having been slapped around by his master, the slave waited till

78. *Tutte le opere di Matteo di Bandello*, ed. Francesco Flora, vol. 2 (Verona, 1943), pp. 374–78.

night and cut the master's throat. What astonishes Bandello about this case is that the slave had been with this master for more than thirty years and still had not learned loyalty. When brought to the old town hall of Milan for justice, the slave laughingly and rudely said, "Quarter me and do to me the worst you know, for if I have received a slap, I am fully avenged for it."[79] These taunting words evoked another slave owner's nightmare: the slave with nothing to lose, the slave who cut one's throat for the one slap too many. Bandello wrote that the Genoese understood all this, for when they had male or female slaves who deserved to be punished, they sold them or sent them away to the salt mines on Iviza in the Balearics, and this was what led him to tell the Maiorcan story. Two other things are worth noting about this story. Bandello correctly stated that Giovanni Pontano told this story in a work on obedience, and that the slave owners in Naples knew how to keep slaves in line.

This story's language highlights fear of Moors, concern about slaves who can instantly turn violent, and advice on how to instill obedience in slaves. Loyalty was, as Bandello and Petrarch believed, hard to find, but most owners were willing to settle for the outward forms of obedience which at least guaranteed their personal safety. The frame of Bandello's story allowed him to make an astute comment about slaveholding in Genoa, where he lived for a while. He also gives us a rare glimpse of slavery in Milan. But his story concerns vengeance, and the fact that a slave who is prepared to die for it may be able to obtain it. How were masters to give slaves a reason to go on living, besides the hope of killing their owners? Well, there is no sign of manumission in any of this literature, even though the legal evidence shows that it did occur. A hope for eventual freedom is not part of the literary slave's universe. Instead, Bandello suggests that more pain might do the trick, even though he puts words in a laughing slave's mouth, words that dare the Milanese authorities to quarter him. If fear of this punishment, and whatever the worst they could do, were not enough to keep a slave from murder, then just how much could pain accomplish? Maybe, Bandello seems to suggest, the Genoese were right to pass on their problem slaves to other owners, to work them to death in the mines.

Bandello has another story about two faithful slaves belonging to the sultan of Ormo, an alleged island off the coast of Ethiopia. This story takes place somewhere in the Muslim East, where male slaves might become rich and powerful—as in the Ottoman Empire, safely distant from Italy. The details of the story are not relevant here, except that the slaves came from the

79. Ibid., p. 373: "Squartatemi e fatemi peggio che sapete, che se io ho avuto uno schiaffo, io me ne sono altamente vendicato."

fabled realm of Prester John, by the sixteenth century believed to be located somewhere in sub-Saharan Africa. These slaves, Maometto and Caim (presumably Muslim), demonstrated to their owner "a faithful and loving servitude" and in fact turned out to be more loyal than the sultan's treacherous oldest son.[80] Eventually the two slaves, who refuse separate orders to kill one another in exchange for even more riches, then eliminate the usurper (the sultan's son) and restore the kingdom. So it was possible for slaves to be proverbially loyal, but in a constructed oriental rather than in an Italian setting.

Giambattista Basile (ca.1575–1632) collected Italian folk tales in Neapolitan dialect, which were published after his death as *Lo cunto de li cunti* (The Tale of Tales), and are better known as *Il pentamerone*. These tales did not have much influence in Italy outside the Mezzogiorno until they were translated into Italian and published by Benedetto Croce in 1925. They are one of the first great collections of folk tales in any Italian dialect and earn Basile the reputation of being the Grimm of the South. Basile's occasion for this collection is a frame story that sets the stage for telling the folk tales, and a slave is one of the main characters, but she remains nameless.[81] A princess named Zoza laughs at the wrong old woman, who curses her by saying that the only husband she will ever find is Taddeo, a prince himself cursed with a death-like sleep. He can only be awakened by a woman who can fill a vase hanging over his tomb with tears in three days. He will then reward his savior with his love. After many interesting adventures Zoza reaches the tomb, starts crying, and collects her tears in the vase. Watching all this is a certain cricket-legged slave (*gambi di grillo*) who knows all about Taddeo and his curse, and who plans, at the last minute when the vase is almost filled and Zoza is asleep, to complete the task and capture the prince's love. The slave's plan works, and Taddeo arises from his tomb, "grabs the mass of black flesh" (*massa di carne nera*), and marries the slave. Zoza sees how she has been cheated and says "that two black things have placed her on the naked earth (i.e., left her with nothing), sleep and a slave."[82]

Meanwhile, the cricket-legged slave has become pregnant and quite demanding, and Taddeo is at his wits' end to keep her satisfied. With every new request, she threatens in a crude way "to punch herself in the belly and

80. Ibid., p. 604: "una fedele ed amorevole servitù."

81. Giambattista Basile, *Il pentamerone*, ed. and trans. Benedetto Croce (Bari, 1957), pp. 3–12.

82. Ibid., p. 8: "che due cose nere l'avevano posta sulla nuda terra, il sonno e una schiava."

crush [the fetus she calls] Giorgetiello" if he does not comply with her wishes.[83] Her final demand is to be amused by stories, so Taddeo summons ten women to tell her tales, and hence this collection. The slave, called black, barbarous, hideous, ugly, and other things, is herself becoming the object of Zoza's own plot, but we may leave the story here.

This is an incredibly revealing way to construct an occasion for a collection of stories. The frame story, where the nameless black slave ensnares the handsome prince, perpetuates stereotypes about blacks, and shows just how durable these images of bad black things had now become in parts of Italian culture. Again the slave is a domestic enemy: plotting, devious, and evil—willing to harm a baby in the womb in order to gratify her whims. What a trick to play on a prince, to saddle him with this incongruous match. Zoza, temporarily undone by two black things, constructs an image of sleep and a slave—oblivion and nightmare—that make plots when the victim is totally vulnerable. This is exactly how domestic slavery threatened masters.

In another story, Basile describes how the innocent Lisa, whose real identity was unknown, had been turned into a slave by her evil aunt, herself described as "all bitter like a slave."[84] To become a slave meant this: the baronessa cut Lisa's hair and then beat her with the tresses, dressed her in a tattered gown, and beat her about the head every day, leaving eggplants under the eyes, marks in her face, and her mouth looking as though she had eaten a raw pigeon—bloody. Lisa's true identity was eventually revealed, and this abuse ended. Perhaps inadvertently, Basile gives us a vivid impression of what it was like to be a mistreated slave, down to the swollen purple bruises under Lisa's eyes. This Cinderella-like tale is the occasion for describing how debased a slave might become. The baronessa, no heroine, supplies a final clue about the slave's status. When Lisa's uncle, not knowing her real identity, makes a kind gesture toward her, the aunt objects, saying that this big-lipped slave (*schiava musuta*) did not deserve to be treated like everyone else; it was like everyone pissing in the same pot.[85]

The same issues of color and slavery interested Matteo Ricci (1552–1610), the Jesuit missionary from Macerata who was active in China from 1583 until his death.[86] Ricci considered the Chinese to be whites, except for

---

83. Ibid., p. 9: for example, "mi pugni a ventre dare e Giorgetiello acciaccare."

84. Ibid., pp. 207–12: "La schiavotta"—"tutta fiele come schiava."

85. Ibid., p. 210.

86. For a recent, insightful account of Ricci, see Lionel Jensen, *Manufacturing Confucianism: Chinese Traditions and Universal Civilization* (Durham, N.C., 1997), esp. pp. 33–146.

those in the south, who, living near the torrid zone, had become dark (*fosco*).[87] Ricci may have been thinking of his native Italy, with darker people in the south. Unlike Italy, China was a "kingdom filled with slaves, not taken in warfare from other kingdoms, but from its own, indigenous people."[88] This contrast may have struck Ricci because he would have known that what slaves there were in Italy came exclusively from other countries, except for the few children of slaves. In China people sold themselves or their children into slavery for a variety of reasons. What struck Ricci was the sale of children by parents unable to support them—sold for the price of a pig or a broken-down horse. Because China generated its own slaves, it also supplied other kingdoms with slaves, but by these means God brought many of the slaves to Christianity, since the Spanish and other Christian peoples were among the purchasers. Ricci concludes that "the population surplus, poverty, and the burden of raising the children, and the very liberty which these slaves [presumably as converts] have among them [the Christians] easily excuse their sale."[89] Since Ricci goes on to discuss the Chinese practice of infanticide, he clearly believed he had good reasons for thinking that sale into slavery was a preferable outcome for these unwanted children.

The Capuchin priest Giovanni Antonio Cavazzi spent some time as a missionary in central Africa, and an account of his experiences was published in Bologna in 1687. Even as slavery was waning in Italy, news of slavery elsewhere came home, and Italians observed and participated in foreign slave systems. One of Father Cavazzi's tasks was to teach slave owners the obligation of putting their slaves to catechism so that they could be baptized and become good Christians before embarking for America.[90] Cavazzi thought that the number of slaves in Congo was about equal to the number of free people, which made the kingdom from his perspective an unusual society.[91] The slaves belonging to the Portuguese lived in fear of being sold

87. *Fonte Ricciane*, ed. Pasquale D'Elia, vol. 1 (Rome, 1942), para. 136.

88. Ibid., para. 157, for this and what follows: "questo regno pieno di schiavi, non presi in guerra di altri regni, ma de' suoi proprij naturali."

89. Ibid.: "Ma il vendere figliuoli facilmente scusa la multitudine della gente, povertà e travaglio de allevarli, e la molta libertà che tra loro hanno questi schiavi."

90. G. A. Cavazzi, *Istorica descrizione de' tre regni Congo, Matamba, et Angola* (Bologna, 1687), p. 166.

91. Ibid., pp. 163–65, for this and what follows. John K. Thornton, *The Kongolese St. Anthony: Dona Beatriz Kimpa Vita and the Antonian Movement, 1684–1706* (Cambridge, 1998) recounts the story of how an African woman became inhabited by the spirit of Saint Anthony of Padua and began to explain to the Italian Capuchin monks in Kongo how they misrepresented the true African origins of the Holy Family and Saint Francis.

off and taken to New Spain. Slaves suffered from so much terror that some ran off into the forests, and others killed themselves. According to Cavazzi, the slaves believed that they would be killed, and their bodies transformed into oil and charcoal, although Europeans often tried to explain exactly where oil and charcoal came from. Cavazzi saw that in traditional African slavery the children of slaves remained quasi-free and often lived outside the households to which they belonged, though bearing the marks of their owners. Slaves of the hearth worked in perpetual servitude in the household. Only those slaves taken in war really risked being sold to the Portuguese. So the slaves belonging to Africans seemed to Cavazzi to be pertinacious, rebellious, lazy, and badly treated, but there was a big difference between this local slavery and the genuine terror the Portuguese inspired. These Italian Capuchins in Africa, perhaps as good-hearted as the friar Cristoforo whom Alessandro Manzoni portrayed as the enemy of tyranny in his *I promessi sposi*, gave the Italian reading public a vivid portrait of slavery in the wider world. In this way slavery still remained a lively image in Italian minds even while slaves in Italy were becoming rare.

The Milanese nobleman Cesare Beccaria (1738–1792) is best known for his short book *On Crimes and Punishments*, first published in 1764. He was a leading figure in the Italian Enlightenment who served the Austrian government and wrote a great deal about the economy. He is deservedly famous for his arguments against torture and capital punishment, and his support for speedy justice with penalties proportionate to the crimes. These "enlightened" attitudes toward justice won Beccaria accolades across Europe, but there was another side to his humanity. For example, he thought that theft without violence should be punished only by fines, but of course the poor committed many of these crimes. For them, Beccaria recommended "the only type of slavery that can be called just, that slavery of one's labor and person, for a time, for society."[92] Imprisonment was temporary slavery and Beccaria had no problem with that. He was even more explicit when he considered perpetual slavery (*la schiavitú perpetua*) as the reasonable alternative to torture or execution. Slavery was preferable to torture because it induced as much fear but was less violent.[93] Slavery was a better deterrent than execution to capital crimes because slavery was just the beginning of punishment: it comprised "the entire sum of the unhappy moments" of a lifetime, unlike execution, which was the unhappiness of a sin-

92. Cesare Beccaria, *Dei delitti e delle pene*, ed. Franco Venturi (Turin, 1965), p. 52: "quell'unica sorte di schiavitú che si possa chiamar giusta, cioè la schiavitú per un tempo delle opere e della persona alla comune società."

93. Ibid., p. 60.

gle moment.[94] Thus, one of his best arguments against capital punishment *required* the existence of penal slavery. To Beccaria, transporting criminals far away was useless slavery, because penal servitude should be local to benefit society.[95] Though Beccaria does not mention the convict galleys of the Venetian and Genoese republics, he intends that free people should be able to see the hard life of those condemned to a life of slavery in the galleys in order to deter them from crime, and that they should also see how this slavery benefits society because then they will favor this harsh punishment over executions. The Italian states had no overseas colonies left, so it was not practical anyway to transport criminals, as the English would soon do to distant Australia. Just enough slavery remained in Italy, and the memory of its language endured, so that Beccaria could envision it as the reasonable alternative to execution. Beccaria believed that taking away someone's legal personality and turning that person into a slave was better—more moral and efficient—than taking his or her life. It was still possible, we note, to separate a person's work from his or her body by turning the body into a thing and not viewing it as a creature with rights.

The playwright Vittorio Alfieri (1749–1803) wrote elegant tragedies on classical themes—the one on Brutus was dedicated to George Washington—and he is also well known for an engaging autobiography. Born in Asti, Alfieri had a complex relationship with the kingdom of Sardinia (Piedmont), which he saw as a repressive state, and he called himself a friend of liberty. By 1784 he had decided to leave the kingdom for good. Once he got out and breathed the fresh air of liberty, he still felt more like an ex-slave than a free man. Alfieri remembered well the remark Pompey supposedly made when he fled to Egypt: "He who enters the house of a tyrant becomes a slave if he was not one already."[96] Even Alfieri, a rich nobleman who had seen much of Europe, could still in the right circumstances think of himself as a slave. Alfieri was not a royalist, but he did detest the republicanism of the French Revolution, and in particular he hated French rule in Italy, which he saw as slavery.[97] For these views he became a hero to Italian patriots, and his works were viewed, rightly or wrongly, as nationalistic and anti-French. Alfieri was basically nonpolitical, and as an author he was more angry about pirated French editions of his plays than anything else. He compared these publishers to slaves who, unable to whiten themselves (*imbiancare sé stessi*) were content to dirty or blacken others (*sporciare gli al-*

94. Ibid., pp. 64–65.
95. Ibid., p. 72.
96. Vittorio Alfieri, *Vita*, ed. Giampaolo Dossena (Turin, 1967), p. 224.
97. Ibid., p. 261.

tri). In the context of the language of Italian slavery, these are rich comments. With respect to the Sardinian monarchy in Turin, Alfieri could think of himself as a slave, and there was no shame in that, since the state deprived him of liberty. But these other slaves, French publishers, evoked the color line, and Alfieri did not learn this from his classical models. Down in Genoa, the first place outside Piedmont Alfieri visited, there were in his youth some North African slaves in the state arsenal, who were dark, but not capable of being whitened. To be blackened was still to be dirtied. The Italians knew the racial slavery of the Americas from books, but some of their own language still remained—enough to let them make sense of Alfieri's image of slaves whitening themselves by dirtying others.

The effect of the French Revolution on Italian consciousness is a vast subject that cannot be addressed here. Slavery provides a unique perspective on these other issues, and also provides a wonderful opportunity to look at the question of how the language of liberty intersected (or did not) with the older discourse of slavery. Let us begin with the image of light, so often tritely associated with liberty, or by its absence with slavery. Words about liberty, equality, and fraternity made up waves of light (photons, particles) that swept across the Italian states. The Convention had abolished slavery in the French colonies in 1794 because slavery was incompatible with liberty. In Italy, as we have seen, there was an older language about slavery, color, the Muslim world, and all the rest, and this wave was also present. For a time in the 1790s these waves were intersecting in the same place, but to what effect? In the physical world waves of light intersect all the time before our eyes without apparently affecting what we see before us, just as what we see does not distort what others in the same field of vision are viewing. And so the light of liberty, could pass through the light of slavery, and not be changed, and not change slavery. This effect is to be seen in people like Thomas Jefferson, and in "enlightened" countries, like the new republic in America, where everyone knew that slavery endured. This image of light can help us to avoid facile condemnations of past people or societies that did not see things as we do, and also remind us that posterity, when perspectives change, will see appalling gaps in our own perceptions. In France there was no slavery to abolish, but in parts of Italy an increasingly anomalous slavery endured. Would it remain impervious to the light of liberty (as in America) or might the various waves somehow collide and alter both the meaning of liberty and the fact of slavery? This is the problem the Genoese faced.

Genoa was by 1797 a historical relic, an aristocratic republic in which the vast majority of citizens had no voice. A Jacobin revolt broke out on 22 May, and one group of rebels, in addition to freeing debtors in the Malapaga prison, then broke into the Arsenal and freed the convicts and slaves chained to the oars of the galleys moored there. Invited to join the revolt, some of the released did so, while others wisely disappeared into the crowd, not wanting to be recaptured.[98] After a series of disorders, the old republic, under the vigilant eye of Napoleon in Paris, voted itself out of existence and established a French-style Convention on 14 June.[99] A month later, the new government planned a big festival for 14 July to celebrate the anniversary of the taking of the Bastille, and the restored liberty of the new Ligurian Republic. The best account of this day comes from the journal *Avvisi di Genova*, no. 27, published on Wednesday, 19 July 1797.[100]

In the Piazza Acquaverde, outside the old walls of Genoa, there was a tree and an altar dedicated to liberty. A parade advanced from the center of the city to this place. The centerpiece of the procession was the Carriage of Liberty, which was followed by sixty-eight chained North African slaves. The reporter described their arrival at the altar as "the most tender moment that can be imagined." The chains were broken, and the people burst into tears as they saw the slaves regain their freedom. Before the Tree of Liberty, the President of the Republic, Giacomo Brignole, gave the slaves caps of liberty and embraced them in a sign of brotherhood. He told them that they were free from slavery and invited them to return to their countries and tell whomever they met about the humanity and generosity of the Ligurian people. All this showed the slaves how the unhappy Genoese who

98. The best narrative account of all this is Antonino Ronco, *Storia della Repubblica Ligure 1797–1799* (Genoa, 1988), pp. 63–66.

99. Ibid., pp. 79–141 for this and what follows.

100. Biblioteca Universitaria di Genova, *Avvisi di Genova*. The account follows a description of the festivities around the Tree of Liberty, where everyone took an oath to defend the republic. I transcribe the account in full because it is hard to find. "Stavano a piedi dell'Ara i Barbareschi, che incatenati fino a quel punto seguitato avevano il Carro della Libertà. Fu questo un momento de' più teneri, chi si possano immaginare. Allo sciogliersi delle loro catene il Popolo tutto accompagno colle lacrime il pianto di quegli fino a quell'istante infelici individui, che ben si può credere quali segni manifestassero di contentezza per la riacquistata libertà. Furono esse sospese all'Albero della Libertà, ed intanto il Presidente ponendo loro sul capo un berretto a colori della Nazione gli accolse ad uno ad uno fra le braccia in segno di fratellanza. Erano 68. Sciolti in tal guisa dalla schiavitù, andate disse loro, liberi ai vostri paesi, e ridite all incontrarvi che faranno i vostri patrioti, ridite loro qual sia l'umanità, e la generosità del Popolo Ligure, ed insegnate ad essi ad usarne altrettanta verso di que' disgraziati nostri Concittadini, che gemono fra voi nelle pesante catene della schiavitù. La funzione non potè essere nè più tenera, nè più adattata a spiegare il grande oggetto del giorno."

were languishing as slaves in North Africa should be treated. Whatever practical thoughts of exchanging slaves may have been on official minds, the public breaking of chains and unilateral freeing of slaves marked the apparent end of slavery in Genoa.

The correspondent of the *Gazzetta nazionale genovese* on 15 July found himself unable to adequately describe such a sublime subject as what had occurred in the Piazza della Libertà. The author of the article in the *Giornale degli amici del popolo* of 17 July offered a brief account.[101] He twice explicitly referred to the slaves as Africans. What happened to these ex-slaves, and how the Genoese addressed the issue of liberty in the various constitutions of their short-lived republic, we will consider below when addressing the context of the law. The emphasis on language and on outward signs like chained slaves following a carriage of liberty reveals that in July of 1797 the continued existence of slavery was seen by enough people as incompatible with liberty to bring about the end of the slavery of African men in the galleys. And they ended it in an exceptionally public and vivid way. In this case, the light from France did change the way the Genoese saw their institutions. The captain who took the ex-slaves back to North Africa reported that the Genoese had not expected any payment in return, and they did not get anything. The captain revealed that in November 1797, 105 Genoese remained slaves in Algiers, and thirty-five in Tunis.[102]

The Romantic poet and essayist Giacomo Leopardi (1798–1837), from Recanati in the Marches, passed his early years in a family-imposed isolation that left him only with his books as a way to participate in the world of learning. The fruits of this solitary and depressed study are contained in his *Zibaldone*, the thousands of pages of notes published many years after his death. Racked by ill health and a loveless fixation on love, Leopardi confided his deepest thoughts to his notebooks and also worked out his ideas for poems. Penned up in a dreary palace in the middle of nowhere, Leopardi spent a few days in April 1821 worrying about the connection between slavery and liberty. Others (he must mean Aristotle) had concluded that "the true and perfect liberty of a people cannot maintain itself or exist without the practice of internal slavery."[103] Leopardi thought this to be false, but for complex reasons; he believed that the abolition of slavery stems from the abolition of liberty. In other words, he too believed that slavery was necessary for a free people. Despite contemporary debates in

101. I found both these periodicals in the Biblioteca Universitaria di Genova.

102. F. Zamboni, *Gli Ezzelini*, pp. clix-clx, contains the notice of this report.

103. *Tutti le opere di Giacomo Leopardi*, vol. 1, *Zibaldone di pensieri*, ed. Francesco Flora (Milan, 1953), pp. 609–17, for this and what follows.

England, France, and America on this issue, Leopardi drew his argument from classical sources. He accepted, as most now did, that in a state of nature people were born free and equal, but in society things were different. For Leopardi, liberty and equality (two of the watchwords of the French Revolution and soon to become the slogan of Mazzini's Young Italy) were not naturally compatible since genuine liberty for the best people required that society be hierarchical and that inferiors serve their betters. Slaves were outside the law and did not share in the advantages of property, equality, and liberty; they were outside the nation, like another race (*razza*), subordinated and subaltern to the free and equal race. The jobs that degraded free people and diminished their liberty required slaves to perform them. Roman and Greek history confirmed all this. The necessity or use of slavery for a free people was not based on their liberty, but on their equality; slaves fulfilled the base functions so that free people would be equal in their access to leisure for the higher things. Leopardi concluded with a remarkable observation about the caste system in India, which he believed existed without slavery precisely because prescribed inequality got the hard jobs done and preserved the liberty and equality of the upper ranks. Likewise in China, where sons followed their fathers' professions, there was liberty (for some) but not equality.

In his bookish isolation from the world, and thanks to his noble background which saved him from physical work, Leopardi still knew that his style of life, his liberty, depended on social inequality and the hard work of others, be they Italian peasants in the Marches or the generic slaves he liked to view as a kind of second race of humanity. As an aristocrat, he was no hypocrite about this; without citing Aristotle by name, he knew well that the good life for some meant misery for others. In his terms, liberty needed inequality. It was not on account of these beliefs that Leopardi became identified as the poet favoring the rise of the Italian nation. Leopardi used the Italian language to create a style of poetry so astonishingly fresh that nothing he privately thought about hierarchy and subordination hurt his reputation. The idea of slavery, so embedded in Italy's past, taught him permanent lessons about human equality—that for the best to be equals (and have the time for poetry) others had to do the dirty work. And they would not do it selflessly, just to please their betters.

Giuseppe Mazzini (1805–1872), Italian patriot and ardent republican, theorist of the Risorgimento, passed most of his life as an exile. After his youth Mazzini seldom saw his native Genoa. Mazzini's basic humanity, his strong belief in liberty and equality, his insistence that Italy cease being a mere geographic expression, and educate and employ its people—all these characteristics, plus his sincerity and modesty, make him an attractive thinker and person.[104] Perhaps because he was born in Genoa just eight years after the city sent its last North African slaves home, but also because he was steeped in Italian language and culture, slavery comes up in almost everything he wrote. He could not stop thinking about liberty and equality. His major political works, from his first publication in 1829 to one of the last in 1871, discuss "slavery" (*schiavitù*) in revealing ways. In his earliest published essay, on Italian literature, when beginning a list of those writers who were ridiculed as dreamers but were really just in advance of their times, he singled out for praise those who opposed the slave trade and slavery.[105] Mazzini remained an abolitionist for the rest of his life. Slavery served in Mazzini's writings as a convenient leitmotif for evoking the experiences of Italians living under foreign rule.

Mazzini went beyond a conventional approach to slavery in an address to Italian workers published in 1840. Italians working for wages were like slaves, in the sense that the choice between hunger and a salary was no choice at all.[106] Italian workers were even worse off than some of their fellow laborers in the rest of Europe because their country itself was also enslaved. In a country where so many could not read, where there were no legal associations or educational institutions for the workers, even an official catechism in Milan encouraged people to behave toward their sovereign (the Austrian emperor) like faithful slaves kowtowing to their owners.[107] To which Mazzini replied, "Italian workers, our brothers! We are not slaves nor do we want to be slaves." The employers/masters regarded everyone else through the distorted fantasy that they, the masters, came from a different race (*razza*), born to command, while the millions of others were destined from birth or capture to serve. Mazzini concluded from slavery that there should be no masters or slaves, but that people should be brothers (and sisters) valuing liberty, equality, and humanity.

A brief work, *A Prayer for the Plantation Owners*, that Mazzini wrote in 1846 shows how complex the language of slavery had become after texts and translations had broken down the barriers between languages. Mazzini wrote, in English, to a correspondent on 26 October that he had found that "to write one or two pages on abolitionism is just the same to me as to have to prove that the Sun gives light and warmth."[108] His English was good

104. See Dennis Mack Smith, *Mazzini* (New Haven, Conn., 1994).

105. *Scritti politici dell'Ottocento*, vol. 1, ed. Franco della Peruta (Milan, 1969); here *D'una letteratura europea* (1829), p. 271.

106. Ibid., p. 469.

107. Ibid., pp. 471–72, for this and what follows.

108. *Scritti editi e inediti di Giuseppe Mazzini*, vol. 30 (Imola, 1919), p. 249.

enough to write clear letters, but what at last came into his mind was a prayer, which he had to write in French to send to America to be published in English in a Boston periodical. (He must have regarded French as the common language with his abolitionist friends there.) Also in October, he wrote a letter in Italian to his mother back in Genoa telling her that he had written on request two or three pages on the emancipation of the blacks.[109] He did not have the time to make her a copy now, but promised to send her one; he did not do so, however, so we have no version in Italian by his hand. To make his work more widely known, it was published in Italian in a Genoese journal in 1854, translated from the English version! So his fellow Italians read a version two removes from Mazzini's original French. What all this shows is that, for intellectuals like Mazzini, command of several languages brought to their native Italian a rich heritage of experiences. A prayer offered in French by the Italian Mazzini on behalf of the souls of American planters was soon read in Italy as a prescient condemnation of the world sketched in *La Cabanna di Zio Tomasso*.

The prayer combines Mazzini's deep spirituality and his practical grasp of politics.[110] He judges the slaveowners as sinners against God and humanity, worshiping at the idols of profit and sugarcane. His main argument is that slavery violates the unity of humanity and impedes the natural progress of history from slavery to serfdom to wage labor to unionism. The last vestiges of paganism, ironically, still survived among the planters of the American republic, and this deeply offended Mazzini. Violence formed the root of slavery. Mazzini believed it was wrong to own people made in the image of God. He used the story of Cain and Abel to show that two human races (Fr. *races*; It. *razze*) existed: the condemned race of the violent, and "our" privileged race of law. It is refreshing to see Mazzini use the concept of race as a way to distinguish the saved from the cursed—not by color or by origin but by moral judgment.

Mazzini's belief in the common humanity of all peoples was the touchstone of his thought. He does not recognize, explicitly or implicitly, that slavery ever existed in Italy. The broader context of slavery in the world allowed Mazzini to use all his languages and beliefs to reach an international audience. In one of his last works, published in 1871—again a letter to the artisan classes—Mazzini called the emancipation of the slaves (and he must have had America in mind here) a revolution of liberty, just as the end of serfdom in the Middle Ages had been a revolt of equality, and just as the lib-

109. Ibid., p. 252.
110. Ibid., pp. 285–93.

eration of the workers (presumably a revolt of humanity) would take place (he thought) in his own time.[111] Mazzini opposed the communists, nor was he really a socialist; he was a liberal reformer who believed in private property, republican government, and the rights of labor. Mazzini's highly personal and anticlerical religious views taught him that true Christianity entailed the end of slavery. He had, so he believed, witnessed this outcome in his own time.

Mazzini, with a sense of history, probably growing from his Genoese roots and long exile abroad, remained confident about the inevitability of human progress, even though he never lived to see the Italian republic, which was born only in 1946. Mazzini must have known that there had been slaves in Genoa for centuries up to 1797. Yet in his mind slavery remained a global issue. He knew enough about the rest of the world to admire both John Brown and Abraham Lincoln.[112] Italian slavery did not exist for Mazzini, even in its historical context. To rid the world of slavery would represent part of the worldwide progress toward a better society. If we could ask Mazzini our problematic question—Why is there not slavery?—he would answer: because of the emergence of the Italian working classes, both in the northern factories or the Sicilian estates. He did not simply take over an older discourse on slavery and force it to fit the contemporary realities of an industrializing economy. Mazzini did not play with words, and he knew that no one could buy Italians any more. He believed, however, that the workers had no choice but to work for wages, and this denial of liberty and equality really disturbed him to the extent that the miseries of many working Italians looked to him a lot like slavery. Without the model of slavery, what would these miseries have looked like?

Even as Mazzini was thinking about slavery and liberty, a new generation of scholars was "discovering," in the midnineteenth century, the distinctive medieval slavery of places like Venice and Genoa. The new Italian nation in the late nineteenth century, like Germany, came late to the scramble for overseas colonies. Italian designs first focused on Libya and Eritrea, the leftovers, but in the 1890s, in what came to be the colony of Somalia, the Italians witnessed pervasive slavery. A leading Italian explorer and colonialist, Antonio Cecchi, who was killed in Somalia in 1896, had owned a fifteen-year-old girl.[113] At this time a private company was exploiting the

111. *Scritti politici dell'Ottocento*, p. 837.

112. D. Mack Smith, *Mazzini*, p. 167.

113. Robert L. Hess, *Italian Colonialism in Somalia* (Chicago, 1966), p. 65. The book is an excellent English introduction to the general issues. The best and most

region and waging a halfhearted campaign against slavery. Benadir, a region of what was to become the colony of Somalia, did not yet formally belong to Italy, but this girl represented a revival of Italian slavery; she was a new Italian slave. An Italian official, Giorgio Sorrentino, came across this slave in 1897, and in his memoirs, published in 1912, he described the encounter. The person he met was Fatma, a chocolate-colored girl (a new color here, unfamiliar to the medieval contracts) of the Galla tribe.[114] He characterized her as pretty, thin, with a thick head of hair, scintillating eyes, teeth like pearls, and a sweet smile; she made an excellent impression. Sorrentino freed her on the spot(!). He decided to keep her in his service on the same terms as under Cecchi(!), but she was now free and received a salary. He printed her picture in his book. Much later on in his memoirs, when discussing the Galla, he praised them for their quasi-European features, and said they made good concubines.[115]

The Benadir Company's scandalous inability to suppress slavery and the slave trade was one of the main reasons why the Italian government officially took over Somalia in 1905. The colony's governor, Tommaso Carletti, stated in 1907 that "there are races (I am saddened to find myself in agreement with old Aristotle) that, either by innate intellectual inferiority, or because of historical development, appear destined to be servants, or at least are not capable of unconditional freedom."[116] Carletti seems a poor choice to preside over the end of slavery in Somalia. In his monograph, published in 1912, Carletti was more specific. He began his chapter on slavery with an argument on the naturalness of slavery, and, (shades of Cesare Lombroso), he pointed to ant societies as proof, even to observing that red ants reduced black ants, "that is to say the black race among ants" to slavery.[117] Everything comes together in the mind of this unattractive bureaucrat (typical of those who ended up in the colonies)—the old racism joins with the new. Carletti knew his history well enough to observe that since it had taken the European peoples thousands of years to eradicate all traces of slavery there(!), it would not be quick work to end it in Somalia, where contemporary estimates (1904) put the number of slaves in Mogadiscio at

recent Italian work on colonialism is Luigi Goglia and Fabio Grassi, *Il colonialismo italiano da Adua all'impero*, 2nd ed. (Rome, 1993).

114. Giorgio Sorrentino, *Ricordi del Benadir* (Naples, 1912), pp. 20–21.

115. Ibid., p. 405.

116. Quoted in R. Hess, *Italian Colonialism*, p. 98.

117. Tommaso Carletti, *I problemi del Benadir* (Viterbo, 1912), p. 175: "e la *formica rufescens* riduce in ischiavitù la *formica fusca*, che anche pel colore sarebbe a dire la razza negra tra le formiche."

2,095 out of a total population of 6,695, a proportion of more than one-third.[118]

These figures come from a report Luigi Robecchi-Brichetti prepared for the Antislavery Society of Italy (founded in 1888) based on his travels in Benadir in 1903. He was an abolitionist who understood that history would judge his society harshly if it allowed slavery to continue. Robecchi-Brichetti carefully documented the realities of slavery, even publishing examples of written sales contracts for slaves in Arabic from 1902—as clear evidence as anyone could demand that slavery was pervasive.[119] He wrote that for women slavery meant prostitution, and for men it meant the complete destruction of physical and mental energies.[120] Slavery morally debased people, it negated the natural and inviolable rights of the family, and it irrationally exploited the individual and his home country. Slavery also harmed the society that permitted it. Finally, slavery was a state of things that only rested on an insufficient and shameful justification—not on serious arguments, scientific or moral—but in a deplorable local tradition. Robecchi-Brichetti seems to have taken to heart everything Mazzini wrote about liberty, which he considered to be the most natural and dear of rights.[121] These comments, from a decent man, poignantly illustrate how well some Italians comprehended slavery, its language, and its context.

And so we have come full circle; Robecchi-Brichetti's letters from Benadir coincided with the first national conference of the Antislavery Society of Italy in 1903, where the participants were anxious not to fall behind their fellow Europeans in the cause. One delegate noted that the purpose of their work "was to substitute for the law of force the force of law," a subject we will take up in the next chapter.[122] By the time of its second conference took place in 1907, the society could boast that it had rescued about 2,500 people from the claws of the black slavers, mainly in Libya.[123] At its third congress in 1921 the society had broadened the scope of its interests to include

118. Luigi Robecchi-Brichetti, *Dal Benadir: Lettere illustrate alla Società Antischiavista d'Italia* (Milan, 1904), pp. 70–71.

119. Ibid., pp. 31–33.

120. Ibid., pp. 234–35, for this and what follows.

121. Ibid., p. 96.

122. My main source for what follows is the documents in files from the Archivio Segreto Vaticano, Segreteria di Stato; the quotation is from Anno 1903, Rubrica 204, *Bolletino della Società Antischiavista d'Italia* p. 8.

123. Archivio Segreto Vaticano, Segreteria di Stato, Anno 1907, Rubrica 204, telegram from Filippo Tolli, president of the society, to Pope Pius X.

the fates of indigenes in Africa and America. The preliminary program stated that the main purpose of the society was to "take up the defense of indigenes and to remove all the obstacles that prevent the accomplishment of this and which tend to place the yoke on the necks of the colored races and exploit them"—admirable sentiments from a group that was also starting to look at slave and wage labor in the countries to which Italians had been emigrating for the past few decades.[124] At the society's fourth meeting in 1926, Egilberto Martire claimed, as quoted at the start of this chapter, that it was possible to be black and Italian. Of course, for some the cause of antislavery was just another way to palliate colonization. Well- run colonies and religious missions would become an important reason that there was not slavery, but of equal importance was the good works of those people who objected to slavery on moral grounds.

So, even into Primo Levi's youth, slavery remained an issue. Antonio Gramsci (1891–1937), from Sardinia, was educated in Turin and though originally a socialist, became one of the founders of the Communist Party of Italy. Under fascism he paid for his political beliefs with a long term of imprisonment that hastened his early death. While in prison he kept a series of notebooks. In 1934 Gramsci was pondering the role of the *popolo* in the thirteenth-century Italian communes.[125] Thinking about subaltern peoples, Gramsci wondered if they originally derived from a different race (*razza*) from the dominant group, or a mixture of races, like the ancient slaves. Subaltern groups occasionally had some autonomy, but slaves and the proletariat in the classical world, and serfs and the proletariat in the Middle Ages, were denied autonomy and an organized, collective life. Gramsci saw parallels between the ancient slaves and the medieval workers but their circumstances were not identical. (And he missed the existence of medieval slaves.) Ancient slave revolts, like the one under Spartacus, differed from medieval worker revolts, like that of the Ciompi in Florence (1378) because the latter could form alliances, however temporary, with other groups. (Slave revolts had no friends.) For Gramsci, the modern state had abolished genuine alliances between social groups, and substituted the "active hegemony of the dominant and controlling group," which in turn abolished the autonomy of the others. Thoughts about slavery and working people helped Gramsci to meditate about hegemony and the ways in which

124. Archivio Segreto Vaticano, Segreteria di Stato, Anno 1921, Rubrica 12, fasc. 2. The Archivio Segreto Vaticano is not yet available to scholars consulting documents from the beginning of 1922 to the present.

125. For what follows see Antonio Gramsci, *Quaderni del carcere*, vol. 3 (Turin, 1975), pp. 2286–87.

the masters, whether as owners or employers, eventually dominate what the "lower orders," be they slaves or workers, are able to do. Gramsci has moved well beyond Mazzini's evolutionary approach to slavery, serfdom, and wage labor. His questions about the lack of evidence for revolts by medieval workers (or slaves) will be addressed in the last chapter when we examine the social forces sustaining poverty and slavery—another way of looking at hegemony.

Italian slavery, both in its medieval past and its fascist present, had not receded into oblivion. Even more importantly, the language of slavery remained a lively discourse, keeping alive ways of thinking that would stay relevant long after people thought (or hoped) that the institution of slavery had died out. Think how horrified Mazzini would have been to learn that when his Italy wanted colonies it would turn a blind eye toward people like Antonio Cecchi! The Italians emigrated to Africa (and America) with the heritage of their medieval past and a language well stocked with racial attitudes, enabling some to see color-based hierarchy and slavery in the ants. Hence the language of slavery is the last but steep price any society must pay for having tolerated the institution and profited from it. Long after slaves disappear, the heritage of the words and the ideas they struggle to express is the ultimate reckoning. The hypocrisies, the racism, the sexism, the brutality bound up with the daily practice of slavery live on in language, where they continue to punish the descendants of both owners and slaves indiscriminately. The habits of expression that excused slavery endure as unfinished business, unexpiated sin, in all those societies that used words to exploit the enslavement of others. Thus slavery lives on long after the last slave has died.

CHAPTER TWO
THE LANGUAGE OF THE LAW

It's a strange thing that all our masters, who rule the world, want to bring paper, pen, and ink into everything.

ALESSANDRO MANZONI, *I promessi sposi*

THE LAW

In the December term of 1834 the Supreme Court of North Carolina heard arguments in the remarkable case *State v. Will*, which tested the right of a slave to self-defense in the face of a murderous assault.[1] B. F. Moore, arguing for the slave Will, stressed the humanity and rationality of slaves as people, in whom some instinct for furious anger in self-defense was both natural and desirable, since it was one of a bundle of human qualities, like loyalty, that were worth preserving. As Moore claimed, "Human institutions are inadequate to the task of setting a condition in society which shall impart to its members the highest perfection of philosophic fortitude and the lowest degradation of animal existence, which shall blend into harmony the reasonable man and the passionless brute."[2] A deep student of history, Moore cited Justice Blackstone's commentary on homicide, which noted that in "an edict of the Emperor Constantine, when the rigor of Roman law began to relax and soften, a master was allowed to chastise his slave with rods and imprisonment; and if death accidentally ensued, he was guilty of no crime, but if he struck him with a club or stone and thereby occasioned his death . . . it was a case of homicide."[3] Will's assailant, an overseer, had shot him in the back, so Moore was well beyond clubs and stones and into the area where the instinct to preserve oneself could not be sacrificed without also shedding other human qualities needed to make up a whole person. So a little bit of Roman law,

---

1. 18 NC 122. This case is discussed in Thomas D. Morris, *Southern Slavery and the Law 1619–1860* (Chapel Hill, N.C., 1996), pp. 279–81.
2. 18 NC 138.
3. 18 NC 132.

generally deemed harsh and similar to practices in contemporary Turkey, slipped into a nineteenth-century North Carolina courtroom.[4]

What exactly had the emperor Constantine done? In 319 he issued an edict defining the circumstances under which a master might be liable for homicide in the killing of a slave.[5] Normal beating with a light rod or lashes, even if it resulted in death, was not homicide. Constantine (or his legal advisors) drew the line at intent to kill; signs of this were attacking the slave with a weapon or using hanging, poison, or other immoderate means to assault the slave. In 329 the emperor further clarified these rules by insisting that masters had the right to beat a slave to induce better behavior, and even if the slave died, there should be no investigation to determine whether the owner's intent was to correct or to kill.[6] Simple punishment remained the absolute right of masters, and Constantine wanted to make sure that slave owners knew that the law was not going to pry into their private efforts to ensure the slaves' obedience. As the lawyers interpreted the edict, discipline was no crime; only an intent to kill was illegal. Left unstated but clear enough was that the means of punishing a slave proved the master's intent—a whip or a stick was fine, a sword or a noose evinced murderous thoughts. The emperor did not invoke his new religion as a motive behind these decisions, but he did limit the absolute right of a master over a slave's life. Christianity does seem to be behind Constantine's order that any condemned person (free or slave) should be branded elsewhere than on the face, in order not to disfigure what was made in the likeness of God (celestial beauty).[7]

The lawful limits of violence against slaves endured as a real moral problem throughout the history of slavery. On 1 May 1479, Genoese officials went to the house of Lodisio de Maris Pesagno to investigate the death of the slave Caterina, a twenty-five-year-old Moor.[8] Questioning one Brigid-

---

4. Slavery in Turkey and Rome was linked in *State v. Reed*, 9 NC 455 (1823).

5. *Codex Theodosianus*. Edited by Theodor Mommsen (Dublin, 1970) 9.12.1. The best survey of Roman slavery is Keith Bradley, *Slavery and Society at Rome* (Cambridge, 1994). See also G. E. M. de Ste Croix, *The Class Struggle in the Ancient Greek World from the Archaic Age to the Arab Conquests* (Ithaca, 1981).

6. *Codex Theodosianus*. Edited by Theodor Mommsen (Dublin, 1970) 9.12.2. The key sentences are "Si servus, dum culpam dominus vindicat, mortuus fuerit, dominus culpa homicidii non tenetur, quia tunc homicidii reus est, si occidere voluisse convincitur. Nam emendatio non vocatur ad crimen."

7. *Codex Theodosianus*. Edited by Theodor Mommsen (Dublin, 1970) 9.40.2.

8. Luigi Tria, "La schiavitù in Liguria," *Atti della Società Ligure di Storia Patria* 70 (1947): pp. 206–7.

ina, they learned that Caterina had been found hung from a light fixture in the kitchen. Brigidina had cut Caterina down and she fell to the ground dead. Examining the corpse, the officials discovered that Caterina was seriously wounded everywhere on her body, and especially on her private parts, her backside appearing black from blows and charcoal. Caterina was apparently burned as well as beaten. The kitchen became a torture chamber. The judge, seeing these wounds and accepting Brigidina's statement that the victim had hung herself with a noose, gave leave for the owners to bury the body. And so the officials did their duty, unless any better information came their way later. Perhaps Caterina in a moment of despair committed suicide, or perhaps her torturers went too far. Brigidina's testimony sufficed, and it is likely that no one took any further interest in the manner of Caterina's death. Even Constantine may have hoped for more diligence than this.

An imperial edict of 319, a mysterious death in 1479, and an American court case in 1834 illustrate a central feature of slavery that the law had to face: the place of violence in maintaining slavery. Everyone agreed that in order to have slaves the owners needed the right to impose discipline as they saw fit, with as few questions as possible. But, the law also struggled with the fact that correction could and did go too far, and that premeditated homicide was a social problem that could not be ignored or treated as simply a foolish destruction of one's own property. Violence and discipline were a central legal issue, as was the slave's humanity. The limits of the slave's humanity were always ambiguous, especially when we remember that in ancient Rome, medieval Genoa, and the American South, it was not a crime for a master to rape or sexually abuse a slave. Even in a case in Siena in 1450, where two men broke into a widow's house and raped her slave Lucia, the judge fined the two men for breaking and entering, with no damages to the slave's owner, let alone any justice for Lucia.[9] Yet in medieval Italy, unlike Rome or the United States, slaves could enter into legal marriages, so the lawyers found themselves in the deep waters of power and human sexuality. But everywhere, and beyond a doubt, slavery was worse for women, who suffered all the other violence as well as the possibility of forced sex. In all these matters the language of the law needed to be carefully chosen, word by word. After violence, we will look at the drier but vi-

9. Giulio Prunai, "Notizie e documenti sulla servitù domestica nel territorio senese (secc. VIII–XVI)," *Bulletino senese di storia patria* 7 (1936): 407–9. In 1456 a new law set a fine of one hundred lire for anyone entering a house for the purpose of carnally knowing a slave, but again the emphasis was not on rape. Ibid., p. 414.

tal words of sales contracts, and how this language reveals the buying and selling of humans in its starkest form.

PRAGMATICS AND THE LAW

The law is supposed to be meaningful speech. Pragmatics invites us to explore the right contexts and perspectives to make clear what we are doing when we study the law and legal instruments. Using language to make law and contracts itself generated the contexts, the small worlds of markets and courts. The language of buying and selling will be explored in detail in Chapter 4. Here our interest is in the prescriptive sources, the law, and most importantly the contracts for buying, selling, and freeing slaves. Legal language needs to be as explicit as possible, but "the impossibility of complete explicitness" reminds us that no law or contract can cover every contingency.[10] Much about the law will remain implicit, and context helps to ferret out the lost implicit meanings of medieval Italian slavery. This chapter does not intend to privilege the law over behavior and the economy as contexts for exploring slavery. Far from selling the law as the key for knowing everything else, this chapter situates law and its ministers as another interest group in society. The law's keepers, notaries and lawyers, encouraged people to adopt legal forms for their behavior because it benefited the professional classes administering the law. People followed the law and made binding contracts because it efficiently accomplished their aims, but also because the lawyers and notaries had won the point that their way of commodifying people worked the best. The law accommodated itself very well to the fallen state of humanity. The law's assumption that its language was best and should shape reality made it one of the sustaining forces behind slavery. Occasional subversive lawyers might through argument save an individual slave, but the law's venerable authority ensured that the institution survived over the centuries.

Language is a cultural commodity, an ironic commentary on slaves who in theory possessed no goods except for what the master allowed. Jacob Mey asks the good question: "whose language are we speaking when we use 'our' language?"[11] Did the masters own the language as surely as they owned the slaves? All the early evidence concerning the language of the law comes from legal codes or contracts written down in medieval Latin, which itself was not the same in Genoa, Venice, Rome, and Palermo. The official,

10. See Jef Verschueren, *Understanding Pragmatics* (London, 1999), pp. 26–27.
11. Jacob Mey, *Pragmatics: An Introduction* (Oxford, 1993), p. 288.

stylized language was the preserve of the Church, and soon also of the professional body of notaries, who possessed the arcane skill of writing contracts in a language the parties never spoke and seldom read. Since the earliest evidence from contracts comes from shortly after 1000, and most early notaries were priests, it makes sense that in Italy these contracts were in Latin and not in the vernacular dialects, which were almost never written down. But in the later centuries, why did this legal and business Latin remain so durable, why into the age of Dante and beyond were notaries still using it? This conservatism in usage involved all law and contracts, not just those concerning slavery, so the broader context must provide the answers. Perhaps the notaries, monopolizing the lucrative business of copying, stuck to Latin to preserve their expertise and incomes. Their self-interest is patent, but what about the parties, the ordinary buyers and sellers? Latin's prestige was formidable. Most wealthy merchants and traders eventually had enough scraps of Latin to understand what was in their contracts, which were translations into Latin of agreements made in Italian dialects. The law remained in Latin even longer than commercial acts, so legal stipulations in contracts were more exact in Latin, and sometimes still appeared in that language even when the rest of the document was in the vernacular. The average workers, servants, peasants, or slaves understood nothing of this Latin; it was not "their" language.

Certainly the medieval Latin of a Genoese slave contract was far from the Mongol dialect spoken by the Tartar woman who found herself sold into slavery. But even back in Genoa, the Italian dialect she had to learn in order to survive carried with it a social context with little bits of leverage that might make her lot more bearable, if she could learn them. And so there were pragmatic users of language long before the rise of pragmatics. Jacob Mey concludes his introduction to pragmatics by observing that it is beneficial to the underprivileged, that it emancipates people from social control through language.[12] If so, what more useful tool could there be for retrieving the full context of slavery, and maybe even provide a little retroactive emancipation into the bargain?

The law's language on slavery received exacting and lavish attention from Roman lawyers, whose insights Justinian's sixth-century jurists collected into that monument to jurisprudence, the *Digest*. It would be at least another thousand years before markets and the law together matched the level of sophistication found in Roman practice, whose language subsequently faded in and out of relevance like some intermittent radio signal from a distant past. Even when ruined as a complete system, bits of Roman

12. Ibid., p. 304.

law endured as phrases into either law codes or contracts, preserved both in memory of systematic thought and because Roman solutions still sometimes made sense even when their original context no longer existed. Book 21 of the *Digest*, on market sales, distilled the experiences of centuries of buying and selling slaves into a crisp analysis of mutual obligations, so let us begin with a brief look at what the Romans offered posterity in this matter.

"Caveat emptor" has entered many languages as a piece of Roman wisdom, but the *Digest* begins with an opinion that the seller must inform the buyer about the diseases and defects of a slave, and whether he or she was a runaway, a malingerer, or liable for past damages.[13] Ignorance of flaws is no excuse, and sellers are expected to know their merchandise well enough to disclose its defects. In the murky area of mental disturbances like obstinacy or depression, the law did not recognize a right to cancel a sale unless the seller had guaranteed that the slave was not stubborn or sad. For this reason, the warranty that a slave was not a runaway had to be expressed in the contract, for this inclination was considered to be a state of mind.[14] Even some physical ailments were sometimes defects and sometimes not. Ordinary bed-wetting was not grounds for canceling a sale, unless it was caused by a diseased bladder.[15] In law a pregnant slave was healthy, for it was natural for women slaves to conceive and so the assurance that a slave was well was not affected by whether she was pregnant.[16] The lawyers also understood the difference between a contractual promise and banter during bargaining when the seller had the right to extol the slave's qualities. Saying that a slave was not a thief gave the buyer the chance to return a slave who was one, but commending a slave for being frugal was not a guarantee and would not allow the return of a wastrel.[17] Trying to get back the sale price of a slave who had died raised questions about negligence, and the set period for such returns (sixty days or six months, depending on the type of return).[18] Slave sales were guaranteed under penalty of double the price to the buyer. Roman lawyers thought it necessary for the contract to state the nationality of a slave, for this was an important fact the buyer needed to know

13. In general see Alan Watson, *Roman Slave Law* (Baltimore, 1987). Here, *Corpus Iuris Civilis*, Vol 1, *Digesta*. Edited by P. Krueger and T. Mommsen (Dublin, 1973) 21.1.1: "quid morbi vitiive cuique sit, quis fugitivus errove sit noxave."

14. *Corpus Iuris Civilis*, Vol 1, *Digesta*. Edited by P. Krueger and T. Mommsen (Dublin, 1973) 21.1.4.

15. Ibid., 21.1.12.

16. Ibid., 21.1.14.1.

17. Ibid., 21.1.19.

18. Ibid., 21.1.31.

in order to determine the slave's strengths and weaknesses.[19] There is much more to the law than these simple points, but all of this, in addition to the immense body of rules on buying and selling in general, established a framework for minimizing risk and fraud in the markets.

Lombard law is a sort of halfway house between Roman practice and the revival of urban and territorial law in the central Middle Ages. The Lombards established a kingdom in Italy in the late sixth century, and their rulers issued law codes that tried to bridge the gap between themselves and their "Roman" subjects. None of these new laws mentions buying or selling, or how markets worked. There is a good deal of law on slaves, most of it concerning wergild—the tribal method of compensating owners for various levels of harm done to slaves—or how to punish bad slaves. But the silence on buying and selling slaves, which was certainly still happening, suggests that the Lombards were content to leave in place an obviously efficient Roman system. Even if the system was too complex for their actual needs, legal anachronisms would just slip away and leave the required features of a contract in place. One late edict, by King Ratchis in 745 or 746, deserves notice because it is the only part of Lombard law to address the question raised by Constantine, of masters killing slaves. This new rule seems to have been prompted by a recent incident at the royal court. Any Lombard could bring a freeman or half-slave to the court in order to make him his slave.[20] If he did not get the proper permission from the king or official, and in a fury then killed the man, whether he was slave or free before, he must pay a wergild in compensation to the king and in some cases to the man's family as well.[21] If the slave or half-free person was only injured, he became the king's property. The issue here was not the right to punish slaves, which Lombard law did not discuss and presumably left as absolute, but violating the king's peace in a technical procedure for declaring someone a slave. Although Lombard law recognized some right of self-defense, it limited it to free men.[22] No one was worrying about the legal limits of punishing slaves and killing them only attracted notice in narrow circumstances.

In Apulia and Calabria in southern Italy, areas of Byzantine control lasted until the Normans conquered them in the eleventh century. Rural slavery had declined in these regions in the ninth and tenth centuries

19. Ibid., 21.1.31.21.

20. The half-slave occupied a nebulous place between free and slave, and was destined to disappear as a social category in medieval Italy.

21. *Leges Langobardorum, Monumenta Germaniae Historica*, vol. 4 (Hanover, 1868), *Ratchis leges* 7, pp. 188–89.

22. Ibid., *Liutprand* 20.

largely because domain agricultural cultivation collapsed and the empire was not able to enforce slavery by condemning people to it and by pursuing runaways.[23] A legal manual in Greek from about the end of the tenth century, given by its editors the Latin title *Prochiron legum*, reveals the southern Italian knowledge of contemporary Byzantine law. This compilation distills into simple injunctions legislation by Justinian, Leo III (717–741) and Basil I (867–886).[24] The *Prochiron legum* is filled with references to slaves, resembling the legal codes of antiquity. Even if slavery was waning in the South, texts like this one may have served as models for people in other parts of Italy, though they might have learned about Byzantine practices in other ways, including direct observation. In this legal tract people were either slave or free, though liberty was the natural condition and the first man, Adam, had been created free.[25] These Byzantine laws reflect a society preoccupied with runaways, punishment and torture, and sex between free people and slaves—problems usually endemic in slave cultures. If anyone wounded a slave with a whip or rod and the slave died from the beating, it was not homicide. If the owner immoderately tortured the slave or used poison, he should be punished as a killer.[26] People were allowed to sell their children into slavery.[27] Injuries to slaves belonging to others were damages to the owners and subject to recovery.[28] These are just a few provisions from a collection whose author knew well the routines of slavery. Benjamin Z. Kedar has pointed out that an earlier Byzantine law code, the *Ecloga*, issued in 741, laid down the rule, also appearing in later codes, that "when a married man maintains relations with his own slave," she should be sold away from the province and the state should receive her purchase price.[29] This law, probably intended more to defend marriage than the rights of female slaves, found no imitators in later law codes or practices in northern Italy. Still, the law set the example that in some circumstances it would pro-

23. Jean-Marie Martin, *La Pouille du VIe au XIIe siècle* (Rome, 1993), pp. 210, 255, 298.

24. *Prochiron legum*, ed. F. Brandileone and V. Puntoni, Fonti per la storia d'Italia, vol. 30 (Rome, 1895), pp. i–xviii.

25. Ibid., pp. 191–92.

26. Ibid., p. 256 (a rule of Basil I).

27. Ibid., p. 282.

28. Ibid., p. 284.

29. Benjamin Z. Kedar, "On the Origins of the Earliest Laws of Frankish Jerusalem: The Canons of the Council of Nablus, 1120," *Speculum* 74 (1999): 310–35, here pp. 313–14. The later *Prochiron legum* contains the same provision—see F. Brandileone and V. Puntoni, *Prochiron legum*, p. 250, section 34:58.

tect slaves from their masters. This style of slavery was far more complex than what the Lombards knew, and was a little more humane than Roman type.

But aside from the law, whose language survived, there was still buying and selling of slaves, sometimes by written contract. From a few of these documents which survive from the time just before the regular runs of notarial records begin in the twelfth century, we can see which Roman traditions endured.

LANGUAGE OF CONTRACTS

A precious sale contract survives from Noli on the Ligurian coast near Genoa, dated 9 July 1005, in which Armano, who claimed to live by the law of the Salian Franks, sold to a couple Benedetto and Benedetta a slave (*ancilla*) named Erkentruda, of the Burgundian nation.[30] Nearly five centuries after the *Digest*, which was unknown in Italy in this period, a contract preserved the Roman tradition that it was necessary to record the slave's nationality. Armano also guaranteed the buyer that the slave was not a thief, a runaway, or sick, but sound of body and mind.[31] The contract, which conveyed ownership according to Roman and Frankish forms, stipulated a classical penalty of an ounce of gold for failure to comply with its terms and testified to the good legal knowledge of Giovanni, notary of the sacred palace—a Byzantine title. Down in Siena the notary Ildibrando recorded another slave sale in April of 1064, but here the Latin was much worse, and the legal knowledge slight.[32] A woman named Udiglola sold a slave to a couple Paolo and Alberta, but the contract omits the slave's name and nation yet mentions her late mother Berta. The only trace of Roman contracts here is the double-the-price penalty. All that is left is a bare understanding that writing ratified a sale, and most of the document concerns the woman's right to sell things and her claim that the sale did not result from violence but her free will. An early sale contract from Pisa in 1112 also contained only the double penalty. Another contract from 1114 listed the penalty and the slave's birthplace—Corsica.[33] Finally, a slave sale from Bari

30. Luigi T. Belgrano, "Cartario genovese ed illustrazione del registro arcivescovile," *Atti della Società Ligure di Storia Patria* 2, pt. 1 (1870), pp. 67–68 n. 42.

31. Ibid.: "non fura non fugitiva neque cadiva, set mente et corpore sana ipsa esse dico." He may mean "cadiva" as bad rather than unhealthy.

32. G. Prunai, "Notizie," pp. 259–60.

33. Amerigo D'Amia, *Schiavitù romana e servitù medievale* (Milan, 1931), pp. 221–22.

in 1121 contained the best Latin and the clearest ideas about Roman law. The contract specified the Slavic nationality of the slave and her daughter, guaranteed the sale, and stipulated a large penalty.[34] All these contracts were in Latin, a language understood by none of the parties—the preserve of notaries, who sold their Latin for a fee.

The contracts are older than most medieval law. People made contracts and in particular sold slaves before they set down the abstract rules on contracts and slaves. Beginning with the oldest notarial records in the twelfth century, we have a relatively uniform, regular, and sophisticated way of making a contract. The details of how notaries actually wrote down the words of a contract can be reserved for later. People wanted a written record of a contract because a paper copy preserved somewhere, even if they did not have it and could not read it, conferred legal force on the contract's terms, something much harder to prove in the case of an oral deal. Most contracts concerned selling things, and a written contract was a form of title. Proving that a person was one's slave, in a system where skin color was at first usually no help, required proof, especially if, as sometimes happened, a slave spoke up and claimed to be a free person illegally sold or kept as a slave.[35] So, as useful as written records were for business and property transactions, it was especially efficient to convey slaves through written agreements.

Behind every sale, there was an act of enslavement not ratified by contract. Slaves born into the condition are a separate problem. Here we are looking for the original enslavement. Some such enslavements occurred early on in Sardinia and Corsica, but most slaves in Italy became slaves elsewhere and were transported into Italy. Capturing people into slavery, while sanctioned by civil and canon law, was essentially an extralegal act for which no paper trail usually existed. A Circassian slave named Bandeto was sold as booty in La Spezia in 1444, the sellers noting that he had been taken in war outside the nearby port of Sarzana—but he was already a slave.[36] The rarity of people selling themselves into slavery attracted so much legal commentary for this very reason—here, at least, was an act ratifying a slave's status. This context of language is crucial for understanding how best to prove slavery. In addition, it betrays the uneasy recognition that behind every slave there was a crime out there, somewhere, involving something one could not do on the streets of Palermo or Genoa, or, which was viewed as a

34. *Codice diplomatico barese, Le pergamene di S. Nicola di Bari*, vol. 5, ed. Francesco Nitti di Vito (Bari, 1902), pp. 114–15.
35. For examples from Bari, Genoa, and Palermo, see below.
36. A. D'Amia, *Schiavitù*, p. 269.

horrific crime when done by Muslim slavers raiding the coasts of Italy. Context is important.

The first surviving Genoese slave sale occurs in the oldest extant cartulary by the notary Giovanni Scriba. This sale took place on 28 March 1159, when a Saracen named Peireto changed hands for six lire and ten solidi.[37] A Saracen was a Muslim probably from Spain, and Peireto is plainly not an Arabic name, so already language raises some issues—the terminology of slavery, and slave names. For at least the next five hundred years, slaves continued to be sold in Genoa. These contracts are the best collective source for looking at individual lives, but their broader context raises important questions about the contracts themselves. Nubeloto purchased this slave—how did he find one? This question too opens up a rich contextual vein. There never was any regular slave market in Genoa, though at least one shop with a stock of slaves existed in the late fourteenth century.[38] Almost all slave sales in Genoa conveyed individuals, or a mother and child, so there were few lots of slaves changing hands. Some masters sold slaves for whatever reason, while other slaves came to sale through importers who had brought the slaves to the city to be sold at a profit. A person in the market for a slave therefore had to look around for a purchase, and the importers needed to find individual customers. Two places fit these needs. The docks and city markets were good spots for a person to ask, "Who has a slave to sell?" and the sellers could announce their wares as well. In later centuries for sure, and probably as early as the twelfth, the shops of jewelers and goldsmiths were places to learn about slaves, and by the fifteenth century the law allowed jewelers to sell slaves retail—a revealing synergy of businesses.[39] This kind of search for a slave was difficult for women because their role in the market was usually more private, and wealthy women were not in the habit of wandering around the port and the open-air shops to ask questions about commerce in people. The role of women in slavery is a complex one and the mechanics of the business made it hard for women to participate in it, as buyers or sellers. But of course some did.

Information searches by buyers and sellers in a market with low turnover are complex enough, yet where were the slaves when they were sold, or even just inspected by casual customers who might be in the market for the right slave at the right price? No one would buy a horse or a mule, let alone

37. Mario Chiaudano and Mattia Moresco, *Il cartolare di Giovanni Scriba* (Rome, 1935), no. 529, 1:283–84.

38. Luigi T. Belgrano, *Della vita privata dei genovesi* (Genoa, 1875), p. 86.

39. *Leges Genuenses: Historiae Patriae Monumenta*, ed. by Cornelio Desimoni and Luigi T. Belgrano, vol. 18 (Turin, 1901), col. 680.

a slave, without examining the merchandise. It is possible that many slaves changed hands between people who knew one another and even the slaves—a need to sell and a desire to buy could casually come together. More likely in the case of the Genoese owners and certainly of the importers, they had the slave or slaves with them in the market, readily available for potential customers to inspect. This must have been a humiliating (or liberating?) moment for a slave, to be led through the streets by a master, possibly chained, not as a sign of status, but to be sold. Also, to be present when bargaining set one's price must have been a fascinatingly awful experience. The Flemish soldier Emanuel D'Aranda, captured by Algerian corsairs and enslaved in 1640, recalled how potential buyers "took me by the hand to see if it were hard and brawny by working, and they caused me to open my mouth, to see whether my teeth were able to overcome Bisket in the gallies."[40] D'Aranda, remembering the solemn day he was sold, noted his price, two hundred pattacoons or pieces of eight. No one suggested that a slave had any right to consent to a sale, and it would be worth knowing any case where a humane master took a slave's wishes into account. Slaves appeared in public markets to be emancipated or sold, when not there doing a master's bidding.

There are almost no records of bargaining in medieval markets. All we have are final prices that vary according to the sex, age, color, skills, and defects of particular slaves. For now, the emphasis is on the language of contract and its context, so let us assume that there was a general sense of slave values, and that leaving aside a few dumb or highly motivated buyers and sellers, bargaining produced a just price, as it was supposed to do. A slave might be worth L5 in the twelfth century and L150 in the fifteenth, but problems of real and nominal value aside, the price was always substantial in every period, so people with this kind of money usually knew what they were doing.

In this style of conducting business, when the parties agreed, their next step was to find a notary to draw up a proper, legally binding contract in Latin. This could be done on the spot, because notaries congregated in public places to do their business. Transactions in livestock tend to be speedy because these objects of commerce are mortal, so the seller is usually eager to be paid as soon as possible. Also, once a slave learned that she or he was on the way out of a household, it was best to get that slave out quickly. Even more compelling was the fact that the importers, having invested in slaves months earlier and having endured a risky sea voyage to Genoa,

40. Emanuel D'Aranda, *The History of Algiers and it's Slavery with Many Remarkable Particularities of Africk*, trans. John Davies (London, 1666), p. 9.

wanted at last to realize a profit. A slave was not a casual or impulsive purchase, even for the rich, although there were times when physical attraction prompted a quick decision. Here too, information about the habits of the different "nations" of people, and lessons from the ancient science of physiognomy, helped buyers assess the race and face of their purchases. All these motives point to rapid bargaining. The seller invariably employed the notary, and the contract always took the form "I sell"—that is how title legally passed. Skilled notaries knew more about sales contracts than anything else—sales of land, houses, and commodities in particular and in Genoa of more mules than horses—and a slave sale was not an everyday occurrence for a notary.

Still, a sale was a sale, and notaries knew how to take the results of bargaining in the Genoese or Palermitan dialect and put them into correct Latin legalese. But the parties also knew a lot about the terms and conditions of any sale, and it was the notary's job to ensure that a fair sale was impervious to subsequent legal challenge. (Of course there were other skilled people, the lawyers, whose craft it was to help aggrieved parties break contracts, but let us assume good faith and an ironclad contract.) These sales contracts were on-the-spot transfers. No example survives of a deal promising future delivery of a slave. And so a person changed hands, and seldom does anything in a contract reveal what came with the slave. In one rare instance a notice of a slave sale in Florence on 24 July 1367 records that the price of forty-five florins included the clothing, valued at five florins.[41] As preoccupied as most medieval people were with clothing, it seems likely that a slave came with the clothes on his or her back, and nothing more. The recently imported slaves had nothing else, and there are no signs that the established slaves were allowed to take along any personal property. Sales of mules and horses never mentioned harnesses or saddles either.

To return now to the first sale in the records, we can look closely at what Brun Silvester, a non-Genoese importer, was doing when he sold Peireto to Nubeloto the money changer. The contract was a sale, in which Brun acknowledged that he had received the purchase price of six lire and 10 solidi and that the slave was legally his to sell. At this early stage of written contracts, Brun seems to have possessed no piece of paper that proved Peireto was his slave. The rest of the contract makes six explicit legal claims. These statements were special speech acts, performatives that changed reality and created tangible obligations enforceable at law. (1) The seller gave the buyer complete ownership with no strings attached, and no heirs had the

41. Ridolfo Livi, *La schiavitù domestica nei tempi di mezzo e nei moderni* (Padua, 1928), p. 167.

right to dispute the sale. (2) The seller promised not to interfere in any way with the buyer's possession, under the standard penalty of double the purchase price—a serious incentive to leave the buyer alone. (3) The seller promised to defend the sale against anyone, and this guaranteed title especially against any previous owner who might surface to contest the sale. (4) The seller agreed to fulfill these terms under pledge of his goods and property. (5) The buyer had the right to recover any legal damages or fines from the seller's property. (6) The buyer could exercise this right of recovery without obtaining a legal judgment, and the seller waived the right to challenge the recovery. In other words, if Brun caused problems later, Nubeloto could just take a double penalty of thirteen lire, without having to go to court to establish the claim. All these stipulations reveal an already sophisticated method of producing slave sale contracts, and the contracts appear hard to break. But generations of experience, in Genoa and other Italian cities, will provide an even richer context for understanding slave sales.

The notary Giovanni Scriba continued to refine his craft, and by 25 November 1160 he was using a slightly different and crisper set of phrases, but more complexity was also creeping into the legalese. This time a merchant from Narbonne was selling a Saracen slave named Machomet to a Genoese shipmaster for three lire.[42] Besides the tightened legalisms, two new conditions entered this and some subsequent contracts. First, the seller stipulated that the slave was not known to be a thief, a runaway, or sick.[43] Where did these words come from, and what did they mean? These words are unusual because they appear in the next contract (more on this shortly) but subsequently these issues were not routinely addressed by other Genoese notaries until the early fourteenth century, and then in a quite different form. Perhaps in this case a foreign merchant, whose local reputation may not have been a sufficient guarantee, had to promise more than usual. Possibly these words come from a legal tradition in Languedoc and the merchant insisted on them, but then why would the next group making a slave contract also require these words? Machomet was sold with five Genoese witnesses present. In the next contract, made on the same day, another Saracen

42. M. Chiaudano and M. Moresco, *Giovanni Scriba*, no. 788, 1:423. The Genoese is described as a *carravelator*—most likely a shipmaster. For a valuable analysis of the broader, western Mediterranean context of slavery see Olivia Remie Constable, "Muslim Spain and Mediterranean Slavery: The Medieval Slave Trade as an Aspect of Muslim-Christian Relations," in *Christendom and Its Discontents*, ed. Scott Waugh and Peter D. Diehl (Cambridge, 1996), pp. 264–84.

43. M. Chiaudano and M. Moresco, *Giovanni Scriba*, no. 788, 1:423: "quem furem fugacem non scio vel caduce infirmitatis partecipem."

named Ali was sold by one Genoese to another, with five Genoese witnesses, none the same as in the previous act. So we have fourteen people and one notary involved in the sale of two slaves. The common thread appears to be the notary Giovanni Scriba. Yet in later sale contracts written by him, he did not use these exact words about theft, flight, or illness. So if it was such a good idea to do so, why did he stop doing it, and why did no other notary for so long afterward include these conditions in his contracts?

One anomalous feature in the second contract may solve the problem. Virtually the same as the previous one, it notes, however, that four years have elapsed since the sale.[44] Relying on written records was still relatively recent, and many other sales may have occurred on verbal contracts. Yet this owner thought it was worth his while to have a written contract now. I think the merchant from Narbonne suggested this language, and that the second Genoese group, possibly waiting on line for the notary, heard these new conditions and thought—why not for us too? The key fact is that Scriba never used the exact words again, and to understand this we need to analyze the context and meaning of these words. Peire de Volta of Narbonne did not guarantee that his slave was not a thief, a runaway, or sick; he stated that he did not know him to be such. How could any seller provide a warranty on these matters? Sickness was such a mystery to these people that the possibility of a latent malady was always undeniable. How long into the future would equally unpredictable good health last? Would any future illness be grounds for terminating the contract? Ordinarily not, or else no sale would be secure. The seller was on surer grounds in stating that he did not *know* Machomet to be a thief or runaway; these were observable facts that a person upon his word should know. But what if Machomet proved to be a bad slave?—and these characteristics were typical of what masters described as bad behavior. If Machomet ran away, could the buyer go to Peire and demand his money back because the contract had stipulated that the slave was not a runaway? Here again the answer is no—who could reasonably be held to this condition, and for how long?—and the same problems existed for theft.

Peire of course guaranteed nothing beyond his own good faith. He carefully used the word "know"—what was in the slave's heart or future was beyond certainty. No one could ask Machomet himself to promise anything because he was an object of sale and not a legal person capable of promising (yet). So the words in the contract really meant nothing: they were no guarantee of future behavior or grounds for canceling the sale. They raised the issue of troubling conduct but did nothing about it. These words were a

44. Ibid., no. 789, 25 November 1160, 1:424: "iam sunt transacti anni iiii."

waste of time, a precocious attempt to solve the problem of warranty before it was fully understood. That is why these words do not appear again, though the issues remained. Scriba's last surviving sale of a slave took another look at the problem. Here the seller said he did not know that the slave was a killer, a thief, or a runaway.[45] This contract does not mention sickness, but it raises a deeper fear of slave owners, that slaves might be capable of homicide, and masters thought they were themselves the most likely targets. The unusual common thread here is the Genoese shipmaster Peire, the buyer of both Machomet and Ali—an experienced slave owner who may himself have been the last user of this type of pointless condition for many years.

There is no reason to examine every contract, and even the same notary did not always use the same legalese throughout his career. The notary Oberto Scriba de Mercato is a valuable example because he was active from at least 1186 to 1214, and he was a highly skilled and speedy in his work. His use of legal language in slave sale contracts displays considerable stability over time. His basic contract had the seller promise not to impede the sale, and to defend it under double penalty; and it conveyed both possession and ownership, which were not always the same thing.[46] By 1200 Oberto was routinely adding the new condition, written down right after the price, that if the slave was actually worth more, the seller gave the difference to the buyer as a gift.[47] This is a strange condition, because nothing was ever said about the possibility that the slave was actually worth less than his or her purchase price. The buyer had no obvious recourse if he or she felt cheated—that was the nature of bargaining. But why then worry about concealed value? The buyers must have feared that disgruntled sellers would try to renege on contracts by claiming that they had been cheated, and so the contract now sealed off this last way for the seller to have second thoughts.

Oberto Scriba's surviving contracts are numerous enough to provide some unique words describing the particular context of an individual contract. The standard condition to defend the sale against all men varied by a single word in the sale of a Saracen slave named Asmeto in 1190, and the word is "Christian": the seller promised to defend the sale against all Christian men.[48] This condition appears unique in Genoa, and it must be in this

45. Ibid., no. 837, 10 June 1161, 2:15: "nescio quod sit occidivus fur vel fugitivus."

46. Contracts in published editions for 1186, 1190, and ASG, CN N. 4.

47. ASG, CN, N. 4, "Si plus valet dono tibi."

48. Mario Chiaudano and R. M. della Rocca, *Oberto Scriba de Mercato 1190* (Turin, 1938), no. 244, 12 March 1190, p. 96.

contract because there was a Muslim somewhere having a legitimate claim to the slave. So, if this slave was stolen, as seems likely, the buyer in theory risked that the real owner would turn up and make a claim. It is inconceivable that the Genoese courts would have heard such a case against a Christian Genoese owner, and unlikely that a Muslim making such a claim would escape with his life. It is equally implausible that the new owner would ever take this Muslim slave to a Muslim land, where such a slave could immediately claim freedom.[49] This condition was unique because it did not address legal reality, but at least someone recognized that in another jurisdiction under Muslim law the title to Asmeto was defective.

In 1190 another six words were added to the same condition in a sale; the seller promised to defend the sale of a Saracen named Busso against all men "except the king of Sicily and his forces."[50] Genoa was on bad terms with the king of Sicily, and Busso may have been stolen or war booty. But King Tancred of Sicily was a Christian, and might someday again be a friend of Genoa, and there were Christian courts in Sicily where one might claim a slave. In 1200 a Greek slave named Alexius was sold in Genoa and in this case the seller promised to defend the sale against all men in the district of Genoa— basically Liguria.[51] This geographical limitation is also a unique condition. Alexius was probably from Romania, the lands of the Byzantine Empire which were now confined to the Aegean. He was certainly a Christian— probably Greek Orthodox, but nevertheless a Christian slave in a Christian society. This was not yet a problem, though in the thirteenth century some awkward questions would surface about the propriety of Christians owning coreligionists; hence, this was not the issue concerning Alexius. Again, there was probably a previous owner out there somewhere, in a place on bad terms with Genoa, and the seller was warning the buyer to keep the slave close to home. At five lire the price was about average so the buyer did not even get a discount. These few words in one condition evoke the broader context of slavery, that all slaves were in some sense stolen property. But once safely in Genoa everyone could pretend that title was secure, with a few words added occasionally to a contract just to be on the safe side. The larger point is that many of these experiments in refining contractual terms were failures, and most notaries kept to the dull but reliable words of their predecessors.

Women, buying and selling slaves, appear in significant numbers in

---

49. For some insights into Muslim slave law see Bernard Lewis, *Race and Slavery in the Middle East* (Oxford, 1990), pp. 7–10.

50. Mario Chiaudano and R. M. della Rocca, *Oberto Scriba 1190*, no. 612, p. 242, 1190: "excepto rege sicilie et eius fortia."

51. ASG, CN, N. 4, 239r, "in districtu ianue."

Oberto's contracts. To make a valid contract in Genoa, which followed Roman law, a woman had to renounce the Lex Julia, which guaranteed her certain rights, and she also needed the support of two men, called relatives, counselors, or *vicini* (whether neighbors or relatives is not always clear). These men were present as pseudo-guardians to protect the woman's interests (and also those of her male relatives); they were not there to consent to or guarantee anything. When a woman went into the market to make a big purchase like a slave (or to invest) she was not able to accomplish what men could do alone. Here is an example of the particular problems women faced. Marchisia the wife of Vallo sold a Saracen slave girl named Alaxina for four and a half lire on 8 July 1200. Marchisia had to promise twice that she would make sure her husband ratified the sale, and she also needed a *defensor*, Guglielmo Scarleta, who promised to uphold the sale against anyone, especially Marchisia's husband.[52] A husband might allow a wife to conduct business in his absence, and even leave behind a notarial act stating this. Marchisia had no such powers. Was she taking the opportunity of her husband's absence to get rid of a slave girl she did not want, or was this a routine sale complicated by Vallo's absence? We cannot answer these questions, but we know women were not free agents.

By the early thirteenth century, some new words appeared in the contracts. Color became a way to describe a slave and it remained for centuries a fixture of the contracts. A precocious notice of color appeared in 1190, when a contract noted that a slave was a white Saracen. Perhaps this unusual linking called for special remark.[53] After the conquest of Valencia there was a big glut of slaves in the Mediterranean markets, and some made their way to Genoa. Contracts from October of 1239 described a female, male, and little girl from Valencia as black; a female slave Axia as brown; and another one, also named Axia, as white.[54] This spectrum went from black to brown to white, but other hues also occurred, like olive, somewhere between brown and white. In 1252 one seller said his slave Asmeto was "brown between two colors"—just between black and white, or a subtle shade of brown.[55] The western Mediterranean slaves first raised the issue of color; another woman named Sofla, and described as a black from Ceuta in North Africa, shows that the Genoese had diverse sources of slaves.

What is the context for the words black, brown, olive, and white—when

---

52. ASG, CN, N. 4, 221v–222r, Oberto Scriba de Mercato notary.

53. M. Chiaudano and R. M. della Rocca, *Oberto Scriba 1190*, no. 487, p. 192.

54. ASG, CN, N. 24, pt. 1, 114v–115r, Bonovassallo de Cassino notary.

55. ASG, CN, N. 18, pt. 2, 30v, Januino de Predono notary: "brunus inter duos colores."

they refer to human beings? Sales of mules and horses frequently mentioned color, but never the names of the animals, if they had them. Sales of humans always noted the name, often an ethnic identity like Moor, Saracen, or Greek, and now a color. In the twelfth century perhaps the pool of potential slaves was limited to the central Mediterranean, and the slaves were more or less the same color—even Muslims from Sicily or Christians from Sardinia. The simplest interpretation is therefore that exotic slaves from the wider world diversified the Genoese slave population, so that people found it useful to distinguish slaves by color. In Palermo slave owners faced the same situation and were by the 1280s parties to the first surviving contracts noting color and ethnic origin: in Sicily there were plenty of slaves from Sclavonia (Dalmatia) and still some Muslims and Jews living according to their own traditions.[56] The Genoese knew Palermo well and may have copied the habit of noting skin color from its merchants.

Color alone was not always a useful means of identification when it came to important matters like describing a runaway. Color was a physical characteristic, and by itself it would be helpful in describing a black slave in virtually all-white Genoa. In Sicily, where brown does not routinely appear in the records (perhaps olive substituted), and where there were more people of color, color alone was less useful as a unique feature likely to identify an individual. There are not enough contracts before the fifteenth century to prove a correlation between color and price. Certainly color did not matter for horses or mules; their color was incidental to value. For humans it was probably different, but the brown Axia above was more expensive than the white one—L 7 as against L5s.15—and the black family of three sold for L 15, no real difference in cost when the child's likely low price is discounted. By the fifteenth century prices indicate a market preference for white slaves, at a time when racist attitudes abounded.[57] For the earlier centuries it is the context of the words for colors that might help to clarify their meaning in Italian societies. To be called "white," even to be called a "white Saracen slave" was more positive than the label "black Saracen slave." "White"'s association with purity, fairness, and virginity contrasted sharply as we have seen with the soiled, impure, and demonic connotations of "black." To be called "black" would not be so good for the people so categorized, but were the Genoese and Palermitans already discriminating against darker people, and did the adjective "black" simply ratify an older

56. See Pietro Bugarella, *Le imbreviature del notaio Adamo de Citella a Palermo (1 registro 1286–1287)* (Rome, 1981).

57. Domenico Gioffrè, *Il mercato degli schiavi a Genova nel secolo XV* (Genoa, 1971), pp. 129, 140. See also the discussion of prices and color in Chapter 4.

judgment, making things no worse for slaves? Since we are exploring the origins of western racism, these considerations are very important.

If we view the character of ancient Roman slavery as nonracist, especially in the western Mediterranean, and the character of the slave trade of early modern Europe as profoundly racist, then somewhere in between lay the roots of racism. Initially, slavery in Genoa lacked a strong racial component: there was no connection between color and the condition of slavery. (Between religion and slavery, yes—all the Muslims in Genoa were slaves.) Genoese slavery became incredibly diverse; by the fifteenth century there were yellow Tartar, white Circassian, brown and black Moorish and Saracen, Canary Island, and even Jewish slaves, and soon sub-Saharan Africans as well. The same was true in Venice and Palermo, but emancipations made some people of color into free inhabitants. All these crosscurrents make it impossible to locate distinctly racist values in these thirteenth-century markets. But labels carried their own sting in the context of the words "black" and "white."

At the same time in the 1230s and 40s new words helped to complicate the old problems of warranty regarding the character and health of slaves. Contracts now stipulated that slaves came, in the fullest formula, "with all the faults and defects" that they had.[58] The same language could also be used about a mule, such as one sold for seventeen lire in 1346.[59] Eventually a simpler expression attached to this condition and began to substitute for it—"pro tali qualis est"—the sale was of the slave "as is." These terms shifted the burden onto the buyer, whose job it was to be wary, and to diligently inquire about the plain and not so obvious problems of the slave. Here again, context is vital. An astute buyer was supposed to ask questions like: "Has this slave ever run away? Is she a thief? Has he been treated by a doctor in the last month?"—this last question relevant to a fifteenth-century court case.[60] If the slave ran away or dropped dead after the sale, it was buyer beware. After decades of experimenting on the issue of warranty, the Genoese found a sale "as is" to be the easiest solution. Seeking the best information about the slave required the seller to be honest when questioned, and lawyers could always be found to make a case, say, for the seller of a slave who died of a long-term illness concealed from the buyer. But the

---

58. ASG, CN, N. 31, pt. 1, 323v, 8 October 144, Matteo de Predono notary: "cum omnibus viciis et magagnis super se habentibus de cruribus." In this case the legs were a problem!

59. ASG, CN, N. 167, 161r, Lanfranco Nazario notary.

60. Bartolomeo de Bosco, *Consilia egregii domini Bartholomei de Bosco famosissimi iuris consulti genuensis* (Loano, 1620), no. 301, pp. 493–95.

shifting of responsibility onto buyers could only take place in a context where demand for slaves was high, and the sellers were at an advantage.

In the fourteenth century the legalese remained fairly stable, but ages began to appear in some contracts, for example, one involving—note this precision—a male slave named Benedetto, about fifteen years of age, from the mountains of Barca by Bernice (central Libya).[61] In an unusual lot sale of three slaves, a married couple and a single woman, the notary Benvenuto Bracelli covered all possible problems by employing a formula that stated that the slaves were free of all vices, faults, and defects, and sold as is.[62] A unique provision highlights the enduring problem of what to do about the presumed health of slaves. Archa de Busalla sold his slave Teodora and added the condition that if she appeared to have leprosy he would return the money, but only if signs of the disease appeared in the next fifteen days.[63] There must have been some grounds for suspicion, and also uniquely, the contract described Teodora as present, agreeing, and consenting. Perhaps someone in the family had developed leprosy and the owner wanted to sell this valuable slave before she contracted it. The fifteen-day waiting period is a remarkable concession to the fear of hidden illness, and we would like to know if it rested on any practical knowledge of incubation periods. After the devastating appearance of bubonic plague in 1348, illness became a serious issue for everyone in a world of labor shortages where the prices of slaves increased rapidly. Buying a slave during epidemics was a risky undertaking. The old problems worsened, the plague was a mystery, and guarantees of health were illusory. A female slave named Marta, sold in 1380, was declared "healthy up to today, free of all latent, hidden illnesses"—what more could the seller say?[64] Giovanni tried—when he sold his Tartar slave, also named Marta, in 1386 he declared her to be "healthy, in good condition, free of all faults and defects, apparent and not apparent."[65] What did it mean to claim that the slave was free of unapparent conditions? How could a court enforce this language? In the next century two Pisan sales contracts claimed that the slaves, both women, were not bed-

61. ASG, CN, N. 8, 91v, 10 April 1313, sold for nineteen lire.

62. ASG, CN, N. 289, 77v–78r, 10 January 1362—the three sold for the lump sum of L 150.

63. ASG, CN, N. 253, 164r, 19 August 1314, Parentino de Quinto notary, sold for fifteen lire.

64. Léone Liagre-De Sturler, *Les relations commerciales entre Gênes, la Belgique, et l'Outremont*, vol. 2 (Brussels, 1969), p. 506.

65. ASG, CN, N. 169, 216v, Antonio de Bonizio notary: "sana nitida de omnibus viciis et magagnis ipsius aparentibus et non aparentibus."

wetters, but at this point we have reached a level of finicky exactitude with few imitators.[66]

For Sicily, Matteo Gaudioso has described a similar evolution in contractual terms that produced three standard forms by the fifteenth century.[67] A sale contract "modu di fera" meant that the seller was not responsible for any defects—basically a sale "as is," or as the contracts elegantly put it, "as a sackful of bones" (*pro saculo ossibus pleno*). A sale "ad usum machazeni" followed common market practices where the buyer stipulated that if some specific defects appeared, he or she could return the slave. A sale "alla fratesca" implied total, brotherly good faith in both parties and assumed the sale would be so cordial as to preclude the need for all the fine print. After centuries of legal thought, the words of contracts were now basically settled throughout Italy, with some distinctive regional variations, so we can ask other questions about their context and meaning.

A Genoese sale from 1414 was one of the first to add a new right to the standard clause handing over to the owner the right to have, to hold, *to enjoy*, and to possess a slave.[68] The fact that the slave was a seventeen-year-old Tartar named Maria, sold for the high price of L 107, suggests that sexual exploitation was on the minds of the buyer and seller. A clear example of sexual motive occurs in the *consilia*, or legal opinions, of the early fifteenth-century Genoese lawyer Bartolomeo de Bosco.[69] In the Gogi case, a buyer attempted to recover the price of a slave who had died. Bosco, arguing for the seller, asserted that Gogi had purchased the slave to satisfy his own lust, and had attempted to return the slave woman (alas nameless) only when his own impotence prevented sex. Additionally, Gogi's own negligence in treating a case of skin mites in the slave was just as likely to have caused the slave's death as was any preexisting condition. Another sign of slavery's wider context is the growing trend in the late fourteenth and fifteenth centuries for contracts and other legal records to describe precisely the physical appearance and any distinguishing marks of the slave. The Florentine tax records on slave sales in the late trecento contained such details in order to ensure sellers paid the tax on the right merchandise. Contracts were also

---

66. A. D'Amia, *Schiavitù*, pp. 265 (1427), 273 (1456).

67. Matteo Gaudioso, *La schiavitù domestica in Sicilia dopo i normanni* (Catania, 1926; reprinted., 1992), pp. 87, 102–3.

68. A. D'Amia, *Schiavitù*, pp. 263–64.

69. See my "A Late Medieval Lawyer Confronts Slavery: The Cases of Bartolomeo de Bosco," *Slavery and Abolition* 20 (1999): 56–58, for a fuller discussion of this case, found in Bartolomeo de Bosco, *Consilia* (Loano, 1620) no. 301, pp. 493–95.

more specific, partly because they were more verbose, as B. Z. Kedar has noted about documents in general after the plague of 1348, but also because good descriptions helped to track down runaways.[70] So, for example, when the Genoese merchant Geronimo Spinola sold to a Sienese noble in 1489 a slave girl named Caterina, from the Canary Islands, he noted that she had a greenish mark on her chin and a small cross on her face under her right eye—details that defined this fourteen-year-old girl for life. Although increasingly detailed, the physical descriptions, mostly of women, lack notices of one complicating condition—pregnancy. Even though a sale contract recorded in Syracuse in 1456 noted that the thirty-year-old Russian slave Uliana did not suffer from a lack of menstruation, among other possible defects, it was rare for any document to note that a woman was fertile, infertile, or pregnant.[71]

Why did not the sales contracts consider the possibility that female slaves were pregnant, and make some provision for the offspring? In Genoa, as elsewhere in most of Italy, children followed the status of the mother, a tradition going back to the Romans. Since paternity was a question of guesswork or hope, while maternity was an observable fact, it made sense to attach slavery to the mother's social condition. But what about a pregnant slave? Another type of legal document, the last will, offered a married man the chance to provide for the possibility that his wife was pregnant and might produce an heir for him, changing the inheritance pattern within the family, as a posthumous son might in a family of daughters. Pregnancy was an important contingency in a testament, but not in a slave sale. Did the pregnancy of a slave matter?—especially since whatever child came to light would be a slave "without consent or contract," to borrow Robert Fogel's phrase. Yes, but in unexpected ways. In Venice on 17 July 1394, Marco Giustiniani, as representative for Giovanni Morosini, sold to Franceschino Mudacio a twenty-four-year-old Circassian slave named Marta, described as "pregnant, otherwise healthy," for sixty ducats.[72] Pregnancy could be a defect in a slave, a perilous state that might kill her, and it could produce a child who would create nothing of value for years, possibly die in childhood anyway, and certainly cost something to feed and clothe.

70. On verbosity see Benjamin Z. Kedar, *Merchants in Crisis: Genoese and Venetian Men of Affairs and the Fourteenth-Century Depression* (New Haven, Conn., 1976), p. 108.

71. A. D'Amia, *Schiavitù*, pp. 272–74.

72. *Bernardo de Rodulfis: Notaio in Venezia (1392–1399)*, ed. Giorgio Tamba (Venice, 1974) no. 92, pp. 100–101.

In this case, more was at stake, for on 20 July Franceschino turned around and sold Marta to Marco Giustiniani, for fifty-eight ducats, on condition that when a son, a daughter, or more was born, the buyer would give the child(ren) to Franceschino.[73] (These special provisions for the child were a good reason for a written contract.) On the same day, Marco sold Marta to someone else for the same price, on condition that whatever was born be given to himself or Franceschino![74] Sold three times in four days, Marta was probably pregnant by Marco Giustiniani, who caused a blizzard of paperwork to get rid of the slave, keep the baby, and conceal his part. If a slave became pregnant, and was not married, and the owner knew he was not the father, he had a disgrace and some violated hospitality on his hands. Silence on the question of pregnancy makes a lot of sense in this context.

How did the slave contracts protect a person from being illegally sold into slavery? In some places, like Norman Sicily, the law severely punished anyone selling a free person as a slave; in this kingdom the seller became a slave.[75] Matters were not always so clear. In 1127 a man named Lupo, along with his advocate, appeared before a judge in Bari.[76] Lupo claimed that he was unjustly being held as a slave by a father and son; they in turn asserted that Lupo was the son of a deceased slave named Maria, who had come into the family as part of a dowry. Lupo insisted that he was born free, and that his mother, a Bulgarian whose name he did not know, had been a free servant in the house, but that is all he remembered. Without any documents to help settle the case, the judge sought out witnesses. He found two people who swore that Lupo's mother was the Bulgarian, and another woman stood up in court and swore that she knew that Lupo's mother was a free person. The judge ordered Lupo to be treated as a free man, and he repeated the legal maxim that no one of the Christian religion should be held as a slave without a legitimate reason, except those born of slaves. The judge imposed no penalty on the slaveholders, who surely had committed more than an innocent error.

A contract's language usually safeguarded the interests of buyers and sellers, but since the consent of the slave was almost never an issue, how could the unjustly enslaved person be protected? Obviously, only the buyer was in a position to help. Here is an example of the problem. In late 1328 a Genoese named Baliano was in Palermo trying to sell as a slave a Greek

73. Ibid., no. 95, pp. 103–4.
74. Ibid., no. 96, pp. 105–6.
75. James M. Powell, *Liber Augustalis* (Syracuse, N.Y., 1971), p. 149.
76. *Codice diplomatico barese*, 5:128–30.

from Pera named Mauro.[77] Unfortunately for Baliano, a powerful local noble and official, Guido Filangeri, wanted to buy the slave and he asked Mauro if he was Baliano's slave. Perhaps Filangeri was already suspicious, but more likely this was part of the ordinary questioning that accompanied buying a slave. Mauro said he was no one's slave, and Filangeri put him and Baliano both in prison while he investigated the business. Filangeri questioned four Genoese merchants and one ship captain, and they all said the sale was bad and evil because the Greek was a free man. The captain said that he had known Mauro to be free for a long time: Mauro was a sailor in his galley and had been going around the world for about four years. This key testimony convinced Filangeri to free Mauro; Baliano's fate is unknown.

How could Mauro be wandering around Palermo with Baliano, who was trying to sell him as a slave? Language does not come up as an issue, but it hardly ever does. Mauro was a Greek from Pera, the Genoese colonial settlement across the Golden Horn from Constantinople. Sailing in Genoese galleys for some years, he probably knew enough Genoese to get along, and somehow he was able to understand and respond to questions asked him in the dialect of Palermo. Baliano was a crooked and happily stupid fellow, but he must have figured that slaves often denied they were rightfully slaves, and who paid any attention to their slavish complaints? How could he prove Mauro was a slave? Luckily for Mauro, Filangeri figured out how to prove he was not one, but if these other Genoese had left port or were in on the game, Mauro might have been in deep trouble. For so many other people, stolen into slavery anyway and lacking the language skills to defend themselves, there would be no moment of justice, just chains or a few scars or brands to "prove" their status as slaves. Since bills of sale were not yet routine, clear title depended on the good faith of the seller. Despite all the legalese in the contract, Mauro's case reminds us to try whenever possible to hear the words or language of slaves.

LANGUAGE OF FREEDOM

Another type of notarial contract was the act of manumission by which an owner freed a person from the chains and yoke of slavery. This form of emancipation existed alongside an older one—manumission in church. Freeing slaves of course occurred under ancient slavery, and Constantine

77. *Acta Curie Felicis Urbis Panormi*, vol. 5, *Registri di lettere ed atti (1328–1333)*, ed. Pietro Corrao (Palermo, 1986), pp. 77–78.

granted to Christians the right to free their slaves in church, with the bishop's approval and a minimum of formalities.[78] Although this style of freeing a slave had mostly yielded by the central Middle Ages to more formal, contractual arrangements, it still happened, and reflected the belief that freeing a slave was a charitable act revealing one's inner intentions. The style of manumission in Bari preserved traces of this old custom. There, a slave being manumitted processed around the main altar in a church as a public display of freedom.[79] But Christianity, along with Islam, obliged no one to free his or her slave. All faiths enjoined masters to treat their slaves with humanity and compassion.[80] In legal terms, a manumission was a speech act that changed the slave's reality. The existence of this escape hatch did not mean the law's framers harbored doubts about the morality of slavery. The prospect of eventual freedom for a few deserving slaves was a legitimate incentive and safety valve in the system.

Again, a standard format for an emancipation appears in the cartulary of Giovanni Scriba, whose customers freed a number of slaves by will or by special act. Emancipations usually stated the owner's motives, which concerned God, healing the owner's soul, and the remission of sins.[81] Eventually the slave's good service also counted as a reason for freedom, but the main weight continued to fall on the owner's charitable intentions. One of medieval Italy's most famous slave owners, the Venetian traveler Marco Polo, freed his slave Pietro in his will written in 1324. Polo stated that he was doing this "so that God may absolve my soul from all guilt and sin"—surely a sign of some scruples about slavery.[82] Without yet revealing any public doubts about the legality of slavery, people still believed that freeing a slave sacrificed a piece of property and as charity this act pleased God and benefited the soul. So there must have been some qualms about the propriety of slavery. When the widow Marina Zancaruolo made her will in Venetian Crete in 1331, she stipulated, among other bequests contingent upon her residual heir dying, that up to three hundred hyperpers (a considerable sum) be spent on purchasing male and female slaves, and then freeing

78. Fabrizio Fabbrini, *La Manumissio in Ecclesia* (Milan, 1965), p. 51.

79. *Codice diplomatico barese*, 5:62. This example is from 1103.

80. F. Fabbrini, *La Manumissio*, pp. 212–14.

81. Clear early examples in M. Chiaudano and M. Moresco, *Giovanni Scriba*, no. 867, 2:31, 28 July 1161, and no. 1070, 2:134–35, 4 August 1163.

82. Marco Polo's will has been published many times. I use here the one in Henry Yule, *The Book of Ser Marco Polo* (London, 1929) vol. 2, pp. 513–15: "ut Deus absolvat animam meam ab omni culpa et peccato."

them.[83] Special circumstances on a colonial island apply here to an apparently Greek woman whose charity might have freed some Greek slaves. But the point is that to free slaves, one had to buy them first, no matter how charitable one's intentions. A manumission from Polizzi in Sicily noted in 1461 that God had created humanity from base earth in His own image and likeness, and this old truth prompted reflections on a common humanity as a reason to free a slave.[84]

Still, one Genoese owner admitted he freed a slave for God and one hundred solidi, and as we will see, money or other rewards certainly also prompted some owners to free slaves.[85] In the earliest surviving Genoese emancipation, from 1161, the owner freed Giovanni from the yoke of slavery, granted him the grace (of freedom) that nature merits, removed the stain of slavery, and sent him on his way, free in God.[86] Another early emancipation gave the slave the freedom to go to the four corners of the world and the right to make contracts and conduct business.[87] Other basic rights usually conceded included the *peculium*, the slave's personal property, if any, and the rights of a free Roman citizen, including the ability to make a will. Although few emancipations explicitly mention it, Oberto Scriba was careful to note in an act of 1204 that he made two copies, one for the owner and the other for the ex-slave.[88] These written words became proof of freedom, and every emancipation also contained a heavy monetary penalty on the owner if he or she tried to revoke it without just cause. In an early and legalistic emancipation from Pisa, on 12 December 1172 the owners of Furata declared before a judge that they freed her by their own will and without violence, prompted instead by a love of God and a desire to reward her good service.[89] This Pisan couple also renounced the right of patronage—the enduring obligations, including gratitude, that an ancient Roman slave owner had a right to expect from his freedman or freedwoman. Emancipations usually ignored or renounced this right, but they frequently imposed other, serious conditions.

83. Sally McKee, *Wills from Late Medieval Venetian Crete 1312–1420*, vol. 2 (Washington, D.C., 1998), p. 539.

84. M. Gaudioso, *La schiavitù*, p. 126: "considerans quod summa providencia omnipotens dei ad suam ymaginem et similitudinem umanum genus de limo terre formavit . . ."

85. Mario Chiaudano and Mattia Moresco, *Il cartolare di Giovanni Scriba* (Rome, 1935), no.1150, 2:173, 22 June 1164.

86. Ibid., no. 867, 2:31.

87. Ibid., no. 907, 2:49, 17 September 1161.

88. ASG, CN, Cart. N. 4, 94r.

89. A. D'Amia, *Schiavitù*, no. 12, pp. 228–29.

We do not know what percentage of slaves were ever freed, but it seems to have been small. The owners' motives remain elusive, but we must accept the common claim of spirituality that prompted some of them to give away this peculiar form of property. Unusual circumstances in the Genoese merchant colony in Pera, near Constantinople and since May of 1453 under the control of the Ottoman Turks, show how an Italian faced special incentives to free a slave. Agostino di Taggia owned a Circassian slave named Margarita.[90] Her brothers Acmat and Mustafa, both Muslims, petitioned Agostino to free their sister. Back in Genoa Agostino would not have had to face this request or the brothers—who most likely would have been enslaved on the spot. In Pera, Agostino, claiming to have been moved by the requests of the three siblings, on 3 August 1453 manumitted Margarita on condition that she continue to serve him and his family for three years. If Margarita was also a Muslim, she might have claimed her freedom immediately, since no Christian could own her in a Muslim land. Yet nothing is stated about her faith. Agostino was lucky to get anything in exchange for freeing this slave, and he claimed no spiritual motives for the manumission.

Wills provide another view of what owners intended, and this Genoese evidence is rich. Instead of just the legal formulae, we have some personal language to explore. Safran de Clavica freed his slave Vera if she found a husband, with the counsel of his wife Bonaventura.[91] In 1248 an owner freed his slave Mussa only if he agreed to become a Christian.[92] In 1307 Margarita the wife of Guglielmo de Celvo freed her slave Elena, and stipulated that her husband should receive his legacy only after he made sure the slave was freed.[93] These kinds of conditions suggest desires to control slaves, by making them convert, or marry, or in a few cases become nuns, but in any event to control the expression of their sexuality.

But far more commonly, the conditions, both in wills and emancipations, concerned money or continued service, and these appear early. Arnaldo de Narbona emancipated his slave Maria Nigra (Black Mary) in 1186 on the usual terms, but he required her to serve him for an additional ten years.[94]

90. Ausilia Roccatagliata, "Notai genovesi in Oltremare: Atti rogati a Pera (1453)," *Atti della Società Ligure di Storia Patria* 39 (1999): 101–60; here pp. 134–35.

91. Margaret W. Hall, Hilmar C. Krueger, and Robert L. Reynolds, *Guglielmo Cassinese* (Turin, 1938) no. 239, pp. 97–98, 23 February 1191.

92. ASG, CN, Cart. N. 26, pt. 2., 19v.

93. ASG, CN, Cart. N. 138, 194r–v, 195r.

94. Mario Chiaudano, *Oberto Scriba de Mercato 1186* (Turin, 1940), no. 342, pp. 130–31, 20 December 1186.

Sometimes the deal seems to have been relatively advantageous. Petrina Borrino in 1307 freed her slave Giovanna, who was about twenty years old, on condition that she stay with Simona Embriaco as a servant for the next six years in exchange for food, drink, a bed, and nine lire salary for the years of service.[95] So at twenty-six Giovanna would have a small nest egg and unconditional freedom, and she presumably had a safer life working for a woman. The other common condition was a straight payment. In a number of emancipations from Palermo in 1298–99, most freedoms came in exchange for cash payments roughly equal to the purchase prices. This is clear in the case of Azziza, who was freed in exchange for four ounces of gold to be paid over the next two years, exactly the price her master originally paid.[96] So he was allowing the slave in effect to purchase herself. In this case Azziza also had to wash cloths once a week for her ex-master, so he also got free laundry for two years. One condition in Genoa highlights the dangers possible in being just a bit too specific. In 1252 Giovanni Bucino freed his slave Giovannetta provided that she serve his wife for ten years. If his wife died, Giovannetta should serve his children for five years, including whatever time would already have been served.[97] Inadvertently, these conditions gave the ex-slave a powerful reason to murder the widow sometime early during the term, and cut her service in half. Possibilities like this, and a general fear of hopeful slaves, led Genoa to abolish emancipations by will in the early fourteenth century, as we will see later.

And so the masters sent some slaves free into the world to take whatever road they wanted (as one document put it) with some strings attached. A few emancipations contain some special parting words or acts. When Giofredo Zaccaria manumitted his slave Catalina, a Cuman, in 1354, he specifically granted her all rights as if she had been freeborn in Genoa.[98] Here, citizenship meant more than vague Roman rights. A Sienese owner in 1441 bid his slave Maddalena de Caffa farewell with these words, "Be free and a Roman citizen, released from any and all slavery to me."[99] In his will of 1393 the Venetian noble Pantaleone Giustiniani ordered his slaves Calli and Costa to be freed, and wanted the contract of their servitude—the sales

95. ASG, CN, Cart. N. 138, 370r.

96. Pietro Gulotta, *Le imbreviature del notaio Adamo de Citella a Palermo (2 registro 1298–1299)* (Rome, 1982), no. 344, pp. 267–68.

97. ASG, CN, Cart. N. 27, 259r.

98. ASG, CN, Cart. N. 288, 206 r–v, Benvenuto de Bracelli notary: "sic in Ianua nata fuisse sive a natalibus liberis."

99. G. Prunai, "Notizie," pp. 403–4: "Esto libera civis romana et ab omni et qualibet mea servituti exempta."

contract—to be cut up and placed in their hands, thereby literally destroying the words of their enslavement.[100]

Three final documents show some special and revealing conditions. In Palermo on 27 January 1287 Catapano de Marino sold to the Saracen Salah an olive-colored Saracen slave named Fatima, and on the same day Salah freed her without conditions.[101] Salah rescued a woman from slavery to a Christian, an act probably only possible in Sicily, and not for long, as the power of the indigenous Muslim population waned. The Sienese knight Bartolomeo di Tuccio freed his slave Margarita and their son Vittorio in 1382, freely admitting he was the father. Sometimes parenthood or just a sexual relation accounted for the emancipation, though in this case the father waited until the boy was ten. Perhaps struck by the meaning of slavery in the person of his son, Bartolomeo had included in this emancipation some unusual sentiments—that before God there was no accepting of people (as property), and that by natural law all people are born free.[102] It was easier to concede these points when one's own flesh was enslaved. Vittorio went on to assume a respectable position in Sienese society, and was named *capitano del popolo* in 1413, a rare documented case of upward social mobility for an ex-slave, albeit one with a noble father.[103] Also in Siena, on 2 October 1495, Antonio Bichi freed his slave Caterina, whom he had purchased six years earlier for fifty-two ducats, and who had served him well.[104] As a gift, he handed her fifty-two ducats on the day of her freedom, and he also found her a husband, Cola Gobita, described as "ex partibus indianis"— perhaps a Canary Islander, as this is probably too early for him to have been a Caribbean Indian. The couple agreed to work for Antonio for fifteen years in exchange for food and clothing. But still, Caterina experienced something few slaves ever knew—she held her considerable price in her own hands. Bichi's actions are curious—apparent guilt about slavery mixed with the paternalism of "finding" her a husband.

These emancipations occasionally allow us to hear as well as imagine the ex-slaves. One chance to hear an ex-slave is on the day he or she was both slave and free. On 27 May 1314, Tomasso Archerio, for the benefit of his

100. G. Tamba, *Bernardo*, no. 12, p. 21.

101. P. Bugarella, *Adamo*, nos. 90, 92, pp. 68, 69.

102. G. Prunai, "Notizie," no. 14, pp. 273–75.

103. Maria A. Ceppari Ridolfi et al., *Schiave ribaldi e signori* (Siena, 1994), pp. 3–12. These details are in the documented part of the fictionalized account of this episode, in a book that consciously tries to blur the line between history and fiction, and hence must be used with caution.

104. G. Prunai, "Notizie," no. 56, pp. 430–32.

soul, freed his slave Martino.[105] In the next notarial act, Martino de Mauro-castro (a Black Sea port near the mouth of the Dniester), declared that he had been made free that day, and promised to serve Archerio for four years from this Christmas, or else the manumission would be canceled.[106] Martino acquired a name (in this case a revealing toponymic) and the ability to make a contract to have a legal voice. He was compelled or obliged to give his master something in exchange for his freedom. Such conditions were common in emancipations, either included in the master's notarial act, or as here, promised by the slave as his or her first act as a free man or woman.

Here is another more complex example of a slave's voice. At about midday on 18 June 1314, Giovanni Bonvillano sold to Raimondino de Castronovo for seventeen lire a slave named Nicola Greco de Salonika, with all his faults and defects, as is.[107] By now the notary Parentino de Quinto was routinely recording the previous owner, so Giovanni stated that the slave had been sold to him by an Antonio de Moneglia, as in a legal instrument by the notary Januino Vatacio. All this took place in the canonry next to the hospital of San Giovanni, near the port and one of the commercially busiest and spiritually most respected places in Genoa. In the next act, occurring at the same time and place, Raimondino freed his slave Nicola in a standard contract, which also gave Nicola all his *peculium*, whatever personal property the slave had.[108] In turn Nicola promised to stay with Raimondino, to serve him on land and sea, and to perform all necessary services for six years. Nicola claimed to be more than eighteen years old (the age required to make these promises) and he swore to observe the terms. Raimondino called himself the emancipated son of Jacopo de Castronovo, and by doing this he is noting his own legal majority, probably recent, so he was around the same age as Nicola.

There are many ways to use this language to explore behavior. Raimondino bought a slave in order to free him on the same day. This is unusual, and raises the question of how long Raimondino knew Nicola before he bought him. There must have been some relationship between the two. The very mention of *peculium* in the purchase contract indicates that Nicola was in a favored state for a slave and he must have known he was being sold for the last time. Raimondino loaded every possible incentive for Nicola to be a loyal worker for the next six years, and it only cost him seventeen lire,

105. ASG, CN, Cart. N. 253, 106r, Parentino de Quinto notary.
106. ASG, CN, Cart. N. 253, 106r.
107. ASG, CN, Cart. N., 253, 122r, Parentino de Quinto notary.
108. ASG, CN, Cart. N., 253, 122v.

a cheap price for such service. Raimondino might have kept Nicola as a slave and promised freedom after six years. This too would have been a powerful means of control, but he did not. Raimondino might have added to the emancipation the rather typical condition that if Nicola did not serve loyally and well, he would be returned to the status of servitude and his freedom canceled. But there was no threat to return Nicola to slavery here. In fact, Nicola was on his oath but nothing more. Raimondino's behavior seems calculated to get the maximum of gratitude and loyalty from Nicola, and to rely on these emotions to provide the incentive for Nicola to work hard for the next six years. And all this was done in public, where people could observe the arrangements, and it was all very smart on Raimondino's part.

Nicola Greco de Salonika, clearly a Greek who knew the town he was from, had a full name the day he was still a slave, another unusual feature of the contract. His promise to serve on land and sea indicates a merchant's career for the master and six years of quasi-apprenticeship for the servant/companion Nicola, who probably brought a useful knowledge of Greek and the eastern Mediterranean to his new job. Merchants, frequently accompanied by a slave, servant, or apprentice, learned their trade by doing it, and so no doubt the pair soon took to the sea to make their fortunes. If Nicola kept his eyes open, and made some money of his own on the side, he could eventually become a merchant and enter Genoese society while still young enough to enjoy it. And he had a name, often the only words we surely know about a slave, besides his or her price.

THE WORDS OF THE LAW

Jef Verschueren has observed that "strategies of language use are ways of exploiting the interplay between explicitness and implicitness in the generation of meaning."[109] Users of language are constantly negotiating how explicit they need to be in particular contexts. A conventional style of language is, from one point of view, an efficient compromise about the boundaries between the implicit and explicit. These insights are especially valuable when we look at the law as language, as an instance of what M. Bakhtin called a speech genre or speech community.[110] Only the most obtuse positivist could view the law as only explicit, without a context or conventions of expression that change over time. One of the benefits of pragmatics is

109. J. Verschueren, *Understanding Pragmatics*, p. 156.
110. Ibid., pp. 151–56.

that it encourages a fresh look at the law. Explicit meanings are seldom as clear as the literalists believe. Only a historical approach to language and the law can recover what is implicit in old law, what the lawmakers took for granted centuries ago. Laws are a special genre of writing or speech, often opaque to outsiders. Since so much of Italian law remained in Latin for so long, the genre also privileges the language itself as well as the force behind the words. Legal phrases like "I marry," "I sentence you," or even "I promise" are special types of speech acts, called performatives in pragmatics, because they change realities or accomplish something real when someone utters them. Knowing what the law says about slavery is vital, but how the law says it is also critical to our understanding of what choices were made, what negotiations took place, when people put their intentions into words.

Back in 1905 the distinguished Milanese historian Ettore Verga set himself the task of finding an instance of a slave sold in Milan to a Milanese, and he succeeded. Why he wanted to find it is just as interesting as the discovery. Verga was struck by the complete absence of slavery from all Milanese law, but his instincts told him that slavery existed and that the law's silence was misleading. Soon he found that about 1487 Gaspare Ambrogio Visconti purchased in Milan a four-year-old black slave named Dionisio, originally from the slave market in Tunis.[111] A person was a legitimate item of commerce in Milan, but one would never guess this from reading the law. By not prohibiting slavery, the law implicitly permitted it. Throughout Italy Roman law, the common law unless superseded by local law, did not question the legitimacy of slavery. Dionisio's story means that a contextual reading of the law is essential to understanding how slavery actually worked as a legal institution.

The phenomenon of slavery without explicit law occurs first in the best early collection of law for any Italian state, the statutes of Pisa. The brief (legal primer) of 1162 for the consuls of the commune casually lists male and female slaves among those essential moveables and immoveable items exempted from taxes.[112] This reference is the only legal evidence that slavery existed in Pisa in 1162. Notarial contracts amply demonstrate this fact for Genoa, but in Pisa this type of record does not survive from this period. The late twelfth-century law code of Pisa notes that slaves were allowed to

---

111. Ettore Verga, "Per la storia degli schiavi orientali in Milano," *Archivio storico lombardo* 32 (1905): 188–95, here pp. 194–95.

112. Francesco Bonaini, *Statuti inediti della città di Pisa dal XII al XV secolo*, vol. 1 (Florence, 1854), pp. 4–5.

marry but they nonetheless remained slaves.[113] Emancipation of slaves was also legal. The marvelous contemporary commercial code of Pisa, the earliest and most comprehensive for all of Europe, does not mention slavery at all. Hence the best early legal evidence is almost useless on slavery, especially without the documents of practice, the contracts.

Frederick III of Sicily legislated in 1310 on slaves in a systematic way and "aimed to bring slave ownership more in line with Christian values."[114] This law was relatively humane for Christian slaves, and hence a powerful incentive for Muslim and Jewish slaves to convert, which was perhaps its implicit purpose. The law also used religion to encourage "slaves to be submissive to masters, pleasing them in everything without being fraudulent or disobedient, but in all things attending with good faith . . ."[115] In order to foster human kindness the law prohibited masters from whipping Christian slaves and from cutting or branding their faces—clearly the old influence of Constantine here. Frederick also made clear that nothing prevented a master from punishing, in a light, careful, and kindly way (*juste, leviter, et benigne*) any runaway, deceitful, or impudent slave, and putting a slave in chains was also legal. This law code also confirms the existence of two practices that must have been widespread across Italy.[116] First, the law required that all children of slaves, no matter the religion of the parents, be baptized as Christians. The penalty for breaking this rule was severe: the infant would immediately become free—a powerful incentive for the owner to make sure the baptism occurred. This rule naturally ensured that the children of Muslim and Jewish slaves would not follow the religion of their mothers. Second, the law prohibited masters from putting Christian slave women to work as prostitutes. The penalty was a year in prison for the master and freedom for the slave, but this law omitted, almost certainly intentionally, Jewish and Muslim women from its protections. In Sicily a ruler's

113. Ibid., vol. 2 (Florence, 1870), pp. 790, 792. See David Herlihy, *Pisa in the Early Renaissance* (New Haven, Conn., 1958), pp. 13–14, for more on these law codes.

114. Clifford R. Backman, *The Decline and Fall of Medieval Sicily* (Cambridge, 1995), p. 259 for the quotation, pp. 259–61 for what follows. For the background to this legislation see M. Gaudioso, *La schiavitù*, pp. 41–45.

115. C. Backman, *Decline*, p. 261: "servos enim oportet dominis suis subditos esse, in omnibus placentes non contradicentes, non fraudantes, sed in omnibus fidem bonam attendentes . . ."

116. Here I rely directly on *Capitula Regni Siciliae*, ed. Francesco Testa (Palermo, 1741), pp. 78, 81.

own spiritual values and sense of proper kingship profoundly reshaped the legal structure of slavery, but we cannot know how successful he was in having these intentions carried out.

Genoa's good sources again provide the richest context for interpreting the law's language on slavery. The statutes of Pera, redacted around 1300 for the Genoese colony near Constantinople, largely reflect practices back home in Liguria. This law revealed the two major concerns the Genoese had about their slaves.[117] First, the famous provision that slave owners could not free slaves by last will and testament, lest the slaves hasten the deaths of their masters, emphasizes that a main part of the implicit and explicit context and meaning of the law was fear of slaves. Second, the law imposed draconian punishments and fines on anyone helping a slave to run away, or transporting a slave without the owner's permission, as well as provided rewards for people assisting in finding slaves without proper passes. On Venetian Crete a similar set of laws from 1349 rewarded people who found or captured runaway slaves, and placed huge fines on anyone encouraging a slave to flee.[118] The colonial setting on Crete also revealed that Orthodox monasteries were suspected of harboring runaway slaves. The perennial issue of runaways also appeared in provisions in more comprehensive statutes from the next century.

On 29 March 1403, Jean Le Meingre, called Boucicaut, marshal of France and royal governor of Genoa, accepted and approved a revised set of statutes for the city. Nowhere in this code is there a place where the law on slavery appears as a considered whole. Instead, nearly all notices of slavery occur in the rules on guilds, and in the criminal law. The law was chaotically organized, but in any event ordinary people do not learn social rules by reading the law. Lawyers do that, and people needing to know the law consult lawyers and pay for it. Slaves very rarely had this opportunity, so they must have learned the rules from their masters, from other slaves, or by witnessing exemplary punishments of transgressing slaves. But the law indicates that the Genoese controlled how slaves worked and what they did. Labor is the key to understanding how a society can master the problem of how to live well, and these rules on slavery are a guide to how the Genoese intended to make some people work and live for the benefit of others. Yet the slave code of Genoa is partly a misnomer, since we must assemble it from the scattered references in the law. So we cannot assume that any person or group had grasped the overall significance of slavery in Genoese so-

117. Vincenzo Promis, "Statuti della colonia genovese di Pera," *Miscellanea di storia d'Italia* 11 (1871): 513–780, here pp. 714–15.

118. Paola Ratti Vidulich, *Duca di Candia: Quaternus Consiliorum (1340–1350)* (Venice, 1976), pp. 129–32.

ciety. But for now, let us consider the new, comprehensive code to extract the general legal language of slavery as it existed in Genoa around 1400.

To start with the laws on the guilds, a few seemingly incongruous provisions merit scrutiny. No banker, goldsmith, or any other person was allowed to buy silver, pearls, precious stones, or gold from any male or female slave or servant, or any boy or girl younger than fifteen.[119] This mixture of slaves, servants, and adolescents—those in the power of the others who lived well, the free self-supporting adults—were obvious candidates for stealing and so the law tried to prevent them from benefiting by such thefts. The officials in charge of taxing the possession of slaves, and retail merchants, were not permitted to buy for themselves or anyone else any male or female slaves without the Mercanzia's permission.[120] These officials were naturally in a position to gain from their special knowledge of slaves and their availability. Buried in the rules on butchers is the vital (to slaves) provision that any male or female slave who married with the master's consent was not thereby free.[121] Only the express will of the master freed a slave. This rule is not in the section concerning marriage (civil law), but why here? Perhaps the original case involved a slave belonging to a butcher, in whose heavy, dangerous trade slaves sometimes worked. We do learn that slaves were allowed to marry, in a town where women slaves would soon outnumber the men about forty to one, and the belief persisted that Christian marriage somehow implied or granted freedom. The reality was different in Genoa, however, where emancipation was legal, but not to be confused with permission to marry. The law is silent on selling married slaves and their children apart or as an unbreakable unit, so both these practices must have been legal. Yet again, given the overwhelming numbers of female slaves, very few would ever get married anyway.

Sellers of used keys were not supposed to sell their wares to any male servant or slave or any other person except the master or mistress of a house.[122] In this case gender mattered; the law assumed that women slaves or servants were implausible purchasers of used keys. More ominously, the rules of the apothecaries stated that only a master of a shop could sell, give, or transfer arsenic, with a stiff penalty of up to 100 lire.[123] Also, the apothecaries were not supposed to teach their trade to any Tartar or Turkish slave,

---

119. *Leges Genuenses*, vol. 18, col. 564.

120. Ibid., col. 570.

121. Ibid., col. 584.

122. Ibid., col. 643.

123. Ibid., col. 675–76. For more on poisoning as a type of behavior, see Chapter 3.

under penalty of 50 lire. Other slaves might learn the trade, but even if freed, they could only work as day laborers and never be heads of shops. Even an ex-slave was not to be trusted with selling arsenic. Orlando Patterson found that in colonial Jamaica poisoning was "the means usually employed for exacting vengeance on the master."[124] The Obeah men with their knowledge of herbs and poisons evoke Turks and Tartars. Poisoning was on the minds of Genoese slave owners, but they were especially concerned about those slaves from the east, the Tartars and Turks. It is also clear that emancipated slaves were not fully accepted in Genoese society, and here too the owners' collective guilt was projected onto the victims.

Nothing makes this more clear than another odd rule set down in the middle of the rubrics on guilds. Any manumitted male or female slaves who got involved in or were suspected of prostitution, adultery, theft, or aiding those who behaved badly and thereby earning the hatred and contempt of their neighbors, could be expelled from the neighborhood if three-quarters or more of the residents agreed.[125] If the ex-slave refused to leave in the time allotted, he or she was to be locked out of the house. There were former slaves in town, and the Genoese believed that freeing a slave was a charitable act pleasing to God and benefiting the soul. Some of these former slaves perhaps fell into bad company, troubled respectable people, and set a bad example for slaves. It is unusual to give neighbors the right to throw someone out, and this provision did not apply in general to suspicious characters, just former slaves. Prostitutes, another second class group, had to live in a specified neighborhood.

To finish the section of the law concerning trades, sellers of precious stones were allowed to sell slaves—an interesting synergy of luxury businesses.[126] Rules prohibited cloth merchants from buying any clothing or other things from any slave, garbageman, servant, or person of bad or dishonest reputation.[127] The buyer lost the merchandise and the purchase price. A similar rule warned the coppersmiths not to buy any metal—tin, lead, copper, or bronze—from a slave or garbageman; the penalty here was a small fine and loss of the purchase.[128] Not as serious as poison or used keys, used clothing and old pots still constituted ways that thieving slaves could acquire money they were not supposed to have. All these provisions show just how embedded slaves were in the general context of Genoese life.

124. Orlando Patterson, *The Sociology of Slavery* (Rutherford, N.J., 1969), p. 265.
125. *Leges Genuenses*, vol. 18, col. 645.
126. Ibid., col. 680.
127. Ibid., col. 714.
128. Ibid., col. 713.

Rules on overseas trade also mentioned slaves as items of commerce. Owners of galleys were not allowed to transport slaves out of Chios, a Genoese colony in the Aegean. Apparently it was hard to keep slaves on the island—so tantalizing close to the Ottoman state.[129] Merchants traveling aboard ship were always allowed to have one slave as a servant. The government set rules on how many slaves different types of ships could carry: one-masted ships could load thirty slaves; two-masted ships, forty-five slaves; three-masted ships, sixty slaves. These commonsense regulations reveal a lot of experience in shipping slaves, and a sensible reluctance to transport slaves by galley—too little cargo space and frequent tempting stops for food and water. Overall, these parts of the law reveal that slaves were familiar objects of commerce and suspicion in late medieval Genoa.

Only one part of Genoa's complex civil law noted slaves. The new code included an old provision, set in the law since 1300, that prevented masters from freeing slaves by will.[130] Here again, practical experience must have caused this fear of murderous slaves. The absence of slaves from the civil law of course shows that they were not civic people, citizens. Instead they were, for almost all real purposes, socially dead and simply things, the talking tools that Aristotle envisioned. Why after 1300 the apparently innocuous custom of freeing slaves by will was no longer tolerable to the Genoese remains a mystery. Perhaps, as was the case in some Southern American states, the implicit purpose was to preserve the property of the heirs, apart from the explicit fear of poisoning.

The criminal law contains the most somber aspects of the slave code, revealing how free people were also part of the system. In Genoese law rape was a capital crime, but in some cases a quick marriage could save the culprit from death.[131] The rape of a slave or a "dishonest woman," however carried a fine of fifty to one hundred lire. In the case of a slave half the fine went to the owner, making him or her in effect a beneficiary of the rape. Free women of bad reputation found no friend in the law. B. Z. Kedar's recent edition of the canons of Nablus, the earliest Frankish laws in the Holy Land, contains this remarkable provision: "a man who rapes a female Saracen he owns should be castrated; she should be seized on behalf of the fisc."[132] Perhaps the harsh realities of a newly established colonial society

129. Ibid., cols. 782–83.

130. Ibid., col. 882.

131. Ibid., col. 922.

132. B. Z. Kedar, "On the Origins," his translation on p. 314 of the Latin text on p. 333: "Siquis Sarracenam suam vi oppresserit, ipsa quidem infiscabitur, ipse vero extesticulabitur."

required stern measures to keep the Franks from outraging the majority Muslim population. Whatever motives prompted this rule, people like the Genoese would certainly have been familiar with it. Yet this type of protection was never extended to Christian slaves in Genoa, let alone Muslim ones.

To return to the Genoese code, a section on pregnant slaves required anyone causing a free servant or a slave to conceive to pay the master 25 lire.[133] Once again free women found their status perilously close to slavery. If the pregnancy killed the slave woman, the "father" had to pay 50 lire, and for an additional 25 lire he got to keep the baby. The law admitted that all this was difficult to prove, but the owner's oath sufficed, and even the slave's oath was valid provided she was of good reputation. If the father could or would not pay and was himself a slave, he was to be whipped through the streets as far as Capo Fari, lose an ear, and be returned to his master. Two minor issues concluded this section of the law. Anyone impregnating a slave in a house where he was staying paid a fifty-lire fine, whether the slave died or not; violating Genoese hospitality was a serious offense. Finally, if a master impregnated a slave, the slave was not thereby free, another telling parallel to the earlier confusion about slavery and marriage.

Genoa's criminal law on theft was harsh, ranging from whipping through loss of an ear, loss of the nose, and death for the first offense, depending on the amount stolen.[134] Also, the perpetrator had to restore the goods or spend time in prison. A slave committing the same theft suffered no penalty without the owner's permission, provided that the slave acted alone. (Thus do property rights conflict in interesting ways in slave societies.) But if the slave committed the crime with another slave or a free person, then the law took its ordinary course. Property rights still conflicted, but the master's control over a slave remained absolute so long as no tiny sign of conspiracy threatened the rest of society.

Above all, the law's framers intended to control what they called the excesses and malice of slaves.[135] Since the fear of God did not control their

133. *Leges Genuenses*, vol. 18, cols. 951–52.

134. Ibid., col. 932.

135. Ibid., cols. 959–62. The key passage on beating is in cols. 960: "Et quia necessarium est dominos et dominas seu possessores ipsorum sclavorum et sclavarum ipsos seu ipsas corrigere et castigare; ex quibus sepius contingit quod ultra intentionem ipsorum dominorum aliquando debilitantur vel moriuntur, et aliquando ipsi servi se precipitant vel in se manu iniiciunt . . ." Note the careful gendered language—men and women own male and female slaves, but it is beyond the intention of the men that punishment go too far.

natural savagery, only true discipline kept them in line. This aspect of the law reveals the clash of values and hypocrisies that any slaveowning society must face when it incorporates its repressive needs into a rational system of justice. Slaves were under curfew and not supposed to be out at night. Complications set in when the law sought to explain the right to correct slaves, the true discipline. A slave was not to be wounded or killed unless he or she tried to defend himself or herself. If a slave was killed while attempting self-defense with a weapon, the owner suffered no penalty. Also, there was no penalty for anyone killing a slave who was attempting to enter his house at night. If a citizen wounded an unarmed slave who was behaving aggressively, there was no penalty provided that the slave did not die. If the slave died, a judge decided an appropriate punishment. But the law reiterated that if the slave had been armed, there was no penalty. Society had to balance the right of masters to punish as they wished with the need to prevent deranged masters from stirring up all the slaves by murdering with impunity. The legacy of Roman law endured.

Genoese law observed that it was necessary to punish and beat slaves, and this candor reveals much of the violent circumstances of any slave system. If anyone beat or corrected a male or female slave without using a weapon, it was presumed that the intent was to correct, so there was no reason to punish the master, even if the slave died. So it was permissible to beat a slave to death, as long as it was with a whip or a stick and not a sword. This is the law at its most subtle, because people knew, as the law stated, that it often happened that, beyond the master's intention, slaves became broken down or died from beatings, even sometimes throwing themselves down or laying hands on themselves first. This last phrase is difficult to interpret; it seems to mean that during a beating slaves might simply curl up on the ground or wrap their arms around themselves for self-protection and to try to show that they were not in any way threatening the master. Even this passive submission did not incriminate the killer, provided that he or she only intended correction. So careful here is the law to make sure that the slave cannot control the outcome. Everything depended on what the master intended and what he or she used to beat the slave.

If the passive slave was beaten with a weapon or a metal object, and died, the judge decided the penalty. Then this section of the law, the last in the code, turned to clearing up the difference between a slave and a servant, critical when it came to beating someone to death. If a servant raised a hand against his or her employer, family, or possessions, a master suffered no penalty for whatever he or she did. If, however, anyone killed a male or female servant outside the law, that is, in circumstances the law did not excuse, he or she should be punished according to the law. So, the difference is that a servant was mostly a servant in the eyes of the law, and a slave was nothing at all when the right to rule by force was at stake.

The plan or draft for a Ligurian constitution proposed on 16 November 1797 drew on French precedents but also reflected the long local experience of self-rule, admittedly by a narrow oligarchy. The section concerning the rights of people in society stated that the purpose of society was general happiness.[136] The aim of government was to assure people the enjoyment of their rights, which were liberty, equality, property, and security. Liberty meant the right to do everything not harmful to others or society. Equality was the right to be treated the same in law with no distinctions by birth or heredity. Property rights allowed everyone to gain by the fruits of his or her labor and industry. Security resulted from society defending the rights of every individual. These lofty and admirable sentiments defined freedom, and abolished slavery without even mentioning it, so that language about equality, liberty, and work guaranteed that the law no longer stripped a person of all that his or her labor yielded. The constitution omitted abolishing slavery by name, perhaps because its framers preferred to believe that it was better to plan a free future as if slavery had never occurred. If so, they had forgotten how language itself made such a pretense impossible to sustain for very long.

136. *Progetto di Costituzione per il Popolo Ligure*, pamphlet published in 1797 in Genoa now in a collection of the Società ligure di storia patria, details here on p. 4. The special values were *la libertà, l'eguaglianza, la proprietà*, and *la sicurezza*.

CHAPTER THREE
THE HUMAN BEHAVIOR OF SLAVERY

The touchstone of a man's work is his life.

ALESSANDRO MANZONI, *I promessi sposi*

Sometime during the night of 19–20 June 1605, a slave named Mustafa ran away from his owner, who the next day went to the Genoese authorities to have a proclamation issued.[1] The purpose of this public notice was to recapture the slave, and the owner had to provide a detailed physical description in order to identify his property. The exploitable irony here is that slaves, when sold, taxed, or pursued by the law, were among the best-described people in the medieval past. Mustafa was about twenty-one years old, white, a Hungarian of big stature without a beard. He had been wounded on his right shoulder with a sign or mark from a harquebus bullet (*il segno d'una ferita di archibugiata*)—presumably this scar also warned people that Mustafa was dangerous. The slave also had a collar and chain around his neck, probably because he had run away before. Mustafa dressed in a shirt and yellow trousers in the Hungarian style, and he wore a black felt cap. He escaped with a sack containing bread and some extra clothing. The clothing, which was rather distinctive, could be changed. Mustafa's body, minus the iron collar, was a slave's, engaged in the characteristic behavior of running away.

This chapter takes up the biology of slavery, the human body itself, and how these bodies reproduced, survived, were branded or disfigured, portrayed in art, and eventually buried. The behavior of these bodies, under the stress of enslavement, will also demonstrate individual strategies for survival resulting in outcomes ranging from murder to suicide to motherhood, or in Mustafa's case, as in so many, an unknown fate. Free people displayed the behavior of owning a slave, and justifying the existence of slavery. These behaviors, alas all too human, also form part of the overall conduct of slavery.

1. Luigi Tria, "La schiavitù in Liguria," *Atti della Società Ligure di Storia Patria* 70 (1947): 247.

Actual descriptions of slave bodies provide a good place to pick up these themes. We have already seen some of these problems when looking at the language of slavery and how markets valued different types of bodies. This method, beginning with what we can describe, the bodies, as a way to approach the more elusive subject of behavior, is analogous to how physicists study black holes. So little of slave behavior escapes the controlling gravity of how masters dominate the sources that we must painstakingly comb every possible source to uncover the activities of slaves. This approach will also tie together the themes of gender, color, money, and appearance, and illuminate how the pressures of the economy and social attitudes came to focus on the bodies of slaves. In the example of Mustafa, his body was aged twenty-one years or thereabouts. Age is almost invariably one of the first things we learn about the body of a slave, and it is a puzzling descriptor unless people were really very good at estimating ages, or the slaves themselves knew how old they were. What is the importance of these ages? Upon recapture, would Mustafa have gained his freedom by claiming to be twenty-five, and hence not the Mustafa who was sought? Not likely. So we need to ask a lot of questions about the ages of these bodies. Color has already emerged as both a linguistic and economic barometer of status and price. Mustafa was white—a fact worth knowing, but what did it mean in this period, before the nineteenth century, the supposed beginning of racialist categorizing of people? Color was more than simply another way to define property, like a white dog or a grey horse. Looking at the language of color and race reveals that in the Middle Ages there were already clear ways to see color as a proxy for other information about a person. Long before the supposed nineteenth-century construction of race, previous models existed. Classifying bodies by color merges into another description—ethnicity, and no one has convincingly argued that ethnicity too is a modern constructed category. On the contrary, ethnography is an old subject, and Mustafa was called a Hungarian, down to his clothing, because people understood the bundle of cultural traits that the term signified. To say he was Hungarian is not to claim (today, or in the seventeenth century) any unique biological attributes of Hungarianess. Although certain hereditary diseases and blood types run in particular ethnic groups, no one should state that being a Hungarian was, or is, a biological fact about a person. In this period, when most of Hungary belonged to the Ottoman Turks, being a Hungarian staked a complex identity, as Mustafa's Muslim name partly suggests. So ethnic labels, slippery terms that change over time, reveal less about the bodies of slaves than do the simpler terms, like color.

The size of the body, its bigness or smallness in stature, or whether it was fat or thin, contains information about the conditions of slavery. Little is known about body size and shape in the Middle Ages except what studying skeletons reveals. Unfortunately, slave skeletons are rare. Eighteenth-century Genoa had a graveyard for Muslim slaves, but it lies under the modern port at Foce and probably should not be disturbed anyway. Body size was never quantified but instead varied around the local definition of average—slaves were typically bigger or smaller, by a lot or a little, than average. This is still helpful information about bodies since it records the bodies as the masters saw them—large and dangerous, small and manageable.

The only fact known about Mustafa's face is that he did not have a beard, but in general slave faces received the most attention. Hair and its color, ears (pierced or not), eyes and their color, the shape of the nose, the size of the lips, the dimple in the chin, not to mention moles, freckles, warts, and scars, all gave the face its distinctive identity. Faces could also be stupid or cunning, windows on the soul—and medieval people anticipated Cesare Lombroso by many centuries in their zest for finding traces of character and criminality in facial features. In 1367 Petrarch, living in Venice, wrote a long letter to a friend on how times change. One telling example was the large number of slaves, whose Scythian faces tainted Venice. To Petrarch, these Tartars were repulsive and annoying, and he knew them by their faces.[2] By the early modern period a vast literature had emerged on physiognomy. Giovan Battista Della Porta's classic sixteenth-century book on physiognomy emphasized the face and its color. Physiognomy anticipated modern racist thinking, and it relied more on the color of the bodily humors than on ethnography to explain human differences. So, for example, a white body reflected a timid, cold character, and blonds were malignant, barbaric, and ignorant.[3] Since the color of the face revealed temperament, it's not surprising that a black face seemed melancholic and fearful, while a mixture of white and red, a pinkish face, evinced the best temperament—smart and noble.[4] This early modern synthesis on physiognomy incorporated the best ancient and medieval scholarship on the subject. But in the Middle Ages faces were primarily like fingerprints, often guaranteed to be unique. It is odd that Mustafa's owner thought to tell the police only that

2. Francis Petrarch, *Letters of Old Age: Renum senilium libri I–XVIII*, trans. Aldo S. Bernardo, Saul Levin, and Reta A. Bernardo (Baltimore, 1992), 2:371. Latin text in Franciscus Petrarcha, *Operum*, vol. 2 (Basle, 1554, reprint Ridgewood, N.J., 1965), p. 964: "inextimabilis turba seniorum, utriusque sexus, hanc pulcherriman urbem [Venice] Scythicis vultibus." I am indebted to Benjamin Z. Kedar for this reference.

3. Giovan Battista Della Porta, *Dell'fisonomia dell'uomo*, ed. Mario Cicognani (Parma, 1988), pp. 457 (white body), 445 (blonds—shades of Niceforo here). The Latin edition of this work was first published in 1568, the Italian edition in 1610.

4. Ibid., pp. 458–59.

Mustafa's face was white and beardless and provided no other details, but he probably believed that the collar and chains framing the face were enough to make it easy to spot him.

These bodies also changed over time in important ways as life experiences marked them. As in Mustafa's case the wounding or scarring of slave bodies identified them as such, or made a point about their behavior—usually about running away, or in this instance perhaps capture on a battlefield. The marks intended to punish and humiliate slaves drove home the point that the slave's body was totally subjected to the master's power. Having a body incised in nonaccidental ways is also a behavioral fact about slavery that reveals how some slaves and masters conducted themselves. Someone had shot Mustafa, and the scar left on his shoulder marked him *as the kind of person* who got shot. Beyond purposeful disfiguring of slaves, so many of them were scarred that something systematic was happening to their bodies, especially their hands and faces. Without many good descriptions of free people, the general level of physical scarring remains unclear, but given the dangerous nature of much artisanal and farming work, and the lack of good medical treatments (notably stitching), it would not be surprising to see a lot of scars on medieval people, slave or free. But inquiring about the nature and distribution of these scars will be worthwhile. Other accidents, and time, left some slaves with weakened or missing limbs and other physical problems that limited the ways they could use their own bodies. Finally, some apparently voluntary markings, tattoos and ear piercings, lent distinction to some slave bodies. Perhaps most of these markings originated in the slave's youth, before enslavement occurred, but it is still useful to explore the relatively small area of control a slave had over the way his or her body appeared.

Pregnancy is part of the problem of describing the female body, but also relates to behavior. From a legal perspective a female slave had no right of consent when it came to satisfying the sexual appetites of her master, so it was legally inconceivable that a master could rape his slave, even though this happened all the time. There is a very delicate question concerning whether it was ever in the slave's best interests to become pregnant, and how this behavior, coupled with the fact of motherhood, constituted a strategy for surviving slavery, no matter how demeaning it might appear to outsiders. Becoming pregnant by another slave, or by a free man, or by the master also gave a female slave hard choices about what parent was in the best position, or most likely, to help her child.

This chapter investigates slaves' behavior by emphasizing how trapped people accommodate and resist the demands placed on them for work, obedience, and sex. Nearly all the evidence comes from the owners. The slaves do not even describe their own bodies. Evidence of behavior, despite these barriers, still survives, and it is often mirrored, however imperfectly, in the ways masters use to justify owning people. Owning a slave is also a type of behavior, one the vast majority of Italians never experienced. But they lived in societies that justified slavery and they participated in legal systems that enforced it. The experience of living in a slave-owning society is also a type of behavior worth studying.

DESCRIPTIONS OF SLAVES

An important tax source from late trecento Florence contains 357 notices of slaves, with a few repeats.[5] For the purpose of registering a slave with the authorities, the law required the new owner to provide the name of the seller, the price, and most valuable for present purposes, a brief physical description. Scholars have mined this source for price data, and in a cranky way Ridolfo Livi used it in his search for different racial characteristics among modern Italians. These descriptions, often more detailed than the ones in typical sales contracts, strike me as the most informative collective portrait we have of any premodern slave population. Learning about the physical appearances of slaves, and what their bodies can reveal about life experiences, are good places to begin exploring the behavior of living as a slave.

Let us observe the slave body from head to foot, but a few general comments about appearance merit notice. The source naturally gives the impression that the slave was the sum of his or her personal parts. The record noted distinguishing physical characteristics that could be used to prove that a specific person had been registered. So the owner atomized, or anatomized the slave as a bundle of details, and perhaps saw the body as just that. One striking feature of these descriptions is the way they break down the body into its constituent parts. The canons of Renaissance poetry also dissected the body to extol its beauties; here, the pragmatic need to identify property required looking at the same parts for more complex legal and economic reasons.[6] One owner noted that a child of twelve had a beautiful body, but that may have been because it was difficult to describe children, partly because they lacked distinguishing physical features, and also because they were still changing and would soon outgrow any physical description.[7]

5. Ridolfo Livi, *La schiavitù domestica nei tempi di mezzo e nei tempi moderni* (Padua, 1928), pp. 146–247. All references to individual entries are by number in Livi.

6. I am indebted to David Wallace for this observation.

7. R. Livi, *La schiavitù*, no. 227.

Another owner observed that his slave was phlegmatic, but temperament almost never figured into the record, probably because it was not usually apparent at first glance.[8]

The description almost invariably noted three general characteristics—what we would call ethnicity or nationality, color, and stature or size. Almost all these slaves were Tartars from the northern shores of the Black Sea, although occasionally some conflating of the terms "Tartar" and "Russian" occurred to describe the same person. Greek, Circassian, Bosnian, Albanian, and Turkish slaves were rare in Florence. I will look at the construction of ethnicity in more detail below. At this time and place the market was delivering mostly Tartar slaves, nearly all of them women, to Florence.[9] The owner volunteered the slave's color, and possibly the slave was present during the declaration, so that the notary who wrote down the details could have corrected the owner's description or suggested ways to be more exact. Florentines saw the Tartars as coming in six colors: black, brown, olive, fair, reddish, and white, and they frequently qualified these terms. The continuum makes some sense except for the "fair" category, because the word used here, *flava*, usually means blond and might refer to yellow-skinned people in this context. But the numbers point to some clear distinctions: black 2, brown 18, olive 161, fair 11, reddish 5, white 45. Clearly, the ethnic group the Florentines called "Tartar" was a constructed identity and contained a lot of variety. The consensus was that Tartars, predominantly Turkic peoples, were usually olive-colored, though there were more white ones than black, brown, red, and yellow/fair combined. Olive was in between white and brown, and observers sometimes had difficulty in figuring out just what shade a person was. The only other categories of color with meaningful numbers are for Greek women: olive 17, brown 2, white 5. Most slaves were olive-colored, and it would be worth knowing how the Italians described themselves. In every case but one, in which a person is described as olive, the color is attached to the skin.[10] This emphasis on skin indicates that color was not considered a deep characteristic of a person and hence by itself carried little ethnic baggage, especially when one group like the Tartars displayed so broad a spectrum of colors. Stature, although a commonly noted feature of the slave's body, is not so informative

8. Ibid., no. 272.

9. Iris Origo, "The Domestic Enemy: The Eastern Slaves in Tuscany in the Fourteenth and Fifteenth Centuries," *Speculum* 30 (1955): 321–66, contains a few illustrations that suggest how Italian artists depicted Tartars—see Plates 1–4.

10. R. Livi, *La schiavitù*, no. 83.

since a big majority were simply average, with a few tall ones, and some adults and most children called short. In height, the slaves struck the Florentines as mainly like themselves. In the same vein, a few slaves were called fat, but this condition was not common. Rarer still was a thin slave, so malnutrition does not seem to have been a problem—not surprisingly, given the high and increasing price of slaves in the late trecento.

The head always seemed a person's most distinctive body part, especially the face, as the ancient science of physiognomy taught. One owner simply noted that the slave had "a face quite like ours, *facie admodum nostre*"—presumably this Tartar woman looked like a typical Florentine.[11] But this familiarity was rare, and these eastern slaves struck people as a clear "Other." To start at the top, it is curious that only a few times was the slave's hair color recorded, and only once was there anything about its style or length. Perhaps hair color was not an important, identifying fact about a slave because the hair was mostly hidden from public view, unlike skin color. The forehead offered no special marks except for a unique dimple, but the eyebrows were commonly noted—here the most interesting fact was if they had grown together or not—again useful for identification. Noting the color of the eyebrows was as rare as stating hair color, even though the eyebrows were in plain sight.

The eyes offered more opportunity for comment. Eye color, not hidden from view, was frequently mentioned, but the range of color is puzzling. Black eyes occurred a few times, and blue once, but mostly the owners described the eyes as "pale," probably a miscellaneous blue-grey category—a common color for human eyes in Europe and west Asia. Far more important was the shape of the eyes. The Florentines frequently described Tartar eyes as "concave," by which they probably meant "slanted" or "hooded," too. This is the best way they could find to distinguish Mongol eyes from their own. The descriptions of the eyes did not note anything about the eyelashes or eyelids. The word used most commonly to characterize the eyes, "*suffornati*," does not exist in modern Italian, but it conjures up images of "underdeveloped" or inset eyes. These eyes were so common for Tartars that it really did not add more information to describe the eyes—the ethnic label carried that data. The frequency with which the Florentines mentioned the shape of the eyes suggests that it, along with skin color, was the most outstanding feature of this type of slave. Another aspect of the eyes engaged observers—the outside corner and fold of the eyes, referred to as the tail. Moles and especially scars in the tail of the eyes were often men-

11. Ibid., no. 161.

tioned, again indicating that people's attention focused on the eyes when identifying a person. There were so many small scars around the eyes that many of these slaves must have endured rough childhoods.

In general there was not much to say about the ear. Only one perplexing comment, that someone's ears were small and prominent, provides an overall impression of them. Very frequently, however, the last thing noted about a slave was whether the ears were pierced, which was so common that if the ears were intact, a few owners mentioned it. Pierced ears were a good means, along with other markers, to identify a slave, but there may have been more to it than that. Some girls as young as nine already had their ears pierced—one nine-year-old already had the holes closed, presumably because she was not wearing rings in them.[12] The eastern Mediterranean custom of pierced ears may have marked these children when they were still free, and then was carried over into slavery. Girls usually had both ears pierced, though having one pierced ear was common for both boys and girls, with no trend for the left or right. One woman had two holes in her ear, but multiple piercing appears rare.[13] Only one slave, a Greek woman, had a pierced nose.[14] The nose struck Florentines as flat or snubbed, usually in the case of Tartars, or sharp or aquiline, with people like the Greeks. Once again, the nose served as a proxy for ethnicity, especially for the Tartars, who had the most distinctive faces among the Florentines.

The mouth received almost no notice—it was only once mentioned, when it was described as flat.[15] Lips, occasionally called big, were not commonly mentioned; there was only one harelip in the sample, and there was nothing about the color of lips.[16] Surprisingly, only four slaves had any missing teeth noted, but since the sample was nearly all under thirty and most under twenty, good teeth were probably the rule. A missing tooth was a fairly good way to identify a person, so the records specified just where the gap was. A few notices of a dimple in the chin, or that the chin was pointy, complete the survey of the face. For a male slave, it was useful to know if he was bearded or not, and this is sometimes mentioned, though never the beard's color. The other condition worth noting was the skin's texture, and a large number of these slaves were pockmarked from smallpox, or were just pocked, perhaps from acne or another skin ailment. One

12. Ibid., no. 136.
13. Ibid., no. 266.
14. Ibid., no. 244.
15. Ibid., no. 52.
16. Ibid., no. 265.

face was called dry, perhaps another skin problem.[17] These marks, of course not unique to slaves, helped in the overall identification and perhaps affected price, though it is very hard to disaggregate the elements of price. Finally, distinctive warts and moles were commonly noted on all parts of the face, especially on the broad expanse of the cheeks—again useful for identification because these marks did not change. So the face, with its moles, warts, scars, and pockmarks, told part of a person's story.

These descriptions provide little information about the rest of the body. The occasional slave might be lame or missing the odd finger or toe, but these bodies were usually covered, and distinguishing marks on them would not help to identify the slave to casual observers. Scarring was noticeable on hands and fingers, and here the effects of domestic labor, especially cooking and chopping wood, left their traces on the women. In a few cases distinctive marks or tattoos appeared on the back of the hand. A thirteen-year-old boy from Russia had five black marks in the form of a cross on this part of the body.[18] Another slave from Russia, a young woman named Marta, had black marks in the form of a cross on her left hand, and a Tartar named Maria had a cross of black points on the ring finger of her left hand and a black cross on her left arm.[19] These marks were rare, and probably not associated with baptism, or some owner's whim. Perhaps out in Russia and the Tartar East, some parents tried to advertise Christian status for their children in order to save them from Christian slave raiders, or just to get the children better treatment in cases where the parents sold them into slavery.

One eighteen-year-old slave named Maria, sold as pregnant, cost forty florins, which included whatever child or children she bore.[20] Who knows what circumstances prompted this rare sale of a pregnant woman, whose child followed the mother's status. Many slaves were sold as children; the youngest, a girl of seven, along with her mother, but a Greek girl named Franceschina, also seven, went alone in the market.[21] The Florentines, for whatever reason, found it hard to describe these children, since their stature was, as a few admitted, small, and their bodies were generally unmarked by scars. The one constant feature, skin color, helped a little, and some girls of nine or eleven already had their ears pierced. By the time the child reached

17. Ibid., no. 339.
18. Ibid., no. 15.
19. Ibid., nos. 39, 296.
20. Ibid., no. 37.
21. Ibid., nos. 231, 311.

twelve, there was usually more to say; thus, little Caterina, a Tartar, had olive skin, an ample face, eyebrows almost joined together, a sizable nose, a few freckles, and pierced ears, all for forty florins.[22] Another white-skinned Tartar girl of twelve, Caterina, had a sharp nose and a beautiful body, an ambiguous asset in a female slave, and possibly a calamity for a child.[23] How much work a nine-year-old slave girl might do in the household of a wealthy Florentine the sources do not reveal, but as an investment these children, past the dangerous years of infancy, must have seemed a reasonable purchase, and they were often just as expensive as mature women in their twenties. Most of the male slaves sold, boys in their early teens or younger, cost a bit less than the girls. Young males posed the same problems of description; what could one say about a boy of eleven, except his name and skin color? Some of the boys also had pierced ears, and few had beards. At least none of these children was called thin, and surprisingly few were pockmarked, but their small bodies stood at the beginning of slavery, still subject in all ways to the master's whims.

The behavior of running away deserves special treatment, but notices of escaped slaves, along with sales contracts and tax records, become a reliable source of information about how slaves appeared to their owners. For example, on 17 March 1329, Guido Filangeri, the praetor of Palermo, wrote to officials throughout Sicily informing them that two of his slaves, Guglielmo and a woman named Armenia, had fled.[24] He did not describe the male slave but noted that Armenia was olive-skinned, had a mole on her face, and was a little squint-eyed. It's hard to believe that these scrappy details would be enough to help track them down. When a judge asked the officials of Palermo to spread news around the island about his runaway, he was more informative.[25] This slave, named Matteo Brunetto, was now a Christian, about twenty-two years old, and of the Saracen "race," probably from Djerba in North Africa. He was tall and a little *curbis* (bowlegged?) with big shins. According to his master, this slave, taking bad advice, stole himself by illegally taking himself from his master's possession, an interesting way of stating the slave's temperament—he was a thief.

In a letter written in 1454 the Genoese humanist Jacopo Bracelli sought the government's help in tracking down his slave Valentino, who had escaped with two other slaves (both owned by noblemen) and was heading

<hr>

22. Ibid., no. 189.
23. Ibid., no. 227.
24. *Acta Curie Felicis Urbis Panormi, Registri di lettere ed atti (1328–1333)*, vol. 5, ed. Pietro Corrao (Palermo, 1986), pp. 144–45.
25. Ibid., 7 July 1329, pp. 194–95.

with them for Venice.[26] In elegant Latin style he described the slave as not older than twenty-two, tall, from the Sarmatian nation—an archaism indicating his origins on the north shore of the Black Sea, so that he was probably a Tartar. Bracelli pronounced himself willing to ignore this "juvenile error" if the Genoese ambassador in Venice was successful in tracking down the slave, an unlikely feat. In 1388 the Florentine poet Franco Sacchetti helped by letter to spread the news to a friend in Pisa about a runaway slave named Margherita.[27] From Sacchetti we would expect a rich description, and he does not disappoint. This Margherita was about twenty years old, with brown skin and eyes, with fairly well-developed breasts, that is, not too fat or thin. She was a short woman, and she did not have a very Tartar-like face and she did not speak "our language" very much. Margherita had just fled the past evening, taking with her some clothing—various gowns, which Sacchetti described in minute detail. In a postscript he advised his friend to look in the bordellos because sometimes runaway slaves were found there. This made sense because prostitution provided a way to make a living and answer as few questions as possible. With perhaps some Tuscan and a face not very Eastern, Margherita might be able to blend into the underworld of Pisa. Sacchetti also told his friend to write to another acquaintance in Lucca for the same purpose, so news of Margherita's flight, appearance, and clothing spread to neighboring cities. Finally, a proclamation against two runaway slaves in Genoa in 1605 noted that they were both white and marked on the face.[28] Perhaps by now it was routine to brand all male slaves.

The cumulative weight of these descriptions reminds us that slaves had bodies. They did not simply live as prices, legal categories, or pieces of property. Owners needed to classify slaves, and they did so in ways that reveal how people saw the human form, and how they constructed ethnic categories based on physical features, including color, and perhaps other things like language. How the slaves saw themselves we will never know, so we must depend on the masters for clues to understanding the behavior of being or owning a slave. Slavery rested on the bodies of slaves and what happened to them.

26. Giovanna Balbi, *L'epistolario di Iacopo Bracelli* (Genoa, 1969), pp. 107–9.

27. Franco Sacchetti, *La battaglia delle belle donne, le lettere, le sposizioni di vangeli*, ed. Alberto Chiari (Bari, 1938), pp. 88–89: "d'età di circa a venti anni, la quale'è di pelo e occhi bruni, assai adatta nel busto, cioè né grassa né magra; è piccoletta, e non ha il viso molto tartaresco, ma inanzi adatto al modo di qua che no; e non parla molto scorta nostra lingua."

28. Società di Liguria di Storia Patria, Carte Staglieno 331/6, copy of proclamation 4 March 1605.

Behavior in the context of slavery involved both slaves and masters. Slaves had children, ran away, worked, committed crimes, and resisted slavery in one fashion or another until they died. Resistance ran the gamut from murdering owners, to stealing, lying, running away, or surly behavior on a daily basis down to mean looks or spitting into the master's food.[29] No doubt some slaves accommodated themselves completely to the system, either hoping for emancipation or just as little pain as possible, and some made it into old age. Slaves were trapped people, and they responded to this condition in a number of ways adapted for their survival, up to the point where some other value or despair overcame the will to live. Slave owners also engaged in behaviors that created experiences for slaves. Masters beat and killed their slaves, bought and sold them, and, with the help of learned theologians and humanists, defended the institution of slavery. Embedded in these defenses are signs that there were critics against whom slavery needed to be defended. All these behaviors constitute the ethology of slavery, the study of a type of human conduct—being or owning a slave. The dynamics on both sides of the relationship need to be treated together in order to understand how many centuries of Italians came to terms with their "peculiar institution."

SLAVE BEHAVIORS: REVOLTS AND VIOLENT RESISTANCE

The absence of slave revolts in medieval and early modern Italy is not surprising. Draconian laws and punishments, the small numbers of slaves, and their relative isolation as workers in small groups in domestic or other labor, all conspired to keep slaves apart, apparently docile, and under the vigilant eyes of the authorities. Only at sea might revolt have resulted in the possibility of successful flight, and I know of no instances of insurrections by slaves in transit. The careful rules on the numbers of slaves to be carried in different sizes of ships suggest that contemporaries had taken every precaution against such possibilities, perhaps because they had actually happened. Still, the masters also controlled the records, and we are not likely to learn about successful small-scale revolts or escapes anyway. Nor was it easy in Italy for bands of runaways to gather in the wilder areas and establish autonomous communities, like the Maroons in the West Indies. Slaves were not numerous enough to defend themselves against the forces of repression, and in most of Italy it would not have been easy for transplanted foreigners to live off the land.

29. Eugene D. Genovese, *Roll, Jordan, Roll: The World the Slaves Made* (New York, 1976), pp. 597–98—but this is also a main theme of the book.

Individual revolts, if that is the right way to express it, did certainly happen, ranging from murdering a master to resisting a beating. Here is a murder case from Venice in 1410 that illustrates the usual costs to the slave who succeeded in killing an owner.[30] Bona, a Tartar slave and servant, belonged to the nobleman Niccolo Barbo and lived in her master's house. When Barbo found out that Bona was pregnant, he beat her with a harness for carrying water. (The source does not indicate who the father might have been.) Bona, according to the legal record of this case, prompted by a diabolical spirit and motivated by a desperate mind, formed the intention of poisoning Barbo. She bought arsenic from a boy, presumably an apprentice, who stayed in an apothecary shop in the neighborhood, and put the poison in her master's food and soup (*minestre*). Barbo died, and Bona confessed to everything. It is not clear what made Bona confess so quickly, but she seems to have been so enraged (and perhaps now satisfied with the outcome) that she no longer cared about the consequences to her of the poisoning. All Bona wanted was to kill her master, and it is unlikely that a single beating would have resulted in this response. More likely, Barbo made her pregnant, and instead of treating the mother of his child with some respect, he beat her in a fury, perhaps because she had failed to take precautions. It is certainly possible that someone else was the father, and that he beat her for the affront to the dignity of his household. It is even possible that Bona was lying about being pregnant and he beat her for that.

In any event, Bona was convicted of murder, and the Venetian state planned a typically graphic punishment. Bona was taken by canal on a barge to Santa Croce with a crier aboard who continuously shouted out her crime. This display alerted all slaves to what would happen to them if they acted on their murderous impulses, and presumably it also reassured owners that the state would defend their interests by keeping slaves in line or if necessary by taking vengeance. Then Bona was tied to a horse's tail and dragged to the Piazza San Marco, the ritual center of Venice, where the noblemen who ran the state usually chose to make their points. In between the two pillars of justice Bona was burned alive according to custom until she was dead and her body reduced to ashes. As Edward Muir has observed, "the government reserved mutilation, sometimes followed by execution, for lower-class persons who in the eyes of society had committed the foulest crimes, who earned their living with their hands, and who had no property

30. I am grateful to Dennis Romano for a copy of this document, which is Archivio di Stato di Venezia, Avogaria Comun, Raspe, Reg. 3646, 84v–85r. He discusses this case in *Housecraft and Statecraft: Domestic Service in Renaissance Venice 1400–1600* (Baltimore, 1996), p. 52.

worth confiscating."[31] This slave was at the bottom of the social hierarchy, propertyless, a servant, and murderous. Even Bona's pregnancy did not save her or even delay execution; her condition appears to have been conveniently forgotten, and the burning so quickly followed the crime that no one wanted to wait around and see if she eventually gave birth.

In Venice this case resulted in new rules on selling poison.[32] About the same time in Genoa, more specific rules on selling arsenic revealed that the Genoese too feared poison in the hands of slaves, especially the Turks and Tartars, fierce and stubborn people.[33] Laws placed in the hands of masters absolute power over a rebellious or resisting slave. Owners became society's first line of defense against the slave, and no questions were going to be asked of any master who destroyed personal property in self-defense. Poisoning was a subtle and fearsome attack on masters. So many Italian slaves worked in domestic service that the opportunities for tampering with food were many, and death by poison was hard to prove. Maybe Bona confessed because she wanted to let Venice know just how she had taken vengeance on Barbo, but there must have been other slaves who settled for the secret pleasure of murdering a master, and getting away with it. Physical attacks were harder to conceal, but the laws reveal that the masters feared above all two possibilities—the covert poisoner, and the slave who struck back during the course of a beating. Genoa's laws on this subject, already discussed, drew fine distinctions about resisting a beating and circumscribed to the point of nullity the slave's "right" to self-defense. And yet, even here, there are signs that masters recognized the basic humanity of slaves in the practical admission that a beating could result not only in more perfect obedience, but also in resistance.

There is also the other side of the equation—masters who murdered or attacked their slaves. The frail arguments of economic self-interest were all the defense a slave had against an owner bent on murder. For the master the crime presumably carried its own punishment—financial loss—but there was no real possibility of criminal sanctions, and maybe only a modest level of social disapproval. The contrasting behaviors here are revealing: many signs of social paranoia about slave poisoners, and no effort to address the fears slaves might reasonably have about masters who turned out to be sociopaths or rapists. This stark asymmetry in the behavior of being or own-

31. Edward Muir, *Civic Ritual in Renaissance Venice* (Princeton, N.J., 1981), p. 246, where there is also a good discussion of the ritual purposes of these executions.

32. D. Romano, *Housecraft*, p. 52.

33. *Leges Genuenses: Historiae Patriae Monumenta*, vol. 18 (Turin, 1901), col. 676.

ing a slave highlights an important lesson—society expected masters to exercise self-restraint based on a rational calculus of self-interest, which for slaves might prompt a violent course unless the law terrorized them into acquiescence. No one believed that a reasonable slave would accept his or her condition without force, but no law realistically constrained a master; his reason was supposed to prevail. And if it did not, the perceived social costs were minimal—the odd slave found hanging from a light fixture.

RUNNING AWAY

Efforts to discourage flight or recapture runaways have supplied good evidence on the slaves' appearances, but what light do they shed on their behavior? The sea was the only way to get out of Italy; crossing the Alps was difficult, and the slave would only be farther from home. Dire penalties awaited any ship's captain or crew who helped a slave escape. Most slaves were women and could not be easily concealed on a ship. Few male slaves had useful maritime skills, and those who did found themselves by the sixteenth century chained to a galley bench and were most unlikely to escape except through death. We have seen a few runaways who tried to survive in Italy, whether by working as a prostitute in Pisa or trying to blend in as just another apprentice in Siena. Most slaves were going to have a very hard time carrying this off, even if they looked and spoke like Italians. Since the Italian slave population did not reproduce itself, there would always be a problem about language for the imported slaves. Yet in a country with very strong regional dialects, where in the fifteenth century common people from Venice and Florence would find it nearly impossible to understand one another, a slave's inadequate command of the language was not necessarily going to identify one as a runaway. Besides, there were plenty of free migrants in Italy who also faced language barriers, and even some historians have consistently misidentified Slavic migrants as slaves or runaways.[34]

Ethnic identity proved a greater challenge to slaves on the run in Italy. The prevalence of Tartar slaves in the North made Tartar nationality an ethnic badge, so that a Tartar was a type of person who would attract notice and questions. But there were at least a few emancipated Tartars living in Venice and Genoa, and the slaves must have known this and perhaps hoped, if it was impossible for them to return to the Black Sea, that it might be possible to go to another Italian city and pretend to be free. Bracelli's Tartar

34. Giulio Prunai, "Notizie e documenti sulla servitù domestica nel territorio senese (secc. VIII–XVI)," *Bulletino senese di storia patria* 7 (1936), is an example of this confusion; many of the documents he provides actually concern Slavs, not slaves.

slave Valentino and his compatriots, on the run to Venice, made an astute choice. A Tartar who could speak some version of Italian could survive in Venice, where not too many people would care about missing Genoese property. The Genoese ambassador would see lots of Tartars in Venice, and could not question them all; and the authorities were not yet able to expect people to have papers. It was not inconceivable that a slave could buy or concoct the right papers anyway. So running away was not an irrational act, and the success stories do not leave obvious traces in the records.

The laws, which carefully regulated and punished the behavior of free people who dared to help slaves, suggest that people understood that successful runaways needed help. The early Genoese Statutes of Pera, redacted around 1300, reflect an exemplary ferocity. This law lumped together those who stole slaves or helped anyone who did, or harbored a slave without the master's permission.[35] The law inflicted on a free person a fine of 50 lire or more (several years of artisan wages) plus the value of the slave to the owner, and the loss of a hand. Amputation was a dreaded penalty for any working person, and a powerful incentive to avoid helping a runaway slave. The same penalty awaited anyone who transported a slave without the owner's permission. The next part of the law turned a keener eye on those who transported by land or sea a slave without the owner's permission.[36] Aiding a slave in this manner was a more serious crime—both in Genoa and its eastern colonies a slave who escaped by sea was gone, but this could not happen without assistance. Anyone so helping a slave faced a fine of 100 lire, and if he could not pay he lost a foot. Here is the contemporary sense of justice at work; for harboring a slave, 50 lire and a hand; for transporting one, 100 lire or maybe a foot. There might have been the occasional shipowner who was innocently inveigled into carrying a runaway slave, and here a stiff fine was lesson enough. The law also states that it was necessary to have a pass (*podixia*) from an owner in order to ship a slave, and the pass was supposed to have an official seal on it. Anyone shipping a slave without the proper form paid a hundred-lire fine and was proclaimed twice a year in the city, which was presumably damaging to the reputation of any shipowner or captain. These wealthy people were not going to lose a hand or foot over this matter; they could be counted on to support the social order and slavery. The free people who could not afford to pay were more dangerous and for them the law reserved its real terrors.

But the law also sought to gain the active collaboration of all members of

35. Vincenzo Promis, "Statuti della colonia genovese di Pera," *Miscellanea di storia patria d'Italia* 11 (1871): 513–780, here Cap. 176, pp. 713–15.

36. Ibid., Cap. 177, p. 715.

society in keeping slaves in their places. Anyone who found a slave, without a pass sealed by the master, more than ten thousand paces from the city was empowered to seize the slave. Upon turning him or her over to the master, the lucky person was entitled to 2 lire from the owner, a good bit of money for the average Genoese and an incentive to keep an eye out for suspicious people heading away from Genoa on foot without the right papers. It is of course intriguing that as early as 1300 Genoa had a pass system for slaves outside the city and suburbs. It was desirable to send slaves to market or on errands, and the rich had villas and castles in the countryside that might need the services of a slave. Slavery would become inefficient if slaves could do nothing on their own or not travel without a guard. A system of passes let a slave go about his or her business and also ensured that a monitoring system would be in place to find slaves without passes. Owners had an incentive to follow the rules or else face not so petty harassment as free people seized their slaves and demanded rewards. Passes presume that someone can read or at least recognize them. This was another good reason to make sure that slaves could not read, or write their own passes.

In the revised legal code assembled under French rule in the years 1403–7, some refinements on runaways appeared. Anyone inciting a slave to flee received a hundred-lire fine, and anyone who could not pay lost a hand—another sign that wealthy people were expected to support slavery but also escaped the severe penalty awaiting the vast majority of the population unable to raise 100 lire.[37] Runaway slaves were to be branded or marked on the jaw, a clear warning to everyone about their temperament. The same rules on passes were repeated, except now there were also rewards of 3 lire for anyone capturing a slave even farther from Genoa. A person transporting by sea a slave without a license paid the same hundred-lire fine, except now the commune received two-thirds and the owner one-third. The law also now imposed a stiff penalty on a blacksmith, or any other person, who was to be suspended and stretched if he removed any chains or rings from a slave's body. Collars, chains, and rings impeded an escaping slave, and once again the framers of the laws were eager to make sure he or she got no help. All these rules raise the suspicion that some free people must have been sympathetic to runaway slaves, but we will need more evidence before concluding that this was a major problem for slave owners.

One of the unique features of Italian slavery concerns the early colonial experience cities like Venice and Genoa had in the eastern Mediterranean. From the thirteenth century, in places like Crete, Chios, and especially in

37. *Leges Genuenses*, vol. 18, col. 937–38 for this and what follows.

the Black Sea at Caffa and Tana, Italian merchants first learned about the wider, international slave markets. They also witnessed the older slave systems of the Byzantines, Muslims, and eventually the Mongol cultures, and studied how slavery worked as a legal and economic institution, which they knew something about from Italy and Iberia. Slavery had survived at low levels in northern Italy and thrived in the South, where Genoese and Venetian merchants also witnessed how a wider-scale slave system operated. But this was still Italy, a recognizable if strange culture for northerners in Palermo, whereas the eastern Mediterranean was something out of their experience. Out there, some of the rules on how to behave did not apply. Out there things happened that were crimes, or just did not occur, back home. After all, thousands of Italians experienced the east as merchants, seamen, crusaders, and pilgrims; eventually thousands more settled in the colonial outposts Genoa and Venice established throughout the region. More work needs to be done on how these precocious and ultimately unsuccessful colonial ventures influenced the behavior of the men, and some women, who went East and then brought back different habits and tastes.[38]

On Venetian Crete, a small Italian population dominated the local Greeks and Jews. Slavery probably had a continuous history there since antiquity, and the Venetians had been dealing in slaves since the early Middle Ages. The mixture of these diverse cultures produced a colonial slavery with some hybrid features. A large number of households on Crete owned slaves, an unexceptional activity there. Emancipating slaves by will was also legal and common. In 1335 Marco Fradhelo freed all his slaves, including those who had fled, a remarkable concession.[39] More directly, in a will from 1351 Benedetta ordered that if her slave Soi, who had run away, was ever found, she should serve the sick at the hospital of Santo Spirito for a year and then be free.[40] Wherever Soi was, it is unlikely that this charitable bequest would motivate her to turn herself in and do penance at the hospital in exchange for her freedom. If Soi were still on Crete, maybe she would

38. For one example on how this experience in the east may have affected women at home, see my "The Medieval Family: A Place of Refuge and Sorrow," in *Portraits of Medieval and Renaissance Living: Essays in Memory of David Herlihy* ed. Samuel K. Cohn, Jr., and Steven A. Epstein (Ann Arbor, Mich., 1996), p. 156 (Armenia).

39. Sally McKee, *Wills from Late Medieval Venetian Crete 1312–1420*, 3 vols. (Washington, D.C., 1998), p. 154 n. 120.

40. Ibid., p. 234 n. 182: "Item volo quod si Soi, sclava mea, que affugit michi invenietur, serviat anno uno infirmis ospitalis Sancti Spiritus predicti et postmodum sit libera."

eventually be discovered, and so her owner was being merciful. Free people had intense relations with their slaves. The priest Niccolo Milovani freed his slave Anastasia by will in 1350, and left all of his goods to her three children.[41] If Anastasia was pregnant, this child too was to share in the estate. If Anastasia ever married, she was to receive nothing. Anastasia was certainly the priest's concubine, and this liaison was no doubt easier to conduct on Crete than in Venice. Finally, in 1383 Elena the wife of Francesco Dandolo was ill and pregnant, and when making her will she wanted her slave Maria to nurse her posthumous child and then be free.[42] With poignant realism, Elena added that if her child died before Maria weaned him or her, the slave should receive fifty hyperpers for her redemption. On Crete, with so many slaves and owners, a slave culture was emerging, with behavior similar to other, later island societies in the Caribbean.

Colonial slavery was sometimes worse, sometimes kinder, than what was practiced back home, and some vicious conduct and legal tangles found their way back to the home countries.[43] The revised Statutes of Caffa, collected for this old Genoese colony in the Crimea in 1448, reflect colonial circumstances inconceivable in Genoa.[44] For example, the bishop of Caffa was required to inform the local officials when a slave fled to his house. The law stipulated that the slave was to be baptized within three days, and then handed over to the commune's business agents whose job it was to sell the slave and give the money to the owner. The bishop's house, and maybe his cathedral, served as sanctuary for runaway slaves in Caffa. A slave reaching this refuge was automatically made a Christian (no sign of consent required) but not returned to the owner. Also, there was no way the Genoese could justify handing a Christian slave over to the pagan Tartars. The Church and the government in Caffa, but not back in Genoa, recognized that in some circumstances a slave needed to flee and deserved protection. This would not have worked well back in Venice or Genoa; imagine hundreds of slaves converging on San Marco or San Lorenzo seeking sanctuary.

41. Ibid., pp. 725–26 n. 573 (will in Venetian Italian).

42. Ibid., p. 986 n. 783. The will refers to the posthumous child as male, but when this child is named as principal heir, the will notes that it might be a boy or a girl.

43. For more details on this and other cases see my article "A Late Medieval Lawyer Confronts Slavery: The Cases of Bartolomeo de Bosco," *Slavery and Abolition* 20 (1999): 49–68.

44. Amedeo Vigna, "Codice diplomatico delle colonie tauro-ligure," *Atti della Società Ligure di Storia Patria* 7, pt. 2 (1879) contains the Statutes of Caffa, Cap. 45–46, pp. 634–66 for this and what follows.

Sanctuary could work in Caffa because of two factors. In Caffa a slave could flee to the Tartar hordes or other local communities much more easily than a slave in Italy could find a haven. So it made sense in Caffa to give the slave a chance at internal flight, which at least preserved the slave's value for the owner. The threat of sale outside Caffa, perhaps far away to Italy or Cairo, must have convinced some slaves that it was better to endure hard lives nearer to home than to be sold away with no practical hope of return. Also, in Caffa slaves did not have to become Christians unless they sought sanctuary. Leaving one's faith for the privilege of being sold cannot have struck every slave as a good bargain. Still, any sanctuary was better than none and that is what existed in Caffa. But it was a peculiar sanctuary, surrounded on all sides by the Tartar state or the sea.

Another rule in Caffa stated that if any slave fled there from the countryside or the horde of the Tartars, the slave was free. If, however, the rightful owner turned up in Caffa and claimed the slave, the business agents were to sell the slave and give the purchase price to the master. Here the Genoese were walking a fine line and probably honoring a treaty with the Tartars—sanctuary for runaways from a neighboring state (inconceivable back in Italy) but a practical recognition that if the non-Genoese owner appeared, peace with the powerful neighbor was more important than any slave. The most important problem facing the rulers of Caffa was its status as a colonial city, a multicultural entrepôt filled with Tartars, Italians, Armenians, Slavs, and other peoples. In these conditions it was necessary for the government to ensure the safety of the free population, so there was no room at all for developing an ethnic connection between being a Tartar and being a slave. Everyone practiced slavery without qualms, but slavery was not the same in Caffa as it was in Italy. The law promised that the inhabitants of Caffa could not be sold into slavery, no matter what "nation" they were. In this sense Caffa itself was a refuge, and the city could not function if the local people were vulnerable to capture by slavers, although as we have seen, this was precisely what happened to little Giorgio da Caffa when he was about ten years old in 1450.[45] (It is always necessary to keep in mind the law's prescriptive character and its constant violations.) The statutes also required that no one should collect a tax on any illegal sales, nor should any notary write up such a contract. To make another subtle point, the law stated that no one should buy a man or woman living in Caffa for the purpose of exporting them, under the large penalty of one thousand aspers. This reinforced the general principle that slavehunting was supposed to

45. See Chapter 1, pp. 34–35.

take place outside the city, out there, and only slaves brought into the city should be exported.

The Genoese behaved differently in Caffa and Genoa. Caffa was an emporium for slaves, but it was necessary for political and economic reasons to prevent people from being seized on the streets and impressed into slavery. Not far from Caffa, in the Tartar lands, enslavement happened all the time, or people sold their children into slavery. In theory any sort of person might be brought to Caffa as a slave. In Genoa no one could be enslaved—as in Caffa itself—but the same rule prevailed in surrounding territories like Lombardy and Tuscany. The only white slaves in Genoa were (by the fifteenth century) non-Italians from places like Bosnia, Muslim Spain, and the Caucasus. If the Genoese had come to Caffa with enslaved members of their own people as part of their system of slavery, they would have met on equal terms the Eastern peoples like the Tartars who also practiced slavery, and more important, had slaves from their own ethnic group or "nation." Instead, the Genoese enslaved everyone but themselves and their fellow white Christian western Europeans.

This fundamental difference between the two systems of slavery meant that Italian demand for slaves distorted the local, traditional markets for captive slaves in the Black Sea region. This area became a net exporter of slaves, in a modest way to Italy, and through intermediaries (largely Italian) in a more substantial way to Mamluk Egypt. The existence of these more sophisticated markets, where the local demand for slaves could not be satisfied within Italian or Egyptian society, distorted the Black Sea system and provided incentives for more slave raiding, selling of captives and even children, than there would have been without external demand. The Black Sea was a dress rehearsal for the way English and Dutch traders distorted the indigenous slavery practiced by the African tribes. There is no reason to believe that western European slavers drew on the precocious experiments of their Italian neighbors. But the parallel is clear. There was no slavery in England, France, or the Netherlands, yet their merchants needed slaves to fuel the plantations of the West Indies. Unwilling to enslave their own inhabitants, they turned to another slave system which had no scruples on this score, fed on its originally modest supplies, and created powerful incentives for more self-enslavement in Africa.

Genoa and Venice were fated to lose their colonies and slave trade in the eastern Mediterranean, and not to have any in the New World. This circumstance made Italian slavery exceptional. On Crete or in Caffa, the Venetians and Genoese learned from efforts to control runaways, and yet still draw on local sources of new slaves. They could not offer refuges for runaway slaves if they planned to operate slave markets. Back home, free people needed to be discouraged from helping runaways, and they were probably developing a distaste for slavery precisely because it seemed a small step to start enslaving the local orphans, or the idle, or the potential troublemakers. Genoese and Venetian merchants dealt with societies that already did these things. This is how the experience of runaways, from the perspective of masters who needed to enlist broad participation to support slavery, also made it harder to get popular agreement for the necessary stern measures for keeping slaves in their places.

CULTURAL RESISTANCE

Cultural resistance consists of a bundle of behaviors with which slaves confronted and combated slavery in ways that used covert physical or verbal acts to undermine the institution or just strike back at it.[46] This form of resistance is not a substitute by the faint-hearted for running away or rebelling; it is rather a continuation of the same struggle for personal autonomy by other means. The types of cultural resistance considered here— stealing, lying, and a sharp tongue—reflect the daily struggles of slaves to resist a system that tried to subordinate their wills and actions completely to the wishes of their masters. Some slaves, by the nature of their personalities or the repeated acts of repression they experienced, no doubt conformed to the system and chose survival. Other slaves tested the limits of self-assertion and behaved much as the free wage-earning population did. Both groups were under the thumbs of masters and employers, and even ostensibly free laborers struck back in cultural terms by lying to or stealing from their employers. Slaves, in a more degraded social condition, did not need lessons from journeymen and women and apprentices on how to find within slavery some ways to resist it. The daily humiliations of slavery would have prompted the hope of giving the masters their comeuppance anyway. Some of these ways to resist authority are such a natural part of subordination that we should not be surprised to see wage-earners first using them in Italian cities. This is one of the reasons why certain laws lumped together servants, workers, and slaves as people needing special forms of control. Slaves, as property, differed from other social groups and in some respects were in a privileged position because wealthy owners would not let some punishments fall on their property, while they sometimes could not care less what happened to their free servants. These strange crosscurrents inevitably

46. E. Genovese, *Roll, Jordan, Roll*, pp. 597–98 for some thoughts on cultural resistance.

caused tensions among all those people at the bottom of the social hierarchy, slave or free.

Since none of the evidence comes from the slaves, we must look beneath the surface of the rules masters made to see just what types of behaviors they were trying to stop. The Genoese law code of 1407 provides useful examples of how the law reveals cultural resistance by trying to prevent it. There was no formal slave code in these laws; instead, a series of ad hoc rules show how different groups of masters and employers dealt with particular signs of a common threat. For example, no money changer, goldsmith, or any other person was allowed to buy silver, pearls, precious stones, or gold from any slave or apprentice, male or female, or any boy or girl less than fifteen years of age, with fines ranging from 5 lire to 50 lire.[47] Small, valuable, easily pilferable items like these could disappear from a house into the disgruntled hands of a slave, servant, or young adolescent, three types of potential troublemakers. Keeping these people from stealing was a problem, but it was probably easier to prevent them from benefiting from these thefts by making sure they could not fence the loot. Presumably, despite the fines, which at the top end were substantial, there would always be some way to turn the stolen items into cash. Stealing might also provide the simple and safe pleasure of taking the stuff down to the docks and throwing it into the sea. Cultural resistance was a way of hitting back; the loss to the master or employer was the same; and it could be safer to destroy rather than fence the stolen property.

Dealers in used keys, as we saw in the previous chapter, were not supposed to sell their wares to any apprentice, slave, or servant, or any other person, except the master or mistress of the household.[48] Again, the slaves' company is revealing—just who could be trusted with keys? It would be worth knowing just what the free people thought they needed to lock up, but the slave, sometimes chained, was in a special category with respect to benefiting from a spare key. The cloth merchants were prohibited from buying any things or clothing from any slave, garbageman, or apprentice, or any person of bad or dishonest reputation, under penalty of returning the merchandise and losing the purchase price.[49] Clothing was another item, of lesser value, that was readily available in the households of masters or employers, and again, anything that was easily turned into cash was a problem for the dominant class. The company, again interesting, consisted of slaves and apprentices, lumped together with the unenviable garbage-

47. *Leges Genuenses*, vol. 18, col. 564.
48. Ibid., col. 643.
49. Ibid., col. 714.

men, who might also have a reputation for being thieves, for they were natural objects of suspicion. A similar provision concerning coppersmiths required that they not buy any metal—tin, lead, copper, bronze, or any other—from a slave, garbageman, or similar person, under penalty of loss of the merchandise and a fine of 5 lire.[50] The issue for garbagemen must have been that they could claim (plausibly?) that they had found valuable items in the trash, while in fact they had stolen them. Slaves and "similar persons," that is, those whose behaviors resulted from cultural resistance to hierarchy, had no ready alibi.

Precious and other metals, jewels, clothing, used keys—the masters drew the line at these items and did not tolerate them disappearing from their houses. Such thefts harmed the masters and also put money in the pockets of their "domestic enemies," slaves included. The law's silence (though always a tricky clue) in other areas points to the fact that masters and employers were prepared to tolerate petty pilfering that was part of the acceptable range of behavior, from their point of view. So, stealing food does not come up in the law, since slaves and workers consumed the fruits of their minor crimes. Hunger might be an reasonable excuse, and there probably was not much of a market for used food. The system of exploitation needed some slack, but the habits of petty thievery could easily lead to more serious offenses, so social theory taught.

And some kinds of pilfering were more dangerous than others—of poison, for example. Buried in the rules of the apothecaries was the provision that only the master of a shop could sell, give, or transfer arsenic. His son over twenty years of age might substitute for him in this, but never an apprentice or slave.[51] Poisoning was perhaps not cultural resistance, but the fear of the slave, servant, or apprentice resulted from a wider and more common, if less lethal set of behaviors, and who could set a practical limit to resistance? A summary of changes in the criminal laws prepared in the 1490s contained this new provision. Male or female slaves would be tortured by the state if the owners suspected that they had used potions for various purposes—abortions, poisoning, or love potions—by introducing something into the owners' food and drink.[52] The law elegantly extended suspicion to anything these slaves might do that caused masters or their

---

50. Ibid., col. 713.

51. Ibid., col. 675.

52. *Statuta et decreta communis Genuae*, ed. Antonio Maria Visdomini (Bologna, 1498), appendix on the criminal law, 2v–3r, for this and what follows: "poculum aborcionis amatoreum veneuum [*sic*] seu tosicum," "amisserint seu amittant sensum mentem seu memoriam vel devient a moribus seu vita consueta."

children to lose their minds or memories, or to deviate from their usual habits of living. Malicious (or resisting) slaves might be behind any lapse of memory or strange behavior by a slaveowner. Any miscarriage or weird infatuation occurring in a household might be explained (under torture) by something a slave had done. Whatever prompted these fears, the possibility of slave resistance got the state's attention and threatened slaves with violence over any suspicious event in the master's house.

An episode connected to the arrival of the Bianchi in Genoa in 1399 reveals how a slave's powerful words might affect the free population. The coming of the flagellants to Genoa coincided with severe political and social stress, and slaves were prominent in the local processions responding to the call for public, collective penance.[53] A slave belonging to a nobleman was freed either before or during these events, and she made a remarkable declaration to the free population. The woman said that the Virgin Mary had appeared to her in a dream and told her that the Genoese had not processed in a pure and devout manner. After her claims were investigated, the archbishop ordered a new round of processions. What is worth noting about this story is that an ex-slave's reputation for holiness was so strong that of all Genoese, she was the one who received the message from the next world. This woman understood the power of words. Many Genoese must have been perplexed by Mary's choice of messenger, though perhaps it was more tolerable to receive the message from an "outsider."

A sharp or lying tongue was also a weapon of cultural resistance, but as long as the master held the virtually unlimited right of corporal punishment, it had to be used cautiously. Resisting with words was not necessarily safe, but language could be wounding or provocative. A case from 1442 in Genoa demonstrates the power of language in many contexts. A Circassian slave named Caterina belonged to Bartolomeo Parrisola.[54] Caterina was at a well fetching water when a sixteen-year-old apprentice cutler named Luchino bothered and disturbed her with provocative words. Incensed by this language, Caterina hit him on the head with a rock, and he died thirteen days later. Although Caterina's response was certainly physical, the incident concerns culture and language on several levels. Bartolomeo sprang into action; he hired doctors to treat Luchino, he paid for the burial, and above all with sadness and anxiety he petitioned the government to absolve

53. See my *Genoa and the Genoese 958–1528* (Chapel Hill, N.C., 1996), pp. 255–57 for a fuller discussion of the Bianchi. The notice of the slave comes from Giovanni Stella in the *Annales Genuenses* in Rerum Italicarum Scriptores, n.s. 17, pt 2, ed. by Giovanna Petti Balbi (Bologna, 1975), p. 241.

54. Case in L. Tria, "La Schiavitù," no. 47, pp. 176–77.

Caterina from the penalty for the homicide. What is remarkable is that he succeeded in convincing the state that Caterina did not by her will kill Luchino, but instead was provoked by words to act. The government pardoned Caterina because Bartolomeo had behaved so well and because Luchino's relatives freely remitted their claims—presumably well rewarded by Bartolomeo for this. The doge of Genoa accepted Caterina's all too human response to intense verbal provocation, and in Bartolomeo she had a master who did everything possible to save her from a gruesome, exemplary punishment. That "fighting words" as a defense could save a slave shows the power of language, but doubtless the victim's low social status and his compliant family also explain the leniency here. No amount of physical or verbal provocation would have excused Caterina's response if her master had been the provoker. Caterina must have understood the difference, and while reaching for a rock was not a safe response to insulting words, even against the honor of her owner, she knew enough of Genoese culture to see a path of resistance. Caterina probably knew her master well enough to expect his tireless efforts on her behalf, but she could not have anticipated the government's uncharacteristic leniency. The document mentions nothing about the substance of Luchino's language, but it was probably the lower-class source of those words that saved Caterina.

This episode suggests that once again the widest possible context helps to make sense of language, especially in the delicate area of cultural resistance. Back in 1409 a Genoese ex-slave, Margherita de Rosia, also showed the power of words.[55] Margherita had trouble with wine, and when drinking she said many offensive things about Pietro Lobia. He wanted to shut her up, but Margherita was free to speak as she liked, and Pietro was evidently not a violent man. So he made a substantial gift of 50 lire to Margherita, and in exchange she promised to drink moderately and not become intoxicated, and most important, not to say villainous or injurious things about Pietro, under penalty of forfeiting the gift. Now if Margherita were still a slave no one would pay her for silence, but this ex-slave, free to drink and say as much as she liked, was another problem. No one thought to invoke some clause in her emancipation about good behavior, and no ex-master was at hand to enforce it. Whatever Margherita was saying about Pietro, he was not likely to give us a clue about its substance in the record of his gift to her, which was worth about half the price of a slave, so it must have been pretty bad and probably true.

Within slavery, resistance with words was also possible. Remember Alessandra Macinghi Strozzi's problem with the "bad tongue' of her slave

55. Ibid., p. 162.

Cateruccia.[56] Alessandra was suffering, and frightened, and it was getting so bad that she made the famous comment that it was as if Cateruccia was the mistress and she the slave. Cateruccia accomplished all this with words that show the power of cultural resistance to destabilize an owner. Lying also offered many possibilities for resisting slavery, for costing the owners time and money, for evading work and responsibility. Slaves knew the costs of physical resistance to the masters. Twisting words, harder to prove, offered a wide scope of activity to the ingenious and ironic. And all the good lies were never detected, and did not enter the historical record as such.

These Italian slaves, in general not a self-reproducing population, did not have the chance to create an enduring culture of resistance to be passed down from mother to daughter. Slavery was constantly replenished by new foreigners, and manumissions siphoned off some slaves into the free community. So Eugene Genovese's complex argument for the evolution of a distinctive cultural resistance among American slaves cannot be applied to the smaller, overwhelmingly female, and slowly disappearing Italian slave population. But there are enough stray signs in the records to prove that short of rebellion or flight, slaves used theft and language to retain some vestiges of humanity that occasionally the free population was forced to recognize.

PREGNANCY

Historical records have nothing to say about the motives behind the behavior of becoming pregnant. Slave women certainly had children, but we do not know why. Working back from the existence of children to the motives of their mothers is therefore hopeless, and there are only a few subtle hints about what might have prompted slave women to give more hostages to fortune by having children. In Muslim religious law and tradition, a slave woman giving birth to the child of her owner obtained certain rights not available to the ordinary slave.[57] She gained the status of concubine and her children were free.[58] Nearly everywhere in Christian society a child followed the status of the mother, and no place extended the privileges under Islam for such a mother. From the revival of slavery in medieval Italy so

56. See Chapter 1, p. 33.

57. Bernard Lewis, *Race and Slavery in the Middle East* (Oxford, 1990), p. 8.

58. For some comments on the situation in Spain see David Nirenberg, *Communities of Violence: Persecution of Minorities in the Middle Ages* (Princeton, N.J., 1996), p. 141. In Spain, Muslim women could be enslaved for committing miscegenation (p. 138), yet in Genoa the slave might benefit from such an alliance.

many Muslim women were slaves that they may have brought with them the idea that having a child by the master would improve their status. (This had certainly occurred in Muslim Sicily.) Even if Christian law or religion did not grant any benefits, a child conceived in affectionate circumstances may have cemented the bonds between the free man and the slave woman. Slave women may have thought that having a free man as the father might benefit their child in the long run. Weighed against these hypothetical advantages was the possibility that the man's relatives, especially his wife, might hate the slave and her spurious offspring. In those cases where the child resulted from forced sex, the child might be seen as an awkward embarrassment or a punishment to the master's family. Recent scholarship has shown that medieval women knew far more about contraception than previously thought, and some methods available to them, notably pessaries, were safe and effective.[59] A slave woman therefore had some potential control over becoming pregnant, even when she was unable to resist the sexual demands of her owner or other men.

If motive remains impossible to fathom, some of the results of becoming pregnant and having a child left traces in the legal records, for the irony is that some free men had as their nearest heirs the children they had with slaves. This of course was the hope of the slave woman, who, though property herself, could produce a child who might some day, in some circumstances, have a claim to the master's property. As an heir, the child also attracted the hostility of his or her free relatives who found their hopes for an inheritance frustrated by this interloper. Once again, out in colonial Caffa, where behavior was rougher, some of these issues are less opaque than in the genteel palaces of Genoa or Venice. I have written elsewhere on the case of Niccolino Presani of Cremona, who in Caffa had children by a slave woman or concubine named Lucia, and then, sadly for them all, died without making a will.[60] In Genoa, his Italian relatives tried by every conceivable argument to overturn the legitimation and inherit the estate. In Caffa unconventional unions were common, and men of average means, unfamiliar with the legal niceties required to make a child by a slave one's heir, might easily leave themselves and their families prey to clever legal claims back home. Lucia had children by her owner and moved up a notch in the social hierarchy by becoming his concubine—a legal status conferring some rights on women. Without a good lawyer, how could she anticipate the consequences if her "husband" neglected to take care of his precarious fam-

59. John M. Riddle, *Contraception and Abortion from the Ancient World to the Renaissance* (Cambridge, Mass., 1992), pp. 137–39 and elsewhere.
60. See my *Genoa and the Genoese*, p. 282.

ily? Still, Lucia was lucky to benefit later from one of the best legal minds in Genoa, Bartolomeo de Bosco. This case gave him the opportunity to make two general arguments about Lucia and her children. Before the Fall there was no slavery, and no marriage—all children would have been natural. Once sin entered the world, institutions like slavery and marriage, necessary human innovations, regulated wayward human conduct. The behavior of having a child was natural, whether the mother was slave or free. Having children humanized the slave woman, no matter what anybody said. Second, even in distant Caffa, Roman and Genoese law prevailed. Presani's relatives tried to argue in court that since Caffa was in the domain of the khan of the Tartars, Tartar law should be in force. Bosco considered this claim laughable, and on a more subtle level, he needed to convince a Genoese court that there was no double standard in the behavior of having children. However people acted in Caffa, the same rules were in force as in Genoa. There are of course pluses and minuses to all this—it was just as likely that colonial standards of conduct would debase behavior in Genoa as it was that the more sophisticated style of life in Italy would elevate conduct in Caffa.

Another case from Genoa illustrates the complexities facing a slave woman having children by her owner. Agnese claimed to be the former slave of the late Pasqualino Ratono, and to have had a boy with him named Agostino.[61] As he lay dying, Pasqualino made a will and named as his heirs this Agostino, who had been freed, and a second son named Jacopo, also free and his child by Lucia, another slave of his. (For slave women, competition and rivalry with other slaves was another factor in the decision to have children.) Agnese claimed that she was not mentioned in the will because she had already been effectively freed, and she was in court to get this ratified. A representative of Pasqualino's estate was also in court to claim Agnese as part of the inheritance. It is really possible that Agostino inherited one-half of his slave mother, by his father's will. Agnese was fortunate to get into court and benefit from legal advice of Bosco's caliber, but even he had to admit that Agnese was still a slave, and not even the late Pasqualino's concubine, since it was clear that he had several relationships going, and by law a man could have only one concubine. Pasqualino had brought Agnese with him from Caffa back to Genoa, but he had never troubled to sort out the tangled circumstances of his personal life, beyond freeing his sons. The path out of this mess was clear. Agostino had to free his mother—what free person could own his mother, and even worse, only half of her? In a roundabout way, Agnese's behavior in having a child may have

61. Bartolomeo de Bosco, *Consilia* (Loano, 1620), no. 492, pp. 786–89. These cases do not mention the lawyer's fee.

eventually resulted in the mother's freedom, but the path was certainly arduous. As Bosco himself reminded the court, the laws provided that if anyone carnally knew his slave and she had a child, she was not free because of this. (This law again may have been a faint echo of a local need to correct the misconception of local slaves of Muslim origin.) Agnese must have thought that once Agostino was a free man, he would not forget his mother—probably the real meaning of the phrase "a hostage to fortune."

We know nothing about Agnese's motives and can only presume them from her conduct, not necessarily rational, and from the arguments of lawyers representing her. About male slaves we know even less, and whatever free women had children with them seem to have been quiet about it. Having a child with another slave cannot have benefited any slave woman, so the real opportunities and dangers remained in relations with the master or some other free man. In a strange episode in 1381, the slave Marta Greca went before a notary to swear that she had slept with Stefano Greco of Rhodes, and only him, and had become pregnant.[62] In order to unburden her soul, as she put it, she wanted to ensure that Stefano received the child after birth and that he would be a good father to it. Her master, who seems to have been benevolent, was allowing his slave's child to escape slavery. Both Stefano and Marta, of Greek origin, may have found some solace in a common culture as well as sex. Marta, however, managed to have a free child, and not by her owner. A Florentine slave named Margherita had a child by her master, who sent it to the local orphanage, the Ospedale degli Innocenti.[63] Thirteen months later, in 1466, Margherita stole her baby from a wet-nurse, making clear that the ties between slave mother and child could be very strong. Pregnancy and childbirth, perhaps more than any other aspect of slave life, prove that master and slave found their common humanity in the children they made.

WORK

The behavior owners expected from slaves was of course work, another subject on which we are not well informed. The great majority of female slaves, especially in the fourteenth and fifteenth centuries, were engaged in domestic service. In the details of documents on other matters, we find slaves in the kitchen, out fetching water at a well, cleaning latrines, and working at the myriad of duties that kept a wealthy household going. Fe-

62. ASG, CN, Cart. N. 294, 95v, Benvenuto Bracelli notary.

63. Philip Gavitt, *Charity and Children in Renaissance Florence: The Ospedale degli Innocenti, 1410–1536* (Ann Arbor, Mich., 1990), p. 202.

male slaves worked alongside free servants who did the same things, but whom the law protected from the worst violence that could be inflicted on a slave. Still, wage laborers were paid for what some slaves did for free, beyond their capital costs and upkeep. Free persons who did the work of slaves must have experienced a diminished social status that cannot have pleased them, or resulted always in good working relationships with the slaves. Exotic and costly slaves represented a style of conspicuous consumption that may have protected them from some dangerous work, another point not lost on the free wage laborers who had to do it. Every owner or employer had to calculate the risks and benefits of the capital cost of slaves versus the wages and supply of free labor. After the plague of 1348 free servants might have been harder to find, but slaves too were more expensive. Male slaves also worked in domestic service, and in addition to doing household chores they also appear in stables as people who knew their way around horses and mules. Slaves were numerous enough in Genoa that the commune put them to work in 1380 fortifying the hill of Bolzaneto during a crisis.[64] The labor of slaves was a resource the state might call upon in an emergency.

Of course there was some work that slaves were not supposed to do—in Genoa this included a range of activities. For example, the rules of the port officials, who supervised the public brothels, directed the chief officials to make sure that no female slave belonging to any Genoese or citizen worked in a brothel, under the small penalty of 5 lire for each slave and each offense.[65] If any prostitute or pimp of whatever status, male or female, received such a slave in the stalls, they were to be denounced to the podesta of Genoa, a sign of a serious criminal offense. The city government did not want Genoese slave owners to put their slaves to work in the public brothels, to compete there with the free women who paid for the privilege. Perhaps people believed that such a master was really a pimp, and such a slave had not freely chosen this degrading occupation. In Sicily Frederick III's ostensible reason for prohibiting Christian slaves from working as prostitutes was to avoid coercing a Christian into the sin of fornication.[66] The brothels were potential refuges for runaways, and the Genoese state was discouraging the denizens of brothels from harboring female slaves or giving them a chance to earn a living. The desire to thwart any solidarity

64. Benjamin Z. Kedar, *Merchants in Crisis: Genoese and Venetian Men of Affairs and the Fourteenth-Century Depression* (New Haven, Conn., 1976), p. 127.

65. *Statuto dei padri del comune della repubblica genovese*, ed. Cornelio Desimoni (Genoa, 1885), pp. 30–31.

66. *Capitula Regni Siciliae*, ed. by Francesco Testa (Palermo, 1741), p. 81.

among slaves and prostitutes must account for the harsher penalties facing the latter, as opposed to regular Genoese masters who may have seen profit in prostituting their slaves. The Venetian courtesan and poet Veronica Franco (1546–1591) wrote a letter to a mother contemplating putting her daughter to work as a prostitute.[67] Advising the mother against this course, Franco directly connected prostitution to servitude. The common thread between slavery and prostitution was the loss of control over one's body— something Franco thought contrary to human nature.

In Venice in 1370 the Senate prohibited slaves from learning how to weave silk. The issue here was controlling access to the secrets of the trade: a slave might be sold abroad, and then the "mysteries" of silk weaving could pass to any foreign rival.[68] Genoese law on the apothecaries stated that the masters were not allowed to teach their trade to any Tartar or Turkish slave, under penalty of 50 lire. Masters might teach the trade to other slaves, but even if they were eventually freed they could never be heads of shops. This meant they would never be allowed to sell poison, either as slaves or as free persons.[69] Tartar and Turkish slaves were more threatening, possibly because they came from important states in the eastern Mediterranean that were taking the offensive against Christian states. The statutes of the silk guild, redacted in 1432, allowed members to train male slaves in the trade, but even if the slaves were later freed, they could never be in charge of a shop or an official in the guild, under the big penalty of 100 lire, more than the price of the typical male slave. Slaves and freedmen were allowed to work as day laborers.[70] Almost the exact same provisions appear in the statutes of the dyers' guild from 1426, except that here slaves were in the same class as foreigners; they would never be accepted as equals in the trade, even if free.[71] Both the silk and dyers trade involved some heavy, difficult work appropriate for slaves, and the masters of these guilds, especially those in the silk trade who were rich enough to buy a slave, would not deny themselves the right to train their slaves and put them to work.

67. *Women Poets of the Italian Renaissance: Courtly Ladies and Courtesans*, ed. Laura Anna Stortoni (New York, 1997), p. 177. Prostitution was a "troppo infelice cosa e troppo contraria al senso umano è l'obligar il corpo e l'industria di una tal servitù che spaventa solamente a pensarne."

68. Luca Molà, *La comunità dei lucchesi a Venezia: Immigrazione e industria della seta nel tardo medioevo* (Venice, 1994), p. 172.

69. *Leges Genuenses*, vol. 18, col. 676.

70. Giuseppe Morazzoni, *Mostra delle antiche stoffe genovesi dal secolo xv al secolo xix* (Genoa, 1941), p. 110.

71. ASG, Magistrato delle arti, Busta 178, Fascie 23, 9v.

The masters contemplated the eventual freedom of some of these slaves, but they would never accept that even when free the slaves could then be their equals as heads of shops or guild officials, no matter how skilled or successful they might be. As slaves or freedmen, they were only fit to work alongside the day laborers, the wage-earners. Such a lesson in social status was not lost on the journeymen and women either, who sensed their true value in the eyes of their employers. Domenico Gioffrè suggests that circumscribing the ex-slaves may have also been an effort to keep the trade secrets the slaves learned from benefiting any shops they might set up. But in that case the statutes would have prohibited the freedmen and women from even working anywhere else, and this they did not do.[72]

Medieval and early modern systems of labor embodied a gender division of labor that reflected a broader social consensus about what sorts of behavior were appropriate for women and men. By the sixteenth century, male slaves and convicts figured prominently as rowers in Genoese and Venetian galleys, although in their naval heyday the cities had relied exclusively on free citizen rowers with a strong incentive to row and fight for their city and families. But at all times, naval service fell on the male side of the division of labor, just as only women worked as wet-nurses. Most work did not divide so neatly on one side of the line or the other. Since slaves mainly worked in domestic service, while the vast majority of the free population was not working as domestic servants, the division of labor was not the same among slaves as it was among free persons. Among free domestic servants in sixteenth-century Venice, females still predominated, usually at about two-thirds of the thousands who were in service.[73] Among the servants, the gender balance was more equal, but we lack good data about the earlier situation, when there were more slaves in these positions. In Venice, nobles owned many of the male slaves, and in their households, there was about one male servant for every nobleman and two female servants for every noblewoman.[74] The wealthiest members of society wanted body servants to attend to their personal needs, and the extra slave woman may also have taken care of general household and kitchen duties. It is still puzzling that back in the fifteenth century, when male slaves were cheaper than female ones, there were still so few male slaves working at all in Genoa, and not nearly enough for every nobleman. Unless the style of domestic service changed radically in both cities in the next century, it is more likely that

72. Domenico Gioffrè, *Il mercato degli schiavi a Genova nel secolo XV* (Genoa, 1971), p. 91.

73. D. Romano, *Housecraft*, p. 109.

74. Ibid., p. 108.

people preferred to have free male servants and enslaved females, and as slavery waned they were forced to replace the slaves with free women wage-earners. So the actual gender division of labor in domestic service was probably more balanced than the slave population figures for Genoa would themselves indicate. Especially in the fifteenth century, the richest households still contained a mix of free and slave servants. As some of the laws showed, this situation probably harmed the social status of the free servants who were more disposable than the slaves, since capital cost had to be figured into the decision to hire a free servant or buy a slave.

Several behaviors intersect on this issue of economic calculation. Slaves worked, a type of behavior. Slave owners calculated the costs of owning a slave, and at times it was more profitable to rent out a slave rather than employ one directly. A slave rented out to another employer was in a difficult position—exploited by a short-term proprietor interested in getting his or her money's worth; owned by someone else who planned to benefit from the bargain. Gioffrè's analysis of 208 slave rentals in fifteenth-century Genoa led him to conclude that such deals yielded the owner 7 to 10 percent annually on the capital value of the slave.[75] This was a good rate of return on capital, but there were risks on all sides. A slave with breast milk was a valuable asset, and some masters may have encouraged or even caused slaves to become pregnant with this economic bonus in mind. The rental of a slave named Maddalena, who had milk, ran for four years from 1381 and earned the owner 40 lire.[76] At a common price for young women of 60 lire in these years, the rate of return was a tidy 16 percent. In another contract from 1425, an owner rented his slave Lucia as a wet-nurse and servant to another family for the high price of 60 lire for three years.[77] At an average price of about 100 lire for a young woman, this looks like a 20 percent rate of return. But the renter, whose primary need was milk for his children, had to pay the market price. The owner safeguarded his interests by collecting the entire 60 lire at the beginning of the term, with no provision for returning any of it if Lucia died. So it was in the renter's best interest to conserve this property, but less so as the end of the three years approached. The renter was also obligated to provide Lucia with good and sufficient food, drink, clothing, and shoes, as was the custom for servants. This last phrase reveals the social standards for how to take care of domestic servants, slave or free, and Lucia's owner wanted to ensure that his slave received the standard fare, here the same for a slave or free servant.

75. D. Gioffrè, *Il mercato*, p. 94.
76. ASG, CN, Cart. N. 294, 108r–v, Benvenuto Bracelli notary.
77. L. Tria, "La schiavitù," p. 170.

Another such contract from 1477 differed in some particulars.[78] Although three years' service as a wet-nurse still cost the renter 60 lire, he paid in yearly installments—some advantage to him if the slave, named Maria, died. The renter in this case wanted to keep his right to return the slave, especially in the third year, if she was not providing enough milk for his son. The payment arrangements were also curious; the renter sent a slave named Caterina to work in Maria's owner's house, at a cost of 11 lire a year to be discounted from the 20 lire he owed for the wet-nurse. Clearly wet-nurses were far more expensive than other female servants, so the trade was not equal.[79] As Gioffrè points out about renting wet-nurses, the contracts that give the ages of these women indicate the average age was about twenty-seven and a half, a kind of guarantee to the renter of the slave's responsible behavior and maturity.[80] Institutions also engaged in these rentals, especially hospitals and orphanages. In fifteenth-century Florence the Ospedale degli Innocenti purchased slaves to serve as wet-nurses, rented others, and occasionally sold a slave when it needed cash.[81]

Finally, there are a few signs that some people thought to put slaves to work on the land. In Liguria, with little arable flat land, the most lucrative local farming produced vegetables, fruits, wine, and olive oil. So it was not unusual to see a garden farmer rent two male slaves in 1387, but the slaves themselves, a father and son, were in unusual circumstances.[82] The father Giorgio, twenty-eight years old, was rented for eight years, and his son, Andrea, aged only eight, was rented for twelve years, for a total of 40 lire, paid in advance. The owner, a widow named Giovannina, insisted that the renter take care of these slaves in sickness and in health and feed them well, and at the end of the terms the two slaves were to become free. If they fled before then, the loss was the renter's—an incentive to keep an eye on them. So the owner sent her slaves out of Genoa for good, into the countryside where they presumably learned a useful trade. Giorgio would be free four years before his son, and perhaps he could then buy his son out of the rest of the contract. This exceptional arrangement, and the urban quality of most Genoese slavery, suggest that slavery was uncommon in the Ligurian countryside and that only in rural Sicily did agricultural slavery persist well into the sixteenth century. For example, the parents of San Benedetto of

78. Ibid., p. 183.

79. Evidence from Venice also suggests that wet-nurses were a lot more expensive to rent. D. Romano, *Housecraft*, p. 90.

80. D. Gioffrè, *Il mercato*, p. 102.

81. P. Gavitt, *Charity and Children*, pp. 162–68.

82. Document in L. Tria, "La schiavitù," pp. 152–54, for this and what follows.

Palermo, il Moro, eventually one of the patron saints of Palermo, were "Ethiopian" (which in the period meant that they came from any part of sub-Saharan Africa)—black slaves who worked on a farm where Benedetto spent his childhood in similar work. Again, the small scale of rural ownership of slaves is striking. Jacques Heers has hypothesized that slaves unloaded at Moneglia, east of Genoa, were intended to work in silk cocoon cultivation among the mulberry trees of the Cinque Terre.[83] Whatever the scope of this plausible experiment, it failed, and plantation-style agriculture with slave labor, whether silk in the north or cotton in the south, never developed in Italy.

There is no obvious economic reason why plantation slavery worked in the New World and not in the Old. Robin Blackburn suggests that the main reasons were noneconomic—that the social consensus in Europe valued liberty too keenly to allow Europeans to be enslaved.[84] There are some problems with this analysis; there was a lot of African slavery in Portugal, as Blackburn and others have shown, and Europeans were not at all reluctant to enslave Bosnians and other Europeans.[85] It is likely that Italians would have resisted their own enslavement on plantations, but that would not necessarily have prevented them from bringing Africans or other laborers to Italy to work. Why this did not happen remains a historical puzzle best explored after we examine attitudes toward slavery revealed in the defenses of the practice.

Before turning to the behavior of slave owners and their apologists in defending slavery, we should briefly examine how slaves structured their behavior to survive slavery, or not. Unfortunately, almost nothing is known about how slaves practiced any religion, so whether any beliefs made their lot more bearable is unknown. Wills of ex-slaves are rare, reveal conventional pieties, and cannot serve as evidence on the beliefs of the many who never escaped slavery. Wills from two ex-slaves on Crete confirm this observation. One, by Chali, revealed a very small estate, the bulk of which she left for her soul, for the daughter of her ex-owner to distribute.[86] Herini,

83. Jacques Heers, *Gênes au XVe siècle* (Paris, 1961), p. 238.

84. Robin Blackburn, *The Making of New World Slavery* (London, 1997), pp. 354, 358. Blackburn is very good on this subject, but he is arguing that plantation slavery was largely invented in the New World. Therefore he is not interested in Italian slavery, a subject he does not consider.

85. On slave raiding in Dalmatia throughout the Middle Ages see Daniel Evans, "Slave Coast of Europe," *Slavery and Liberation* 6 (1985): 41–58.

86. S. McKee, *Wills*, pp. 533–34 n. 411.

the other ex-slave, was married, but she too was in modest circumstances and also left most of her things for her soul, and nothing to her husband.[87] In both instances the ex-slaves were concerned about their souls, but no local charity excited their interest enough to name it in their wills. Making a will was an act reserved for free persons, as the testament of Maria, once a slave, demonstrates.[88] Her will, made in 1468, recorded in precise detail the act back in 1459 that had emancipated her. The entire rest of her will consisted of three acts: a legally required legacy to a local hospital; and the choice of her burial site, which was left to the principal heir, the daughter of her late owner. Given the constrained lives of many ex-slaves, this is not surprising; nor is the lack of interest in local Genoese charities, which, however, did include another hospital especially set up for ex-slaves.

Whatever comfort religion provided escaped the records, but a belief in any religion might have been a survival trait among slaves, giving them some reason to carry on.[89] Religion also taught hierarchy and subordination, values masters would like to see their slaves adopt. Above all, slaves were trapped people, with hopes of leaving slavery possibly through emancipation and certainly through death. Walter Burkert has proposed that people in such circumstances try to believe that rituals help to make amends to God for whatever fault, sin, or mistake caused the entrapment.[90] Whether slaves felt guilt or a sense of pollution about their status is impossible to say, but in the obsequious conduct of some ex-slaves we may see some vestiges of guilt. Trapped people mostly want to get away, but sometimes they must sacrifice part of themselves, maybe even something as weighty as their self-respect, in order to accomplish this. When we turn to the behavior of the free population, we will see that justifying slavery also had its costs.

DEFENSES OF SLAVERY

Defenses of slavery, no matter how self-serving or hypocritical, derived from a context and must have been responding to some real criticisms, or at least qualms about how the institution functioned. It may not have been the words of slaves that prompted people like St. Augustine to justify slavery.

---

87. Ibid., pp. 548–49 n. 422.

88. L. Tria, "La schiavitù," pp. 200–201.

89. Survival is a major theme in Walter Burkert, *Creation of the Sacred: Tracks of Biology in Early Religions* (Cambridge, Mass., 1996).

90. Ibid., p. 125.

Pragmatics suggests that a look at the milieu of these justifications can give us a sense of the missing criticism, whatever its origins.[91] Defending slavery was a moral and linguistic choice—a type of human behavior, not a categorical imperative, and in the long history of slavery, it is not surprising that most writers chose to justify the institution. The best-known texts in the Middle Ages—the Bible, St. Augustine, and St. Thomas Aquinas—all accepted the practice. An undercurrent of opposition did exist, though nearly all in the Greek fathers, and hence not likely to be well known in medieval Italy. But defenses of slavery may echo its critics, so a short digression on late ancient criticisms of slavery will help us understand the broader intellectual world in which our subjects lived. Gregory of Nyssa made the most eloquent assault on slavery in a homily written around 380, and here is a sample: "Tell me this: who can buy a man, who can sell him, when he is made in the likeness of God . . . ?" Or even more vividly, "When a man is put up for sale, nothing less than the Lord of the Earth is led onto the auction block."[92] Gregory concludes with a strong plea for the common humanity of master and slave—again forcefully: "what have you got that makes you superior enough to think yourself master of a man when you are just a man yourself?"[93] As Peter Garnsey has rightly emphasized, Gregory of Nyssa was a lonely voice against slavery.[94] John Chrysostom, according to his modern biographer, was uneasy about slavery, and wondered why, if slavery were necessary, God had not provided any slaves for Adam.[95] Still, Chrysostom, like Gregory of Nyssa, did not call on masters to free their slaves.

Hebrew tradition provided another set of choices to make about slavery. The Essenes had abolished slavery in their sect, but the mainstream Hebrews had slaves, both their own brethren and Gentiles.[96] Deuteronomy 15:15–18 reminded the Hebrews that they too had been slaves in Egypt, and required them to free their own Hebrew slaves after six years. This

91. Also an approach followed by Peter Garnsey, *Ideas of Slavery from Aristotle to Augustine* (Cambridge, 1996).

92. T. J. Dennis, "The Relationship Between Gregory of Nyssa's Attack on Slavery in his Fourth Homily on Ecclesiastes and his Treatise *De Hominis Opificio*," *Studia Patristica* 17 (1982): 1065–72, here p. 1066.

93. Ibid., p. 1067.

94. P. Garnsey, *Ideas of Slavery*, pp. 81–82.

95. J. N. D. Kelly, *Golden Mouth: The Story of John Chrysostom* (Ithaca, 1995), pp. 99–100.

96. See I. A. H. Combs, *The Metaphor of Slavery in the Writings of the Early Church* (Sheffield, 1998), p. 54 on Essenes.

model of a lenient, temporary slavery for coreligionists needs to be weighed against Leviticus 25:45–46, which allowed the Hebrews to keep slaves from other nations in permanent bondage, as chattel slaves.[97] But the rules on slavery as set forth in Hebrew Scripture would not become the rules of early Christianity. This result too involved at least some level of choice. Defending or questioning slavery had a long tradition by the time medieval Italians explored the relevant biblical passages and practiced the institution, and the weight of opinion was on the side of those who argued for the legitimacy, even the justice, of slavery.

The late classical thinker with the most influence on medieval Europe was Augustine, and in *The City of God* he offered a famous defense of slavery in Christian society. Augustine's views, well known to Italian theologians and writers from Jacopo da Voragine and Dante to Leopardi, deserve attention here as basic and authoritative opinions on slavery, and as clues to the opinions he was arguing against. Given the nature of the sources, we often have to reconstruct the work of unsuccessful social critics from the canonical views that triumphed. Augustine concluded that "The first cause of slavery, then, is sin, whereby man was subjected to man in the condition of bondage; and this can only happen by the judgment of God, with whom there is no injustice, and who knows how to allot different punishments according to the deserts of the offenders."[98] Augustine conceded that slavery was not natural, but resulted from sin, and justly punished some. Slaves should serve "not with the slyness of fear, but with the fidelity of affection, until all injustice disappears," in effect a life sentence.[99] Augustine does not directly explain why this particular punishment falls on some people and not others, though he suggests that some individuals are slaves to lust, and by extension most of us are compelled by something, so physical slavery of one's being to another is merely a type, and not the harshest, of subordination.

Beneath this analysis there are seven implicit arguments against slavery that Augustine was answering. Turning his own words inside out in this way makes this section of *The City of God* much more revealing. The first anti-

---

97. See in general the excellent analysis of the broad issues in Gregory Chirichigno, *Debt-Slavery in Israel and the Ancient Near East* (Sheffield, 1993).

98. "Prima ergo seruitutis causa peccatum est, ut homo homini condicionis uinculo subderetur, quod non fit nisi Deo iudicante, apud quem non est iniquitas et nouit diuersas poenas meritis distribuere delinquentium." St. Augustine, *De Civitate Dei*, vol. 2 (Turnhout, 1955), p. 682, and pp. 682–83 for what follows. I use here the translation *The City of God*, trans. Henry Bettenson (Harmondsworth, 1972), p. 875.

99. St. Augustine, *De Civitate Dei*, 2:682; *City of God*, p. 875.

slavery argument is that God did not intend for humans to have dominion over rational creatures, that is, over one another. Augustine concedes this point and really had no choice; the famous passage in Genesis giving humanity dominion over the world and its creatures did not mention people as resources to be exploited. Second, slavery is unjust when imposed on the innocent. Augustine of course argues that slavery is an appropriate punishment for sinners, but everyone knew instances where innocent people or big groups were incorporated into a slave regime, regardless of their guilt. (In his heart Augustine believed everyone was already guilty on account of original sin, but that still leaves the question: Why then are some free and others slaves?) The pagans accepted that slavery might result from plain bad luck, so for them fortune explained the injustice of slavery in some circumstances. Christian theologians were not likely to accept this viewpoint, so the answer that no one is really innocent, Augustine's fundamental and boring response to every moral question, would not comfort people who did not believe that they had been justly enslaved.

The third antislavery argument, closely tied to the previous one, is that the slavery of the defeated has nothing to do with justice; it is just the result of bad luck on the field of battle or someplace else. Augustine notes, as did so many others, that the Latin *servus* derives from the preserving of defeated captives, whom the victors might have executed but instead made into slaves, thus destroying their social identity.[100] Here too, Augustine does not let pass the argument that the fortunes of war are not part of the divine plan, so he inevitably points out that defeat in battle and subsequent enslavement are also the just rewards of sin. Augustine anticipates the fourth argument, which is that slavery has nothing to do with the judgment of God; it is a human institution. This is a crucial point because it could eliminate all the religious reasons for slavery and leave it as a human invention, and hence prone to moral lapses and fallibility. Augustine might have accepted this point and freed himself to criticize slavery as another debased creation of human selfishness, but he does not. Instead, he puts forward his idea, in the long quotation above, that everything results from the judgment of God, who is never unjust, and hence sin causes slavery. So Augustine argues that slavery too is part of God's plan, and since the institution comes from God, it cannot be unjust. This internally consistent argument, eerily like what modern economists say about the decisions of the market, is profoundly conservative in that it accepts everything that exists in human history, including slavery, as the just working out of God's plan for the universe.

100. St. Augustine, *De Civitate Dei*, 2:682, *City of God*, p. 874.

Clearly, the antislavery arguments would have had to address the issue of sin. The fifth argument tries to do this by asking why sinners should be masters and devout Christians be slaves to sinners. This is a powerful question, though of course Augustine could simply continue to press his usual explanation and insist that even the devout Christian slave merits, on the grounds of sin, whatever cruelties a sinful master inflicts. Yet he does not so argue, because it was clearly the case by the early fifth century, when he was working on these ideas, that Christians who believed themselves pious owned other Christians. So it could not be sinful per se to own a slave. Augustine contends that evil masters are not free either, since they live under the dominion of some worse sin. He observes about lust that it is "a happier lot to be a slave to a human being than to lust."[101] But has Augustine evaded the point, which is that the master is bad, not that being his or her slave is better than being dominated by worse(?) things like lust? He may have recognized his vacuous reasoning here, for the sixth implicit argument, that there is no slavery in the state of nature, nor was there in Eden before the Fall, gets at the bad masters in another way. If Augustine's hypothetical opponent conceded all his points about sin, then there was still human society before the Fall, without sin or slavery. Augustine has no trouble admitting this was all true; it is his main point. The argument from nature could get nowhere with him, now that humanity bore the guilt and just punishment of original sin.

The question of the unjust master in this world remained, and the seventh and last antislavery argument is that St. Paul was wrong to say that slaves should serve loyally and willingly. This point addresses Paul's words in Ephesians 6:5: "Slaves be obedient to them that are your masters according to the flesh, with fear and trembling, in singleness of your heart, as unto Christ."[102] Is it likely that anyone said that Paul was wrong?[103] Probably not, but Augustine's own response suggests a more subtle point, that Paul *meant* to say that slaves should be loyal until they were freed, which should be soon. In the context of preparing for the speedy Second Coming and the end of the world, that message might have made sense in the first century, but by Augustine's own time no one suggested that devout masters should

101. St. Augustine, *De Civitate Dei*, p. 682: "Et utique felicius seruitur homini, quam libidini . . ."; *The City of God*, p. 875.

102. King James Version except for translation of *servi*, which certainly means "slaves" and not "servants."

103. Fabrizio Fabbrini, *La Manumissio in Ecclesia* (Milan, 1965), pp. 215–17 analyzes this and subsequent passages, where he finds arguments in Paul for a basic human equality.

free their slaves soon. Even the one lonely voice against slavery in early Christianity, Augustine's contemporary Gregory of Nyssa, did not call on the faithful to free their slaves. Augustine could not respond directly to Gregory's point on selling the likeness of God (since he did not know it), though we would expect him to observe that sin had of course changed this original pristine human state into something debased. But having raised the possibility that Paul was encouraging only a brief period for slaves to honor their masters as they served the Lord, Augustine concludes with the somber thought that the slave's duty endures to the end of all injustice.

As a coda to these antislavery points, in the next section of his book Augustine discusses the issue of equality in the relations between masters and slaves. His real subject is the power of the paterfamilias and the ways in which children and slaves resemble and differ from one another. At the back of Augustine's mind two more criticisms of slavery required an answer. First, punishing slaves is unjust because they are right to reject being subordinated. This point relates to some pagan values; if slavery was just bad luck and could happen to anyone, people who became slaves had some right to resist it, especially when it involved cruel punishment.[104] Augustine again argues that until we all reach heaven, "the fathers have an obligation to exercise the authority of masters greater than the duty of slaves to put up with their condition as servants," though he hastens to add that it is just and legitimate to punish slaves in order to improve offenders and keep the peace.[105] The second argument depends on a subtle analogy between membership in a household and being a citizen of a state. Just as citizenship implies some fundamental equality, there should be equality in the household, no slaves and masters. Augustine makes short work of this attack on subordination and hierarchy by insisting on the right to correct slaves, and that "the ordered harmony of those who live together in a house in the matter of giving and obeying orders, contributes to the ordered harmony concerning authority and obedience obtaining among the citizens."[106]

Augustine's formidable powers of reasoning left two attacks on slavery relatively unscathed—the problem of Christians being slaves to unjust masters, and the broader idea of human equality as it related to slavery. Society accepted the slavery of Christians and so did the Church. During the Middle Ages the enslaving of Christians, or the conversion of slaves to Chris-

---

104. See Bernard Williams, *Shame and Necessity* (Berkeley, Calif., 1993) on the general topic of slavery as bad luck.

105. St. Augustine, *De Civitate Dei*, p. 683; *City of God*, p. 876.

106. St. Augustine, *De Civitate Dei*, p. 683; *City of God*, p. 876.

tianity continued to cause problems for the Church.[107] Roman law quickly made it illegal for Jews to own Christian slaves, and similar laws later prohibited Muslims from owning them.[108] In these cases no one prattled on about obeying masters or slavery being a just punishment for sin, but Christian masters were clearly in a different category—why? The other powerful attack on slavery rested on the idea of human equality, but no one apparently believed in this, except maybe for Gregory of Nyssa. The aspiration of some slaves to human equality, however, was not going to disappear, no matter how Augustine tried to ignore it.

Thomas Aquinas, a product of thirteenth-century southern Italy, is another systematic thinker whose analysis of slavery can be used to recover criticisms of it. In his case the scholastic method with its formal style of statements and objections makes the task easier than it is with Augustine's work. Slavery was not the vital part of Aquinas's economic and social world that it was in the late Roman Empire, so Aquinas knew less about slavery and did not write much about it. The first extended discussion of slavery in the *Summa Theologica* appears in the answer to the question: Whether humans in a state of nature are equal?[109] Aquinas concludes that they are, but that there are natural disparities among people like sex and age, and mental differences like wisdom. Even bodily differences caused by diet attract Aquinas's notice. None of these disparities result from natural defects or sin but come from nature itself, not God's judgment. Aquinas next asks if humans in a state of innocence dominate other people.[110] He answers yes to this question as well, but he has to argue first against two propositions—that domination comes only after sin, and that liberty would have prevailed in a state of innocence. Instead, Aquinas argues that hierarchy and subordination are natural social conditions existing even among the angels, who are after all better than people. Aquinas observes that there is no slavery in the natural state. It is natural for everyone to look out for his or her own good, and it is in no one's interest to be a slave. This type of domination, coercing people into the condition of slavery, could not exist in a state of nature.

107. See discussion in Chapter 2 and in Benjamin Z. Kedar, *Crusade and Mission: European Attitudes toward the Muslims* (Princeton, N.J., 1984).

108. For Roman law see Chapter 2, and for example *Capitula Regni Siciliae*, cap. 65, p. 78, which explicitly states that Muslims and Jews cannot buy, sell, or own Christian slaves—a common rule in Christian Mediterranean societies.

109. St Thomas Aquinas, *Summa Theologica*, 4 vols. (Rome, 1923), vol. 3 1.1 Q9 A3.

110. Ibid., vol. 3 1.1 Q9 A4.

Aquinas concludes by observing that humans are naturally social animals, even in a state of innocence, so he repeats that people must be directed for their own good and someone must be in charge. So ingrained was the concept of hierarchy in medieval society, but Aquinas did not accept Aristotle's idea of natural slaves and he knew that slavery rested on force and not sin— an improvement over Augustine, and another sign that owning slaves was a special type of behavior.

Aquinas returns to the issue of slavery as a sidebar to his discussion of natural law, which does not prohibit some things.[111] So it is natural to be naked since nature did not clothe us, but nothing in natural law prohibits clothing. In the same way, common ownership of property, and liberty, are said to be true by the law of nature, so private property and slavery are in this sense not natural, though not prohibited by natural law. Instead, human reason has devised private property and slavery for the benefit of human life, and so God condemns neither. Later in the *Summa Theologica*, Aquinas considers the related question of whether the law of nations, human custom, is the same as natural law.[112] As part of the argument on a broader issue not relevant here, Aquinas distinguishes two aspects of natural law—one absolute by necessity, and the other by human convention not following absolutely from reason. No natural reason explains why one man should be a slave and another free. Slavery is based on utility or usefulness for human society. Slavery pertains to the law of nations and is natural in the second sense, that is by human agreement on what we would call historical grounds, but not by the first. Slavery is not a natural condition.

Aquinas illuminates some contemporary criticisms of slavery. Augustine's mono-explanation, sin, was no longer so convincing, and people no longer knew the reason that some were slaves and others free. Human convention maintained slavery, which was not the inevitable result of divine law or natural differences among people. Utility, a word Aquinas uses in much the same way as modern economists, explained why slavery existed, and also of course the absence of a divine prohibition of it. Aquinas was convinced that no one was a slave by defect or sin, and that self-interest impelled any rational person to resist enslavement. Liberty was the natural state, and although he accepted a basic human equality, for Aquinas the many natural disparities cried out for hierarchy and the need for someone to take command. So the context for criticizing slavery had moved beyond Aristotle's nature and Augustine's sin, but appeals to liberty and equality would not yet carry the day. The worthwhile life for some still meant, now

111. Ibid., vol. 3 1.2 Q94 A5.
112. Ibid., vol. 3 2.2 Q57 A3.

by human convention's idea of utility, that some people who did not much like it would have to do things that benefited others. A person unjustly presented as a slave, as Mauro found himself to be on the streets of Palermo, could object and in his case luck brought a powerful person to correct the injustice. Pragmatics tells us that real slaves had no recourse, except in some limited cases where Christians had been unjustly enslaved. In general, conversion to Christianity, or appeals to equality and liberty, fell on deaf ears. And the reason, going back to Aristotle and remaining unchanged, was always usefulness. Despite slavery's unsavory aspects, its utility outweighed doubts about its ethics. This conclusion, not limited to Italian slavery, would weigh heavily on the Indians and Africans whom the Europeans encountered in the fifteenth and sixteenth centuries.

Vigorous defenses of slavery continued to stress that it was a normal part of life and not contrary to religion. Franco Sacchetti (ca. 1330–ca. 1400) in one of his sermons looked carefully at the question of how baptism affected slaves. According to Sacchetti baptizing slaves was like baptizing cattle because the slaves, similar to dumb beasts, did not intend to become Christians.[113] Slaves resembled cattle, it seems, because they were imprisoned, without free will. Sacchetti also told his fellow Florentines that they did not have to free slaves even when baptized. To free a slave was to take the stick from their backs (an old image here) and would only encourage bad behavior. Sacchetti's use of harsh words and images may indicate that other people remained confused and had scruples about owning Christian slaves.

Ironic words also provide insights on slavery, provided that we carefully examine their context. On September 10, 1552, the Venetian gentleman Bartolomeo Spatafora gave an oration in defense of slavery.[114] As Dennis Romano notes, this oration was a "soggetto giocoso"—a playful subject not meant to be taken too seriously, but it is still a valuable window on the concerns of Venetian slave owners.[115] The tone of this oration shows that

---

113. Franco Sacchetti, *I sermoni evangeli, le lettere, ed altri scritti inediti or rari*, ed. Ottavio Gigli (Florence, 1857), pp. 94–95. The key phrases are " 'poi la maggior parte sono come a battezzare buoi" and "perocchè gli levi il bastone da dosso, e dàgli matera di fare ogni male." Iris Origo discusses these views, "The Domestic Enemy," p. 335, where she notes that Sant' Antonino, archbishop of Florence, expressed similar views on the legitimacy of slavery, if less harshly.

114. Bartolomeo Spathaphora, "In difesa della servitù," in *Quatro orationi* (Venice, 1554), pp. 95–110.

115. D. Romano's useful discussion of this oration is in *Housecraft*, pp. 35–37; he says Spatafora was Sicilian by origin. The oration conflates slavery and domestic service at times, but the defensive points apply to both.

Spatafora used irony as a means to amuse his audience with unexpected arguments for slavery. Spatafora's first argument is that slavery is good because slaves had quiet spirits and hence no worries.[116] This is an interesting notion—that if one accepted slavery, there was not a care in the world, no decisions to make or ambitions to achieve. Slaves did not have to be anxious about surviving. If their masters failed or died, the slaves, as valuable commodities, would be passed through the market to more successful masters, and life would continue as before. Spatafora admits that he does not mean by servitude those held in captivity by the Turks or Moors, or those in prisons or condemned to the galleys. No, he meant those who served a well-off and prudent master, and a fine line separated domestic service and slavery. Spatafora was concerned about the anxiety of owners, and some had ample reasons to be fearful.

The second argument in defense of slavery is that it is good for a person's health and presumably long life.[117] He suggests that it was in the masters' interests to protect their investments by taking care of the slaves' bodies. The image of the pampered slave is an old stereotype, but this is a point about violence against slaves: sane masters would never thoughtlessly destroy their own property. If slaves were cheap, and the task, as old Cato set it, was to speedily squeeze as much work as possible out of them and then discard them, then the slave's health was a resource to be extracted, and not preserved. But Spatafora sees things differently—the slave has physical labor to perform but has tranquility of spirit, while the master, to the injury and inconvenience of his body, has cares and worries. In effect mental work also damages health (no argument in favor of the service economy here). Perhaps the Venetian nobles in the audience chuckled at the idea that liberty was bad for one's health, but they knew that they had taken something from the slaves that they themselves valued.

Third, Spatafora concludes that slavery is good for a pure life; its temptations are limited. If human nature is prone to slip into vice, a well-governed slave has the best chance to avoid sin and merit salvation.[118] Not missing the chance to cite the authority of St. Paul, Spatafora observes that the strength and fortitude needed to endure slavery constitute its virtue. Beneath the apparent irony of these arguments is a kernel of understanding about the context of slavery. Slaves were expensive in sixteenth-century Italy, and Spatafora's case presumes a world in which market mechanisms were working as we would expect in influencing the supply and treatment

116. B. Spatafora, "In difesa della servitù," pp. 97–98.
117. Ibid., p. 99.
118. Ibid., pp. 102–3, for this and what follows.

of costly commodities. All of his points assume that markets work; underneath the specious appeal to morality is a basic understanding of economic self-interest. If the price of slaves were low, slaves would have a lot of worries, and we must presume that one of the certain facts every slave understood was that he or she had a cash price. In this slave world, one's value to society was not an abstraction, it was a market price. All the slave really had was a body. The body's health, strength, attractiveness, capacity to bear children or burdens, were all the slave possessed. In this society the skills of slaves were fairly rudimentary, and no descriptions of slaves provide us with any sense that their skills were noted or especially valued. So on the matter of a healthy body, the interests of masters and slaves coincided. Perhaps this is why so many of the American WPA slave narratives emphasized food; for the slave, food was the key to strength, health, and survival.[119] Also, in Renaissance Italy emancipation remained a possibility, so investing in one's health while a slave might pay off down the road, if despair or bad luck or a cruel master did not intervene.

Finally, Spatafora's temptations take on a different cast in a market setting. Succumbing to temptations, when it ruined one's health, must have been a disaster for the slave as well as the owner. Wine must have been a real problem. For women the risks of pregnancy were also key—counted against pleasing the master and bringing a new slave, or his son and heir, into the world. There was an implicit contract between master and slave about food and health, and at the margins the risk was that it would break down through murder and suicide, which did occur. Above all, good faith required mutual restraint. Spatafora wound up his jests with a long and bland discussion of liberty in Venice, a favorite local theme that must have been hilarious when talking about slavery. But the broader context suggests that Venetian masters were worried, and with good reason, Their unquiet spirits, bad health, economic uncertainties, and impure lives did not make slavery enviable, even to an ironist. Yet by projecting an austere, simple, and practically holy life onto slaves, even irony could not avoid missing the genuine anxieties of slave owners. They knew that the criticisms against bad masters—largely their crimes against the bodies and spirits of slaves, even if slavery was acceptable in moral terms—to some extent involved them all. And if their own liberty was so precious, how could its absence benefit anyone?

119. E. Genovese, *Roll, Jordan, Roll*, pp. 62–63, 540–49.

CHAPTER FOUR
THE LANGUAGE OF THE GREAT
ECONOMY

There was also a fresh order that the shops must be kept well supplied
with bread, under pain of five years in the galleys . . .

ALESSANDRO MANZONI, *I promessi sposi*

This book concludes with the language of the economy because the market is the place where behavior, the law, and
words all come together to commodify people. Markets
are, after all, places where people use words as well as money, and in both
instances suppliers and consumers sometimes worry about the ethics of
their activities. We will turn first to the issue of morality in the economy
and then look closely at the speech act of buying and selling. Then we will
examine those forces, primarily economic, that sustain slavery and finish
with race, the point that ties together these disparate themes.

Manzoni's comment raises at least three important issues about the developing market economy in late medieval Italy, and the other regions of
Europe experiencing similar growth. The government's order about the
food supply suggests the question of how states or some other authority can
coerce people into doing things for the common good, or just for the state.
The governments of medieval and early modern Italy permitted slavery and
fostered the slave trade. Yet no one, except the slaves themselves, was coerced into participating in the buying and selling of slaves. The continued
existence of slavery, however, required considerable violence against the
slaves. Italians witnessed these facts, and this gave a few of them, as in the
case of some Genoese in the 1390s, a way to talk about their own liberty
and keep themselves from becoming slaves, in a political sense, to some foreign power.[1] So legal coercion in the economy opened the door to the

---

1. Steven Epstein, *Genoa and the Genoese 958–1528* (Chapel Hill, N.C., 1996),
p. 249.

broader question of what were the proper limits of coercion, it having been conceded that force and fear had their place in the markets.

Odd Langholm has recently made important points about how medieval thinkers tried, and mainly failed, to deal with the issue of coercion with respect to labor as a commodity.[2] In particular, theories based on appeals to a social contract or the natural state pretended that people interacted as equals, even in the context of a hierarchical society. The pretense of equality crumbles in wage labor, and of course disappears in slavery. In another work I looked at the problem of bargaining over wages when the balance of power was unequal, and I concluded that any bargaining was still better for the workers than none.[3] Yet even theories about bargaining did not pay attention to the roles force and fear had in forcing some people to accede to unjust wages or working conditions, or forcing others into slavery.

Medieval moralists tried to address labor as a commodity by looking for justice and fairness in bargaining and its results, and we will examine this shortly. But they failed to explore force and fear in their most graphic context, slavery, and they did not investigate the question of what actually happened when a person, and not just his or her labor, became the commodity. These lapses, or blind spots, or failures resulted in a developing market economy that accepted a lot of force and fear as normal when it came to slavery, and then was stuck trying to justify circumscribing these methods in other areas of the economy. I will argue in this chapter that turning people into commodities left the Italians (and of course others) with a terrible model for transforming the labor of ostensibly free people into a commodity as well. Market theories failed to explain the role of force, and never, until the modern period, rejected the idea that a person might involuntarily continue to be a commodity. Ships, pepper, clothing, or food did not experience force, need, or compulsion the way people did, and in this sense both slaves and free laborers became commodities in uniquely human ways, in a language context that also requires a closer look.[4]

Another central theme, naturally connected to force and fear, concerns moral responsibility in the economy. The Christian Church raised no moral doubts about slavery, and neither did the highly respected teachers of law and philosophy at Europe's most distinguished law school, the Univer-

2. Odd Langholm, *The Legacy of Scholasticism in Economic Thought* (Cambridge, 1998), p. 180.

3. Steven Epstein, *Wage Labor and Guilds in Medieval Europe* (Chapel Hill, N.C., 1991); this is a general theme of the book.

4. I am indebted to Langholm for some of this analysis of labor, but he did not include slavery in his discussion.

sity of Bologna. And yet, medieval theologians and lawyers debated at length the morality of economic matters like usury and the just price. Since such a debate over slavery never occurred, how did this omission shape the sense of moral responsibility in the economy, in the markets? I will argue that there is no good reason to presume that markets become more moral over time or will by themselves produce moral outcomes. This point about economic justice and morality is important because a prominent theme of modern economics is a worshipful attitude toward free markets as producing the best and even the most moral outcome for all. My colleague John Powelson has recently argued at length that a maximum of power diffusion and bargaining in a market economy results in an absolute minimum of state and legal coercion and hence in moral economic behavior.[5] This reasoning has much to recommend itself, provided that it can be demonstrated in specific historical contexts that moral economic arguments apply *to all persons* to ensure their validity. If, as Powelson also suggests, the classic liberal free market is just an efficient tool, we are obligated to ask if we can rely on this tool, by itself, to produce moral outcomes for everyone.[6]

The existence of slavery for so many centuries argues against the proposition that markets produce moral outcomes, though of course this particular Italian market may have been defective in some way that prevented the usual happy outcome. Also, was the market more responsible than any other social force for the end of Italian slavery? Slavery remains a major problem for those who believe that markets make morality or even foster it. Instead of being a moral result of impersonal market forces, slavery helped to determine the boundaries of the permissible in economic life in Italy, with dire consequences for both morality and the economy. The search for moral responsibility in the economy will lead us again to the language of contracts, because only people, and not markets or commodities, use language. We must get it straight that the idea of a market provides only an organizational context for using language, according to some rules which may not guarantee a moral outcome.

Finally, the epigraph points to a third theme, market failure. In this case the market was not supplying Milan with enough food for its people. Does the existence of slavery also indicate a market failure, and if so, of what type? Even though slavery was a minor part of the economy, did its existence help to spread values that retarded economic development in Italy? In the long term Italy, Spain, and Portugal, the three European societies with the most internal domestic experience with slavery, did not end up in the

5. John P. Powelson, *The Moral Economy* (Ann Arbor, Mich., 1998).
6. Ibid., p. 178.

vanguard of European economic development. Those countries with the most external experience with slavery, England, Holland, and France, eventually outstripped southern Europe in conventional measures of development. I suggest that slavery had a significant role in this outcome, and was not merely a coincidental sideshow. As Powelson has persuasively shown in two recent works, economic development results when power is decentralized, respect for human rights is high, confrontation and violence are at low levels, the law is fairly enforced, and above all when people as individuals or in voluntary groups can use their power to leverage desirable economic outcomes for themselves.[7] In this view, maximizing individual choice in a market in which power is diffused should benefit everyone. How then did slavery for some ever occur? In Powelson's analysis slavery resulted when some people (the enslavers) had too much power, and it would end only with the breakdown of the power required to enforce slavery. It strikes me that the force required to start and maintain slavery was mainly an extra-market outcome, resulting from the decision not to kill a captive, and that the role of force in the economy, both by the state and by private agents, requires much scrutiny if we will ever understand how slavery and free markets coexisted for so long in Italy and elsewhere. The Italian context provides a manageable and refreshingly non-American setting for exploring these questions which have profound significance for other societies and economies.

The epigraph to this chapter requires another word of explanation because it represents so common a confusion about the use of words alone to bring about some economic result. Governments, like the one in Alessandro Manzoni's novel set in seventeenth-century Spanish Lombardy, sometimes try to create supply by simply ordering something to be done, as if the bakers could just make bread out of air to avoid the galleys. Those giving these orders in a command economy understood that much, and simply intended to solve the problem of scarcity by motivating the bakers to find grain and bake bread by whatever means necessary. But such orders seldom accomplish their intended goals, and more typically actually make matters worse. So we cannot expect a desirable economic outcome to result from simply saying that it should be so—or else some state would have long ago outlawed poverty. The point here is that the language of the economy matters a great deal, both in its misperceptions about how markets actually function, and in the ways people find to talk about the way the world should work.

7. Ibid. See also his earlier book, *Centuries of Economic Endeavor* (Ann Arbor, Mich., 1994).

Jacques Le Goff has insisted that there was no economy in the Middle Ages, in the sense that the Church had no economic doctrines and there were no economic thinkers.[8] He suggests that scholars applying modern conceptions of the economy to the medieval period are creating obstacles to a genuine understanding of the past. Some religious issues, like usury or the just price or wage, affected the real world, but the focus of canonists and theologians was usually on sin, and even thinkers who were well informed about economic matters, like Pope Innocent IV (Sinibaldo Fieschi of Genoa) and Sant' Antonino of Florence, were writing mainly about sin, and only incidentally about money. But the absence of the abstract noun "the economy" does not mean that medieval Italians had not carefully observed and conceptualized the world of buying and selling, of letting and hiring, of employing and laboring, any more than the rarity of the abstract noun "slavery" meant that there were no slaves. Medieval Italians did not think or write about the economy or the market as reified constructs, but they wrote a lot about markets in their city law codes, guild statutes, and merchants' handbooks. Le Goff says there was no economy because he wants to distinguish the medieval from the modern understanding of markets. Given the sharp differences in the language used by medieval and modern writers to describe these markets, and the immense changes in their contexts, how can we best enter the mental world of the medieval economy to explore the place of slaves in it? The language of the law has already provided a basis for this exploration as we have seen how it shaped contracts, the basis for exchanging slaves in a market economy. Using language in a market to make contracts also constitutes the backbone of medieval economic thought. Before looking at the language of buying and selling from a strictly market perspective, we must remember that slavery raised some exceptional issues of morality in an economic context. Le Goff might have simply and correctly observed that there were no economists in the Middle Ages, and left it at that. But back then there was a surplus of moralists, and they lived and taught in a world where most people were not yet prepared to leave their moral values at the gate when entering a market to make contracts.

One way to bridge this gap in understanding is to begin with a modern author who discusses economic issues in moral terms that also make sense in a medieval context. Wendell Berry has proposed the existence of a Great Economy, the divine plan for how the world works, and it is a useful tool for exploring the mental attitudes of the Italian people who form the subject of

8. Jacques Le Goff, *Your Money or Your Life: Economy and Religion in the Middle Ages*, trans. Patricia Ranum (New York, 1990), pp. 69–70.

this book.[9] The human economy is what we do, but Berry has a spiritual, or moral idea that humans do not make value, that everything fundamentally worthwhile comes from the Great Economy, from nature and its laws—things we only dimly understand at best. Like many Italian scholastics, Berry insists that every abstract, created value is false and destroys real value, which he identifies as the necessities of food, clothing, and shelter—all of course resulting from human labor. On the humblest level the slaves and the poor needed these things to survive; the wealthy and powerful measured their good life by the refined quality, the luxury, of their necessities. Berry believes that human efforts to create value result in damaging effects like usury and inflation (and I would add slavery), where an emphasis on money and gain leads the greedy to pursue money (and people) for themselves, as instruments for feeding avarice. Berry comes to the economy from agriculture, so he is naturally suspicious of industry, which he sees as lacking in forethought and husbandry, the old virtues the land teaches. He also worries that we do not understand when the human economy goes wrong (as when it buys and sells people) and he sees problems in exploitative attitudes toward nature, and the perpetual competitiveness among us. Modern economists view competition and self-interest as the engines behind the invisible hand's guiding of people and resources into the most efficient activities. Early economists like Adam Smith worried a lot about the place of moral sentiments in the world of getting one's living.[10] Medieval Italians valued cooperation and identified competition as inciting sin, since the desire to win was not neighborly and fed on and gave birth to pride, one of the most perilous sentiments. Slavery certainly is another example of a false value, where the idea of competing against fellow people goes to the limit of nature itself, as people are taken out of nature and society and turned into property.

Berry also takes seriously the Buddhist value of the maximum of well-being with a minimum of consumption.[11] This belief has never been a serious part of Western or Italian culture, where consumption reigns. Even temporary havens from hyperconsumerism, like medieval monasteries and uni-

9. This is a central theme of his work, but see the essay "Two Economies" in his *Home Economics* (New York, 1984), pp. 54–75, here p. 61.

10. See Adam Smith, *The Theory of Moral Sentiments* (Indianapolis, 1984) for a clear and well-known example of how the study of morality should precede an investigation of the markets, and where Smith offers the view that domestic slavery is "the vilest of all states" (p. 282).

11. W. Berry, *Home Economics*, p. 71.

versities, eventually succumbed. It took the steely self-denial of St. Francis of Assisi to reject consumerism in all its forms, and not many people chose his steep path to a moral life of consumption. Berry too is disgusted with the primacy of economic motives, the deification of consumerism and the market with its choices. He is, however, sensitive to basic human activities like working and eating, and he knows that people must combine into communities to guarantee that everyone has something to do and enough to eat. The devil is in the details, however, and we must ask how a sense of community results in a safety net for everyone. The idea of a Great Economy fits a society of believers, an apt description of Italy in the Middle Ages—much of the period covered by this book. Yet Italians were for a long time capable of believing that the divine plans for the universe included slavery for some. That is the problem with vague divine plans or a Great Economy; they can be twisted to fit the world as it is. Appeals to the Great Economy seem to take a long time to save nature or slaves, and medieval Italians, who were more likely than most people to respect the claims of morality in their daily economic activities, accepted slavery as a normal part of the fallen human condition. Once again, the lesson seems to be that the free market, even the great one, has problems with other values like justice and equality.

THE PRAGMATICS OF BUYING AND SELLING

The law provided one context for exploring the language of contracts, and the marketplace was another venue where "the meaningful function of language" turned some people into commodities.[12] M. Bakhtin's ideas about speech genres or communities applied well to markets, where the choices about what words to use mattered to slaves and their vendors. The context for buying and selling slaves shows how people used language in variable, negotiable, and adaptable ways to accomplish performatives, those speech acts that change reality. Besides obvious performatives like "I baptize" or "I resign," "I buy" and "I sell" also changed reality for slaves and determined the language of the Great Economy in this fundamental matter of the human being as commodity.

The contracts for buying and selling a slave almost invariably took the form in which the seller, in the first person singular, declared that he or she, in the present tense, sells (*vendo*), cedes (*cedo*), and hands over (*trado*) the

12. For the definition of pragmatics and what follows, I am indebted to Jef Verschueren, *Understanding Pragmatics* (London, 1999) (definition, p. 8; Bakhtin, pp. 151–56).

slave or slaves at hand. Again, the issue here is not the legal ramifications of these statements, but the language of economics, of exchange. The contract exists because the parties, after bargaining, agreed on the sale. The activities prior to drawing up the contract, which are not documented, can sometimes be inferred from the contract and its context. The seller hired the notary who wrote the contract, and presented the slave as a commodity for sale. A slave consisted of a body and soul, a crucial fact to recognize when the package was for sale. Since a slave's death extinguished all value, one of the rules of this peculiar form of property was that the body had to be alive. Being in the womb counted as being alive for the purposes of being for sale. Some contracts for female slaves dutifully noted the possible body inside the body and included in the purchase price whatever might be born.

A soul resided in the body, and in some offensive way it too was sold. If anyone had asked the right questions about exactly what was happening when a soul changed hands, perhaps some religious objections to slavery would have gained credence. It may seem far-fetched to insist that the soul was also for sale. But this precise point was behind the universal prohibition in Italy against Muslims or Jews owning Christian slaves. Bodies did not vary in relevant ways by religion, but every body had a soul. Souls, however, might be saved or damned, and the Church and the marketplace would not tolerate the prospect of a Christian soul being subjected to the whims, sexual advances, and possible proselytizing of unbelievers. Other commodities did not have the facility for language, which clearly resided in the soul or spirit. If the slave were really a thing, it would not have mattered what religion the owner practiced—the law did not prevent Jews from owning mules. In my view we are dealing with the merchandising of souls, close to the same point Gregory of Nyssa recognized about selling things made in God's likeness and image. Here, the language of contracts suggests that this was more widely perceived (but then ignored) than we might think.

The seller, by stating that he or she sells, accomplished the performative economic and speech act of selling by accepting a price. By bargaining over this price both parties quantified their desire: so many lire or florins or ounces of gold equaled a slave. As contracts in the thirteenth century became more lawyerly and specific, they came to include a legal stipulation of the just price. Markets accepted the scholastic premise that a just price existed and that it was normally the negotiated market price itself.[13] The contract now stipulated that if it varied by more than one-half from the just

13. For references to the vast literature on the just price see Langholm, *The Legacy of Scholasticism*, and Steven Epstein, "The Theory and Practice of the Just Wage," *Journal of Medieval History* 17 (1991): 53–69.

price, the customary amount acknowledged by theologians as a morally acceptable variance, the parties conceded the discrepancy, either way, to one another. In other words, both buyer and seller agreed that their negotiated price was close enough to the market/just price that it would never provide any subsequent basis for invalidating the sale. All these niceties respecting scrupulous theories about the just price ended up affecting the realities of buying and selling in Italian markets, a triumph for the Church's ability to steer economic behavior toward a higher standard of morality. The fairness of the price naturally preoccupied buyer and seller. About the justice of slavery itself, the contracts were silent. So much attention lavished on the intricacies of price demonstrates that the idea of justice or fairness in markets was certainly in the air, so it seems a willful omission not to apply the same standard to the actual matter at hand—dealing in slaves—another sign of the normalcy of this activity.

The buyer, silent in the sale contract, nevertheless accomplishes the performative "I buy" by agreeing to the price at some stage of the negotiation, and then by producing the money. In some cases the buyer did not actually have the money, and so a subsequent contract, technically an acknowledgment of debt, reveals the buyer's voice when he or she promises to pay at a future date. For present purposes, the buyer creates demand and sorts people by ethnicity, color, and price. The buyer has decided to join or to remain in the ranks of slaveholders. No one was required to buy slaves, and it is hard, especially before the plague of 1348, to fathom the economic necessity of owning one. Certainly some artisans owned slaves and worked in demanding physical trades in which slaves would be useful, but the evidence suggests that a need for domestic service or a desire for conspicuous consumption motivated most buyers to purchase slaves. When people bought slaves, we are entitled to presume that their motives temporarily or permanently overwhelmed possible moral worries about the justice of slavery. Of course any troubled owner had the right to emancipate the slave later on. The seller, of course, irrevocably rejected that option.

When one party pronounced the word *vendo*, "I sell," he or she signaled a mental decision and used a word for which there are in most languages surprisingly few synonyms. The same holds for "I buy," another sign that ambiguity was undesirable and clarity the obvious, efficient purpose of the transaction. "I sell" is a performative and establishes a temporary relationship with the buyer. The parties want to accomplish the sale and ideally not interact further over this slave. Perhaps the parties knew one another well, or would have later dealings, but in this matter the entire point of a successful transaction was to finish it so quickly and efficiently that it would never again take up anyone's time. In order to guarantee this economic result, both parties had to exhibit good faith, a legal condition we saw in Chapter 2. Here we are considering a frame of mind that parties to a sale were entitled to presume in one another, on grounds of morality and efficiency. This presumption of good faith, so necessary in economic transactions, is perhaps one of the reasons for the broader and even more critical assumption that markets should be moral. Slavery suggests that looking for morality to result from market activities, or even to influence them, is a big mistake. Most people, however, like to think the best of themselves, and certainly in these Italian markets both contracts and conduct testify to a high degree of self-regard. No evidence indicates moral embarrassment about buying or selling slaves. If, as argued here, slavery helps to determine the boundaries of the permissible in economic life, then clearly slavery was on the moral side of that line in medieval Italy. If moral economic arguments require some basis of appeal to all persons in order to persuade, as in the case of good faith by all, then slaves cannot be persons because they would never concede the justice of their fate, since they did not choose it. All of this reasoning flows from accepting the wider, pragmatic context of what it meant to say "I sell."

As an utterance, "I sell" was not enough to bring about everything the parties to a sale wanted. The next verb, *cedo*, meant placing the slave at the disposition or under the authority of the buyer. This verb moves from the thought of selling to the action of actually doing it. *Trado*, the final verb, completes this intention by physically handing over the property. "I sell, cede, and hand over" accomplishes the task of the seller. But again, does the item matter, is there any difference between a person and a mule? Benvenuto de Bracelli, over the long course of a notarial career in Genoa from the 1330s to the 1380s, probably wrote hundreds of sales contracts for slaves, and dozens for mules.[14] He used the same form of contract for people and mules—the same verbs, the same phrases for just price and good faith. In the 1370s a male slave was about twice the price of a mule—a female a bit more expensive—and that was the difference in the language of the Great Economy.

The mule and the person were both labor for sale, in its most vivid sense a commodity under duress. These mules were big and stubborn animals needing force to make them carry heavy loads over the rocky paths of Liguria. No market theory should ignore the role of force on these creatures (if it even noticed them). So too for the humans. The sellers of commodities, including slaves, might pretend that they were just dealing in items of com-

14. ASG, cartularies I've consulted that contain the work of this notary—N. 242, 287, 288, 289, 290, 293, 294, 295, and for mules N. 293, 108r, 122r–v.

merce. But other objects for sale did not use language, or experience violence and suffer from it. In slavery, we have been looking at the economic language and behavior of bargaining over a person. People selling other commodities, even the mules, also occasionally acted under compulsion, the need to sell at a profit to stay in business, or in some cases for more desperate motives. If these sellers made unwise bargains and failed in the markets, they still had the option of selling their own labor directly in the market, through the relatively new institution of regular wage labor. People having only their own labor in the first place, and no mules or slaves to sell, had no fallback position. They knew what it was like to offer their hands and skill on the market and find no takers. Even this plight was better than slavery because the poorest wage laborer in Genoa or Venice was not a commodity, though this person might starve or by the sixteenth or seventeenth century find himself or herself coerced into working.

Back in the 1220s the emperor Frederick II deported a large group of his Muslim subjects from Sicily to the area around Lucera, near Foggia in Apulia.[15] This Muslim colony provided Frederick and his successors with formidable warriors as well as officials in the royal camera (household) or bureaucracy. The practice of the crown owning public slaves went back to the earliest days of the Norman kingdom of Sicily, and probably drew on Muslim or perhaps even Byzantine tradition.[16] The Angevin ruler Charles II of Naples decided in 1300 to destroy the Muslim community for the ostensible reasons of religious fervor, fear of revolt, and damage to the surrounding territories caused by Muslim turbulence.[17] Angevin documents from this period refer to the many thousands of Muslims around Lucera as "servi" of the royal camera. It must have occurred to the king that these people were in fact his slaves, to be treated as he liked.[18] While the king promised to leave the converts alone, the chaos surrounding the sale of

15. For details on the founding of Lucera see David Abulafia, *Frederick II: A Medieval Emperor* (Oxford, 1988), pp. 145–48.

16. For details on the context of this public slavery see Henri Bresc, "Esclaves auliques et main d'oeuvre servile agricole dans la Sicile des XIIe et XIIIe siècles," in *Figures de l'esclave au Moyen-Age et dans le monde moderne*, ed. Henri Bresc (Paris, 1996), pp. 97–114, here pp. 103–9.

17. Pietro Egidi, *La colonia saracena di Lucera e la sua distruzione* (Naples, 1912), p. 131.

18. Pietro Egidi, *Codice diplomatico dei saraceni di Lucera* (Naples, 1917); this is clear from many documents, e.g., pp. 9, 37.

these slaves swept up some of them as well.[19] The authority on this sorry event, Pietro Egidi, found that a total of about 9,684 Muslims were rounded up for sale, of whom 313 were killed according to the official sources, and doubtless the real totals were higher.[20] At least 9,000 people were sold, so many that slave prices throughout southern Italy were depressed. Egidi concluded that the crown's need for cash was the real reason for these sales, which continued on into 1301. By selling off the Muslims of Lucera in the largest lot sales in Italy since Roman times, Charles II provides a graphic instance of the pragmatics of selling. Even more somber are the lists of those too old or sick for the market, and we can only guess at their fates.[21]

Let us look closely now at the role of force in the economy by exploring the depersonalization of the slaves, the poor, and even economics itself in the world of work.

SLAVERY AND POVERTY

Slavery was not a major part of the economies even of cities like Venice and Genoa, where it remained a secondary factor in overseas trade and local commerce. This fact does not mean, however, that slavery had a minor role to play in the main issue here: the language of the Great Economy. There was a much larger group of people whose economic condition occasionally sank below even that of slaves—for sometimes the poor just starved at no capital cost to anyone. The study of the words used to describe how markets worked, and especially the critical issue of context, demonstrate that studying slaves and the poor together is the best way to understand the issue of justice in the economy. A survey of the literature on these two subjects, poverty and slavery, shows that far more often than not they have been studied separately. In this chapter I want to adjust this imbalance because poverty and slavery together provide a striking look at some key features of Italian economic and moral development. Of course these two institutions have a rich and varied history outside Italy, but Italy provides a useful and unexplored context for analyzing poverty and slavery.

The intersection between these two subjects becomes immediately apparent when we try to define poverty, or the poor people suffering from it. The vast literature on this subject indicates, not surprisingly, that context is

19. Ibid., doc. 498, pp. 245–46.
20. P. Egidi, *La colonia*, p. 203.
21. P. Egidi, *Codice diplomatico*, doc. 455, pp. 214–15.

key, that the social, economic, and ethical definitions of poverty depend on the uses of language in historical settings. In a medieval context, Church and state divided the poor, those living close to either side of bare subsistence and whose survival was in jeopardy, into three classes: the deserving, undeserving, and admirable poor. The deserving poor, the proverbial widows, orphans, and miserable persons, those incapable of maintaining their existence without help, merited support or charity because it pleased God and benefited the souls of donors. A special subclass here was the truly stoical poor who were too proud to ask for help—the "poveri vergognosi" or shame-faced poor. The undeserving poor, the lazy incorrigible troublemakers, should be compelled to work because laziness was sinful and justice demanded the antidote—labor. There was a third category, the truly meritorious and admirable poor, who had volunteered to be poor by renouncing their wealth to follow the example of Jesus. This standard triple approach to poverty is not the issue here; instead, it is the idea of equality as a moral and economic value that yokes together the poor and the slaves.

Amartya Sen analyzes poverty by looking closely at equality and the other moral values that must be weighed against the claims of equality. Sen defines poverty as the "failure of basic capabilities to reach certain minimally acceptable levels," and his capabilities are the freedoms to pursue well-being, as defined in material terms.[22] So the conditions of poverty *and slavery* have in common that they deny the poor *and slaves* the opportunity to live fully, up to the potential of their qualities and special gifts. This is the fundamental equivalence of the two conditions. Sen depreciates equality of opportunity as the best test of equality because he sees people as so diverse in talents that he would rather measure and equate their degree of self-fulfillment rather than simply level the playing field and neglect personal differences, context, and the past. Measuring a person's degree of self-fulfillment, however, cannot be easy, but a slave's was presumably low.

Equality of opportunity is an especially shallow concept for helping the poor *and slaves*, who have been so harmed by adversity that they are willing to settle for very little, far short of what their capabilities might have accomplished in better circumstances.[23] These capabilities differ according to individual talents. And the good of society as a whole, measured here in terms of economic efficiency as a benefit to all, is also a value that sometimes complicates claims for equality, especially in results, however roughly defined. Sen looks at the start of the metaphoric race of life and sees a lot of human diversity—different types of capabilities—and he questions efforts

22. Amartya Sen, *Inequality Reexamined* (Cambridge, Mass., 1992), p. 109.
23. Ibid., pp. 7, 55.

to equalize the end of the race as stifling the most talented at the cost of inefficiencies for all. He emphasizes the long middle of the race, where people discover their capabilities and test their limits. Here the poor and the slaves find their common experience, not in falling behind in the race, so much as in learning that their social contexts doomed them to a poor finish from the beginning. It is not in the interests of slave owners to encourage their slaves to achieve up to the level of their capabilities, for that would certainly include eventual freedom. Perhaps for this reason ancient Roman slave owners held out the prospect of manumission to some domestic slaves in order to motivate the slaves to work hard for several decades before freedom.[24] So the real cost of medieval slavery to society must count the wasted talents of so many condemned to a life of domestic service or rowing, regardless of their capabilities. The meaning of this wastage is a central issue for understanding how using language shapes an economy.

The context that surrounds the poor and the slaves depends so much on language, but not all talk is cheap. There were other real economic costs to confining the large masses of Italian poor, and the smaller group of slaves—to maintaining what Earl Shorris has defined as the "surround."[25] Shorris, along with thinkers as diverse as Sen and the medievalist Bronislaw Geremek, has taken a hard look at the older idea of a culture of poverty and instead refocused attention on those forces, external to the poor *and slaves*, that make it difficult or impossible to escape poverty *and slavery*. Some readers might reasonably object that my equating of the two breaks down here because slavery was a legally defined condition, and poverty just an unfortunate economic outcome for some free people. The medieval cities that provide the bulk of the evidence on slavery, Genoa and Venice, so systematically excluded the poor from any meaningful role in civic life that they were to all intents and purposes a rigorously defined legal class: the inhabitants who were not full citizens, the people who as debased objects of charity accentuated the status of their betters. Hence it seems reasonable to equate the forces of the surround, whether they are legal or traditional, social or economic, with the impediments of poverty *and slavery*.

The subject matter of this chapter is the Great Economy of slavery, so the approach to the forces surrounding the poor and slaves will be eco-

24. See Keith Bradley, *Slavery and Society at Rome* (Cambridge, 1994), pp. 154–65, for an excellent discussion of manumission; the key points are that most slaves were not freed, and there were always others to take the places of those manumitted.

25. Earl Shorris, *New American Blues: A Journey through Poverty to Democracy* (New York, 1997).

nomic, but will not involve the usual stuff of tables and prices—at least not first.[26] Not all the forces of the surround that Shorris identified for poverty are relevant to the problem of slavery, but most are. In keeping with my emphasis on language, I have reclassified these forces according to three rough categories: those that cost money, those that save money, and those that rely on words, leaving aside for the moment the issue of just how cheap talk is. The comparisons about cost also involve language, and must not neglect the poor, or the costs of free labor.

THE COSTS OF SLAVERY

The slave system in medieval and early modern Italy did not cost much to maintain because slaves were a rather low percentage of the population, certainly lower than the poor. Although there were some legal expenses resulting from public efforts to recapture runaway slaves and imprison felonious ones, slave owners succeeded in pushing off nearly all the costs of enforcing slavery onto government. The extent to which the slave-owning class paid its "fair share" of taxes is another matter, but the ordinary expenses of government in places like Genoa and Venice came from excise taxes on consumers, so wealthy slave owners benefited from whatever government did. In Genoa, however, where there were customs levies on importing slaves, a yearly per capita tax on owning them, and a special sales tax when slaves were sold, the state's income from slavery far exceeded the costs of its modest efforts to sustain the institution. So the real daily costs of disciplining slaves and keeping them from running away fell on the owners, who also paid what were in effect luxury taxes on slaves.

The broader economic costs associated with the legality of slavery also merit analysis. Economists define the term "rent seeking" as the "socially costly pursuit of transfers," which in its narrowest sense means the subject of government regulations and who benefits from them.[27] Rent seekers use their power to instigate government rules that foster their interests, traditionally in areas like monopolies and preferential tariffs. Hence rent seeking, at best a zero-sum game or even one that wastes resources, inefficiently redistributes society's wealth by rewarding the powerful. As Gordon Tullock has observed, "most government transfers are not from the wealthy to the poor but from the poorly politically organized to the well politically or-

26. Ibid., pp. 97–200, for Shorris's forces of the surround, most noneconomic.
27. A good introduction to the subject is Robert Tollison and Roger Congleton, *The Economic Analysis of Rent Seeking* (Aldershot, 1995); this definition is on p. xii.

ganized."[28] In our context the poorly politically organized constitute an exact overlap with the poor and slaves. In seeking rents, privileged people reallocate social goods for their own benefit by direct state intervention or by rigging market mechanisms to favor their interests. Rent seeking has some connections to the lives of slaves and the poor. Other slave-owning societies—the American South comes immediately to mind—required high levels of state intervention, even to civil war, to maintain slavery—a classic case of rent seeking by the major slave owners. Nothing of this magnitude occurred in Italy apart from some modest public expenses for police, chains, and whipping; in 1492 the doge and government of Genoa ordered someone to be paid a lira as his fee for whipping a female slave belonging to Baldassare Grillo.[29] The expense is modest, yet the government would not have been so zealous about whipping a servant or employee. In this small matter, some rent seeking took place outside the normal bounds of the employer-employee relationship.

But the main example of rent seeking was of course keeping slavery itself legal, as of course was poverty. Normally, free people are maximizing their capabilities, to the extent that they recognize them and value self-fulfillment as a goal of life. In economic terms, people maximize their utilities by entering a market to offer their skills and satisfy their wants. Slaves cannot do these things, nor can children, whose social status often resembles slavery. Slaves have instead become a means by which their owners maximize utilities or capabilities or happiness. These three words are not synonyms but they cover the range of benefits that enslaving someone else can bring. Another way to use the idea of rent seeking to fathom the true costs of slavery is to weigh what these Italian slaves might have accomplished in life as maximizers of their own capabilities. These lost opportunities deprived their indigenous societies, as well as the Italian ones in which they had become enslaved, of the social and economic contributions they were capable of making. The slave trade constituted an involuntary "brain drain" on those societies providing the slaves.

Slave owners also incurred some slight medical expenses in fighting illness in slaves. Simple prudence dictated that a little money here might save a large investment, but in truth money spent on medieval physicians did the sick little or no good. Medical expenses were still part of the cost of main-

28. Gordon Tullock, *The Economy of Special Privilege and Rent Seeking* (Boston, 1989), pp. 73, 79.

29. Luigi Tria, "La schiavitù in Liguria," *Atti della Società Ligure di Storia Patria* 70 (1947): 221.

taining the surround of slavery, and they were not part of an employer's obligation to a worker, except in special cases where a master had agreed to keep an apprentice in sickness and in health. There were some other minor costs. Masters needed to feed slaves, an obligation the apprentice relationship often shared. Room and board sometimes figured in the pay of other employees, especially servants. The poorest of the poor were available as household servants for no more than food, clothing, and shelter. Pauleta's mother placed her as a servant in 1256 for a term of fourteen years, to perform all services inside and outside the house, in exchange for food, clothing, a place to live, and no wages.[30] A father placed his daughter with a wool worker for twelve years as a servant and pupil, again for no pay, but in this case the child would at least emerge from the experience with a marketable skill.[31] So long as these poor children needed a home, artisan families required few slaves to take care of household chores. There were plenty of such servants on the market before the plague. Servants were more costly after 1348, but so too were slaves. In either period, those deciding to risk the capital costs of buying a slave faced subsequent expenses no greater than those for many servants—just to cover the basics needed for survival.

There was one final cost to enforcing the surround that maintained slavery, although there is no way to calculate it. Whether a person became a slave through capture or through the accident of birth, to be a slave was a piece of bad luck. Slave owners, at least some of them, were uneasy about the possibility that a stroke of good luck might rescue a person from slavery. Any such exit from slavery represented a capital loss which might or might not be compensated. Runaways are not the issue here, though a successful escape was lucky indeed. Slaves were not supposed to be lucky people in the sense that they were not to benefit from the good will of others. Perhaps this view was at the heart of prohibiting slaves to be freed by will in Genoa; slaves should not live in the hope that they would be so lucky. Another danger was love or other emotional entanglements. Perhaps some slave women believed it was lucky to conceive a child with a master or any free man because the tie might bring some good fortune. Conversion to Christianity did not prove to be an especially lucky event for Muslim, Tartar, or Jewish slaves in Italy because it did not bring freedom. Owners self-interestedly opposed the idea of freeing Christian slaves, but even the Church agreed with the owners, possibly because it made no sense to give slaves so much control over their own lives. Who can sum up the expenses of ensuring the bad luck of slaves? Keeping slaves from striking up friendships with good-

30. ASG, CN, Cart. N. 31, pt. 1, 191r.
31. ASG, CN, Cart. N. 55, pt. 2, 5r, 25 January 1272.

hearted free people, trying to prevent women slaves from establishing relationships with free men, making sure that the poor, on the streets or in the brothels, would not dare hide a slave as a way to strike back at the wealthy— all this cost some time, new laws, and uneasy moments. Even if it was just a matter of the collective opportunity cost to masters who might have spent their time in other ways, counteracting the possible good luck of slaves was a real cost of maintaining the surround.

THE SAVINGS OF SLAVERY

One of the many debates about American slavery has concerned its profitability. Medieval and early modern Italian slavery, though a smaller sector of the economy, also existed in an economic context that provided choices about the types of labor to exploit. In the early sixteenth century the de facto ruler of Genoa, Andrea Doria, very closely calculated the costs of using free, convict, or slave rowers in the galleys he leased to the Spanish crown.[32] He also scoured the states of northern Italy for convicts whom he was eager put in his galleys, thus saving governments the expenses of imprisoning people.[33] The large numbers of women slaves in urban domestic service were working not for their masters' profit, but to make their owners' lives comfortable and to display status in the community. Slaves contributed to what Thorstein Veblen called the conspicuous leisure of their owners, but in this age before labor-saving technology, domestic work was productive and saved the owners much drudgery.[34] Possessing these slaves announced one's social power and wealth. Late medieval slavery was practiced by powerful people, not yet rentiers, who still worked at trade and politics. But female slaves did not directly work in financial and trading activities or foster the civic standing of their owners, so we are back on Veblen's ground of display. In this context the value of conspicuous consumption outweighed any considerations of profit, or the opportunity cost of purchasing slaves rather than employing free servants. These issues will receive more attention below, but they are not central to the matter here: how slavery saves money, or how the surround of forces maintaining slavery itself saves more money than it costs to implement. A paradox here is that keeping

32. For details on Doria's slave trading see Edoardo Grendi, *La repubblica aristocratica dei genovesi* (Bologna, 1987), pp. 154–55.

33. See, for example, Mario Lenci, *Lucca, il mare e i corsari barbareschi nel XVI secolo* (Lucca, 1987), pp. 110–30, for details on Doria's requests for Lucca's unfortunate criminals.

34. Thorstein Veblen, *The Theory of the Leisure Class* (New York, 1967).

people in some forms of poverty makes them too weak and dispirited to resist, but also less productive. Hence repression also saves society as a whole
the resources that otherwise would have to be devoted to keeping a sturdy
and assertive poor in their places.

Keeping slaves, or the poor, hungry and pressured saved their owners (in
the case of slaves) and society (for both groups) money and time. It was
pointless to starve one's slaves and lose their capital cost to debilitated labor
and an early grave, though no doubt some savage masters saw things otherwise. Feeding slaves enough to keep up their strength, whether for cleaning
palaces in the cities or pulling at oars, made economic sense. As bad as the
medieval and early modern evidence is for caloric and nutritional intake, it
seems nonexistent for slaves. Plausible economic arguments suggest good
reasons to feed slaves adequately. The Florentine descriptions of slaves revealed almost no fat ones, and yet every morsel of food a slave received
came under the watchful eyes of some free person. Controlling slaves' food
made the point that the owners were in charge of the means of life. The
slaves had no way to keep body and soul together. All their food, clothing,
and shelter came from those with the power to grant or to withhold these
necessities. Perhaps some masters kept their slaves just a bit hungry, to remind them who was in charge. More likely, the masters fed their slaves well
enough to get a return on investment and the prestige value that came from
owning well-maintained people. All this is highly speculative, but it would
be morally blind to omit something like controlling food from the costs of
slavery. Producing too much hunger in slaves risked lethargic workers and
medical bills. To feed them well was another way of teaching a lesson to the
poor, many of whom no doubt envied the slaves' diet. For both groups, it
would be a big error, as Sen has noted, to ignore how the effects of hunger
limit the ability of people to live a life commensurate with their abilities.

Keeping the slaves a bit lean may have saved money; keeping them pressured made them cheaper to control and perhaps more productive. People
who are hurried and pressured do not have the time to cause trouble; they
are so worn down by the trials of daily life that they cannot reflect on what
is happening to them. Men in the galleys were under very stressful conditions—like in a prison, as Samuel Johnson observed, with the additional
risk of drowning. Doria knew just how many years of forced labor could be
extracted from the average galley slave before he was too broken down to
work. Domestic service had its own anxieties, with the added possibility of
forced sex with the owner, or his guests, or even, as we have seen, with people who broke into the house to commit a crime that was not legally rape.
The daily round of chores in the houses of the wealthy presumably kept the
mostly female slaves busy enough with the endless washing, cleaning, and

errand running that never abated. Idleness, temptation enough to the free, and a sin in the poor, was not likely to be a common experience for slaves. Even those slaves lucky enough to be owned by wealthy masters who were mostly concerned with displaying them, had to worry that the owners could easily tire of a particular ornament, or decide to rent her out to someone who needed a job done or had an appetite to satisfy. The pressures of being a milk machine, for example, year in and year out providing food to someone else's children, and worrying about what would happen when the milk dried up, must have taken their toll. Old age must have provoked similar fears in all slaves, most having no family on which to depend and hence subject to the whims of their owners. Add to all this the anxieties about an owner's death or business disasters, or all the other uncertainties facing people who had no legal rights or control over their destinies, and it is easy to see how hurry and pressure contributed to the forces of the surround and also prevented slaves from developing all their capabilities.

The isolation of slaves saved money because it strengthened slavery as an institution. The high cost of female slaves after 1348 meant that no one would own many of them. Male slaves were not common in domestic service, and where they were more numerous, in the sixteenth-century galleys, they had short life expectancies. All these facts worked to keep slaves apart from one another. A feature of the surround that saved money was that it isolated slaves because they were so expensive (women) or expendable (men in the galleys). Without any large communities of slaves—and it was rare for wealthy households to have more than five slaves—the women had no chance to interact with a broader group. The diverse ethnic mix characterizing late medieval slavery also atomized the slave community. Laws that imposed curfews on slaves and limited their movements, as in Genoa, also isolated slaves and made them more reliant on the households that owned them. Their different backgrounds also forced the slaves to learn Italian, or more likely the local dialect, in order to survive. Above all, slaves were not citizens; they were even less significant than the most voiceless and lowest inhabitants of a city. Isolated from civic culture and most legal protections, slaves became socially dishonored persons, the weight of whose troubles reinforced the surround.[35]

The economic and moral calculus behind the decision to free a slave makes manumission either a cost of slavery—some slip through the net—or a saving of money and even more subtly, of the souls of the owners. Manumission is a paradox in the cost-benefit style of analyzing the forces of the

---

35. Social dishonor is a central theme in the now classic study by Orlando Patterson, *Slavery and Social Death* (Cambridge, Mass., 1982).

surround, because it is saving something by being an ostensibly charitable act that must be explored in this context. To look at a specific case, on 13 October 1368 Franco de Canicia freed his slave Jacobina.[36] A manumission was a contract between two people. It was an unusual form of contract because it almost always specifically included a motive for making it, in this case the salvation of Franco's soul, as well as the souls of his departed relatives. Franco obligated all his goods, as in a sale, to guarantee Jacobina's freedom, under the huge penalty of 200 lire, several times her value, if he did not honor this contract. In their simplest form these are the standard terms, though sometimes an owner was less generous than Franco, and something was expected in return from the slave. For example, Tomasso Archerio by notarial contract freed his slave Martino on 27 May 1314, and in the very next act, Martino, now freed, promised to serve his ex-master for four years or else the manumission would be canceled.[37] The threat to return a person to slavery was not always explicit, and the extorting of additional work was not present in every contract, though it certainly cut the cost of manumission. There are enough instances of freeing a slave for nothing except the spiritual rewards that we are required to take this motive seriously. In a rare case, also from 1314, Jacopo Porcello, who freed his slave Fymia de Rosa for nothing in return, told the notary that she was about thirty years old.[38] The ages of freed slaves are so seldom supplied that it is reasonable to suppose that few of them were young. Some manumissions may represent greedy owners washing their hands of an aged slave. By the fifteenth century there was on Genoa's harbor mole a hospital devoted to broken-down slaves; presumably it was a place to deposit the old and feeble. Since the ages of manumitted slaves are mostly unknown, we cannot know in general what was occurring, but we can presume that where long terms of service were required, the slave must have had some life expectancy left. In Fymia's case, the owner presumably gave up many years of service.

Personal reasons sometimes prompted a manumission, regardless of the cost. In 1382 the Sienese knight Bartolomeo de Tuccio freed his slave Margarita and their ten-year-old son Vittorio for family reasons.[39] This verbose contract stated that Bartolomeo, "led by piety and knowing that before God there is no receiving [owning] of persons, and that, by natural law, all peo-

36. ASG, CN, Cart. N. 168, 90r, Lanfranco de Nazario notary.
37. ASG, CN, Cart. N. 253, 106r, Parentino de Quinto notary.
38. ASG, CN, Cart. N. 253, 200v, 27 September 1314.
39. Giulio Prunai, "Notizie e documenti sulla servitù domestica nel territorio senese (secc. VIII–XVI)," *Bulletino senese di storia patria* 7 (1936): 273–75.

ple were born free, and for the health of his soul," freed the two slaves without any consideration or future claim on their services.[40] The contract also made clear that the mother and child now enjoyed all the benefits of Roman citizens. This did not make them citizens of Siena, but it did guarantee some basic economic rights like the ability to make contracts or wills. It certainly cost Bartolomeo some lost wealth to free these slaves, but he acquired an heir and also helped his soul in the next world, and who could set a price on these benefits? Everyone who freed a slave who still had some work left in him or her gave up something material, whether in exchange for the pleasure of helping someone the owner loved, or so as to reward good service in the expectation of future service, or perhaps in some cases on the premise that there was something wrong about slavery. The satisfaction derived from accomplishing any or all of these aims compensated those who decided to go ahead with a manumission.

The health or salvation of the owner's soul was presumably worth obtaining at almost any price. We have already seen that as an act of Christian charity, freeing a slave was meritorious because it was a voluntary renunciation of property, though in this case not to the Church, but to society, which gained one more free working taxpayer. From the owner's point of view, it is hard to measure the gain from this type of charity as opposed to all the other forms of charity—some more expensive than the cost of a slave, most cheaper. Acts of manumission almost always concerned just one slave, or a parent and child, except on Venetian Crete, where testators sometimes freed all their slaves.[41] The owner occasionally associated the souls of deceased relatives with his or her charity, but mostly this was an individual form of charity, and one beyond the means of most people. So there seems to be a one-to-one equivalence: an owner frees a slave and creates a free person—most likely a poor one; in return God heals or maybe even saves one's soul. Although freeing a slave by almost any measure cost money, it resulted in a tangible gain that could only be obtained through substantial charitable giving. And owners could easily attach onerous conditions to the manumission that recovered the entire capital costs of the slave and still obtained the complete spiritual benefits of the act. Furthermore, there was no great pressure to free all one's slaves; just one was was enough. The rhetoric of emancipation gave masters a way to turn what might be

---

40. Ibid., p. 274: "pietate ductus, cogitans etiam quod apud Deum non est aceptio personarum et quod, de iure naturali, omnes homnies liberi nascebantur, . . . et pro salute anime sue."

41. Sally McKee, *Wills from Late Medieval Venetian Crete 1312–1420* (Washington, D.C., 1998) vol. 1, nos. 20, 135, 205, etc.

considered a mark against them, owning slaves who were in many instances Christians, into a chance to display magnanimity. Manumission and the theory of charity behind it lasted as long as society itself did not insist that its own spiritual health required that *all* slaves be freed. No such claims would be made for a long time.

If manumission is a bridge between the costs and benefits of slavery, meanness provides the same link between saving money and our next topic—relying on words alone to maintain the forces of the surround. Meanness is the hard part of life, where no rules are stretched, favors granted, or benefit of a doubt given. It is hard to object to meanness on procedural grounds, for the mean observe the forms carefully, just skirting the line of blatant oppression. Meanness is a type of conduct that leaves few traces in the historical record, but it can be inferred around the edges of ostensibly normal conduct. A new rule in Siena from 1456 imposed a fine of 25 lire on anyone who dared to say anything to a slave that resulted in damages or a lack of service to the owner.[42] This rule penalized a free person who showed any kind of sympathy to a slave. Denying slaves unregulated speech with free persons appears mean-spirited. But most examples of meanness, as we might expect, were not institutional, but personal. Genoese records provide many examples of these. Occasionally, a master does seem to have been exceptionally kind. For example, Pietro Bertono had a servant named Giovanna who was his former slave, and he took the trouble to apprentice her to a trouser maker for two years so that she could learn a useful trade.[43] In this role of committing a nonrelative to an apprenticeship, in legal terms Pietro was acting like Giovanna's father. More typical was Raimundo Besaccia, who freed his slave Cristiana on condition that she continue to serve him or his son for the next eight years, and that she be obedient and not behave dishonestly.[44] This last condition referred to her sexual conduct and was not a common requirement, though the demand for continued obedience was frequently part of manumissions stipulating additional service. As it turned out, Cristiana became pregnant by a certain Giuliano de Insula, so Raimundo on 18 March 1392 exercised his right to return her to slavery for this infraction. Exactly what motivated Raimundo—jealousy, meanness, or second thoughts—is less important than that he enforced a conventional detail of manumission that most people probably thought was a dead letter.

42. G. Prunai, "Notizie," pp. 414 (text of regulations concerning slaves).

43. ASG, CN, Cart. N. 290, 40r–v 13 March 1366, Benvenuto de Bracelli notary.

44. L. Tria, "La schiavitù," pp. 154–55.

Antonio de Vairolo da Camogli extracted from his freed slave Niccolo the promise of paying twelve and a half florins over the next eight years, a sum much higher than the average cost of a male slave.[45] In gratitude for favors received, the blacksmith Giuliano in 1394 gave away to a priest a three-year-old slave named Luchina, the daughter of one of his slaves.[46] Taken from her mother as a toddler, Luchina became a sort of living thank-you note, and faced a puzzling future in a priest's household. Giuliano's conduct to the little slave seems insensitive. There is no point in multiplying examples of meanness or noting examples of good conduct where an owner went out of his or her way to help a slave; the point here is that both resulted from the owners' whims and were unpredictable. It was more bad luck for a slave to have a mean master. Theologians could debate whether the spiritual benefits Raimundo Besaccia obtained from freeing his slave were also annulled when he returned her to slavery. It is an interesting legal problem, for in his case he ended up saving her purchase price by reacquiring her, and beneath a mean act there is often the added bonus to the mean of saving some money into the bargain.

LANGUAGE IN THE GREAT ECONOMY

The focus here is on how Italian societies used words alone to maintain the forces of the surround—the web in which the slaves were caught—and to frame the way slaves fared in the economy. Of course these distinctions between costing or saving money and mere words are very rough, but language itself, apart from cost-benefit analysis, became a powerful tool for fixing the place of slaves in the markets. Language is habitual and people acquire it uncritically; it takes a long time before they challenge assumptions embedded in discourse that has become second nature. Words made ordinary and acceptable what might in other contexts prompt scrutiny of, and perhaps doubt about, the way things were done. Above all, words alone provided the basis for making and expressing moral judgments about the economy.

As suggested, the investigation of meanness is a good way to begin looking at habits—here economic—that the use of words alone can teach a society. In the context of discussing the virtue of fortitude, the biography of San Benedetto il Moro contains a revealing use of words. The humble San Benedetto, by nature a withdrawn, solitary ascetic who passed twenty-seven years working in the Capuchin monastery in Palermo, seems an unlikely

---

45. ASG, CN, Cart. N. 294, 92r–v, Benvenuto de Bracelli notary.
46. L. Tria, "La schiavitù," pp. 156–57.

candidate for insult. But his color marked him as an outsider in sixteenth-century Sicily, and apart from that, what everyone knew about him was that he was the son of slaves. Fortitude is a common quality among saints, and Benedetto first demonstrated it when as a young man he sold his cattle, gave the proceeds to the poor, and became a hermit.[47] This type of voluntary poverty evinced sanctity. (It took fortitude to become poor, and even more to be a slave.) Not only was he joyful in his labors and fasts, but he also put up with a lot of burdens, villainies, and bad treatment. His biographer's best example of these concerns the words of a sacristan who continuously insulted Benedetto. Once, in the presence of many witnesses, he called Benedetto a " slave dog dog" (*schiavo cane perro*), which the author informs us was the strongest possible insult in the Sicilian dialect (probably because of the doubling of the "dog" in Italian [cane] and Spanish [perro]) and of course alluded to the saint's parentage in critical terms. Naturally Benedetto bore all this, and a thousand other spiteful acts, with saintly innocence and humility. To be called a slave, in conjunction with a dog or not, was a deadly insult, and of course in this instance false. "Slave" is a word without positive connotations (unless one is a slave of God—like the pope); to be one was to be the lowest of the low; to descend from one was little better. As we have seen, "slave" continued to carry this baggage even after slavery. The label itself became a badge of dishonor, and even in the absence of slaves, the word still was a vivid name when the institution was not present. When the person was a slave, the insult was just an accurate label, which the person had to endure—and most people are not saints. The word "slave"is a wounding attack or a statement of fact, but it has a big effect whether uttered as an insult or as a label for merchandise in the market.

Earl Shorris identified three topics—the media, intellectual muggings, and ethnic antagonisms—that can aid our search for ways in which words maintained the forces sustaining slavery.[48] Of course modern and medieval societies profoundly differed in these three matters. The media, as currently understood, did not exist ten centuries ago. News traveled slowly if at all, and the shaping of public opinion relied on talk and the slow diffusion of received truths. If there was a proxy for the modern media in the Middle Ages, perhaps the authoritative statements emanating from the Church and the universities gradually persuaded and informed people in ways that created a consensus of opinion on issues. By not condemning slavery or the slave trade, by not using against them the power of words

47. For this and what follows, see Giuseppe Carletti, *Vita di S. Benedetto da S. Filadelfo* (Rome, 1805), pp. 91–92.

48. E. Shorris, *New American Blues*, pp. 185, 188, 191.

alone (its strongest weapon), the Church buttressed these institutions and eased the consciences of those owning or dealing in slaves. Legal commentaries mainly coming from the University of Bologna in the twelfth and thirteenth centuries, mostly from the pens of Italian scholars, strengthened the reasoning supporting slavery.

Many of the great legal minds of the Middle Ages—Accursius, Azo, Baldo de Ubaldis, Bartolo de Sassoferrato—as well as influential theologians like SS Thomas Aquinas and Bonaventure and canonists like Popes Innocent III, Innocent IV, and Gregory IX, grew up in Italy, the home of Roman and canon law. True, "Italy" remained a geographical expression rather than a unified political reality. But the cultural experience of being raised and educated, and eventually teaching in Italy (or, as in the case of some expatriates like Aquinas, in Paris), meant that Italian social and economic life—its regions, countryside, and cities—shaped these people who used words that had a wide influence across Europe. Because of this wider intellectual significance, and the habit of neglecting Italian identity, scholars have not paid enough attention to the Italian context of so much of what we now call medieval intellectual history, especially in the law. The popes who countenanced slavery and made a place for Christian slaves in a Christian society were nearly all Italians. The commentators on Roman law at Bologna, who helped to define key concepts like international law and the law of persons, were similarly from Italy. Though they spoke different dialects and came from contentious states, they were from "this side of the mountains," as the Italian students defined themselves at Bologna, and they knew that this distinguished them from the others—across the mountains and seas.

Once we restore the disembodied language of so much intellectual history to its proper Italian context, where slavery was more widespread than most places in Europe, we can see how the language coming from that context affected the surround. Pope Gregory IX (1227–41) was born Ugolino dei Conti at Anagni in central Italy. Educated at Bologna and Paris, this pope was also a famous canon lawyer as well as the patron of St. Francis. In 1237 and 1238 he wrote two letters to the patriarch of Jerusalem that clarified the Church's teaching on slavery.[49] In the Latin East—the crusader states—where a Muslim slave's conversion to Christianity carried freedom, insincere converts were depriving these states of valuable slaves. Hence owners attempted to prevent slaves from converting. Gregory IX's compro-

49. For this and what follows see Benjamin Z. Kedar, *Crusade and Mission: European Attitudes toward the Muslims* (Princeton, N.J., 1984), pp. 146–49 (texts of letter, pp. 212–15).

mise, if that is the right word, insisted that slaves be allowed the liberty to become Christians and receive religious instruction, but that they would nevertheless remain slaves. In a later letter to the bishop of Majorca, the pope permitted Christian masters to sell Christian slaves, as will seem to them expedient.[50] Although the occasions for these letters came from outside Italy, the pope was simply generalizing ordinary local commercial practices to the rest of the Christian world. Owning Muslim slaves may have been more common on the frontiers of Christendom, but the rules in these medieval centuries came from its Italian heart.

Commentators on the law also contributed to the forces of the surround. Azo (ca. 1150–1230), one of the first commentators on Roman law, wrote on Justinian's *Code*, *Digest*, and *Institutes*—this last a primer on Roman law intended for beginning students. Roman and medieval Italian law on slavery, already examined in Chapter 2, here provides something different—the words necessary to make the practice of slavery appear normal, unexceptional. We have also seen the hegemonic quality of Roman law, this monument of jurisprudence which the medieval commentators mainly treated with respectful awe. The historical weight of Roman law, also a familiar subject, only partly explains the role its prestige played in maintaining the forces of the surround. By commenting on Roman law, medieval scholars entered a sophisticated but almost imaginary world in which their "today" seldom intruded. But their words trained generations of lawyers who directed the bureaucracies of the Church and local governments in Italy. This training, this shaping of opinion, substituted for the media, and merits scrutiny for its effects on the economy.

In two pages of his commentary on the *Institutes*, Azo discusses a fundamental issue—the law of persons.[51] Our concern is the economic importance of his language. Azo begins by saying that everyone is either slave or free, and of course this rules out the idea of equality before the law and accepts slavery as a fact of life. In the law of nations, as Azo observes, violence and force cause slavery. He clearly states that at some point, people become slaves because their captors choose to sell them rather than kill them. Azo mentions but does not stress the traditional "saving" etymology of the Latin *servus*; here, the point is to kill or to sell. Violence makes free people into slaves, and there is no hint that religion shapes or controls this fact of life, though it certainly recommends mercy. Following the *Institutes*, Azo

50. Ibid., p. 215: "prout sibi videbitur expedire."
51. Azo, *Summa Aurea* (Lyon, 1557; facsimile ed., Frankfurt, 1968), 269r–270v for what follows.

knows and discusses that in civil law a nonviolent path also leads people into slavery. A man (*homo liber*) over twenty years of age has the right to sell himself into slavery, to turn himself into a commodity (as we would say) by transferring himself to another for a price (as Azo says). (The gendered nature of Latin makes it clear that women do not have the right to sell themselves into slavery—a curious fact.) I have not seen an example of self-sale in medieval Italy, but it remained legal unless overturned by local statute—which I have also not seen. More important, the idea of selling oneself into slavery remained a fascinating legal and moral puzzle for scholars to explore. The technical issues alone engaged serious attention. Azo ponders whether it is possible for the person to regain his liberty by returning the purchase price. He notes that some say yes, if the owner accepts it voluntarily; others say it is enough if the price is returned, and the owner has no choice but to let the slave go. Azo does not offer an opinion here on whether the slave can control this repurchase. The issue opened the door to serious legal questions about whether the slave could have any property that was not the master's already—the thorny matter of *peculium*.

Besides the possibility of becoming a slave through violence or self-sale, Azo notes a few other peculiar paths into slavery. A person might be recalled into slavery because of his or her ingratitude—by violating the terms of emancipation—and we have seen that this actually occurred in medieval Italy. In Roman law a child could be sold into slavery by a parent because of the family's hunger. In order to keep a family from starving, it seemed reasonable to the Romans to sell a child to preserve the person, now transformed from a potential victim of starvation into a slave of some value. Selling a child meant the family had one less mouth to feed, as well as saving the other family members who could live for a while off the sale price. In theory this too remained legal in Italy, but I know of no instances of it happening, except of course where masters—who were sometimes also the fathers—sold the children of their female slaves.

Free poor people in medieval Italy did not sell their children into slavery. Christian charity may have made this dire path unnecessary, but religion did not prohibit the practice. Poor people sometimes abandoned children to hospitals or charitable people, or just left them on the church doorstep when they were unable to feed them. The poor were unable to profit from selling their children. Instead, the poor when necessary abandoned their children to uncertain fates and relied on the Church and the "kindness of strangers." The social forces that balked at letting the poor sell their own children into slavery in a city like Genoa may not have prevailed everywhere. The parties to such deals may have preferred to keep them secret and out of the notarial cartularies. In thirteenth-century Castile the poor still had the legal right to sell or pawn their children when necessary.[52] What actually happened in Italy remains unclear, but Roman law did not prohibit selling children, and many contracts reveal no second thoughts about the morality of selling other people's children. All this provides another good reason to look at slavery and poverty.

Azo concludes that slavery is the common condition of all slaves, at first glance a trite comment. What he means is that though some slaves are honest and others evil, though some may be freed by their masters and others not, none of this context matters to their enslavement. Other legal commentaries support the same conclusion, preserved by Roman law deep into the Middle Ages, that slavery simply results from bad luck. As we have seen, this powerful ancient idea depersonalized slavery in that the victims of violence became just unlucky, and the oppressors dropped out of the equation. Augustine's stress on sin as the cause of slavery also shifted responsibility away from the owners and once again blamed the victims for their plight. Words accomplished the important task of making slavery banal, supported by the common assumption that people were not equal. The economic consequences are clear—the market was not going to inquire into how a person became a slave, let alone question slavery itself.

Antonino Pieruzzi (1389–1459), archbishop of Florence and later canonized, was also a distinguished Dominican theologian who wrote a *Summa Theologica*. In this work Sant' Antonino pulled together some refinements on the standard teachings on slavery that constituted an authoritative use of the Church's power over words to buttress slavery. Whether or not he originated all these ideas is not as important as the fact that he re-presented this material for Florentines and a wider audience in Italy and beyond. Once again, the point is how Sant' Antonino's writing helped to maintain the forces of the surround, and a few examples will suffice. Sant' Antonino stated that slavery was supported by the law of nations, natural law, and also divine law, and he used Noah's curse of Ham as proof.[53] The actual curse fell on Ham's son Canaan, condemned to be a slave of slaves (*servus servorum*, Genesis 9:24–25). Hence the Bible legitimized slavery, but Sant' Antonino did not make any racial connections to Ham and his descendants—a theme with a long history in biblical exegesis. Sant' Antonino noted that it was good advice to free slaves for remission of one's sins, but this was only advice, and it was not obligatory for Christians to free their slaves. He ex-

52. John Boswell, *The Kindness of Strangers* (New York, 1988), pp. 328–29.
53. Sant' Antonino, archbishop of Florence, *Summa Theologica*, vol. 3 (Verona, 1740; facsimile ed., Graz, 1959), col. 197 for this and what follows.

plained that the conversion of a slave to Christianity did not result in liberty for this reason: baptism affects sin but not the circumstances or obligations of men. The utility arguments Pope Gregory IX had made two centuries ago for why converts should remain slaves had by now found a theological justification—the limits of the power of baptism![54]

Sant' Antonino concluded that it was licit to make captives taken in a just war into slaves. Hence it was a sin for slaves justly enslaved to flee—another powerful religious sanction for the violence at the core of slavery. Christian slaves belonging to infidels or Saracens (Muslims) of course retained the right to flee, for they were all unjustly enslaved. Finally, Sant' Antonino taught that masters should take care of their slaves when they fell sick.[55] The owners were, however, not obliged to take sick slaves to hospital, on this astonishing reasoning. The centurion in the gospel of Matthew had not taken his boy (slave) anywhere, but instead had left him at home for treatment and by himself went to Jesus for a cure. People had to account to God for how they treated slaves, but who would have thought that the centurion story would have provided a reason for masters to treat their slaves at home? Even if hospitals were dangerous places to which the poor were sent to die, Sant' Antonino's use of the biblical passage, wrenched from its context, does not suggest compassion as his motive. His theology crosses the line between using words to sustain slavery and using them to oppress the slaves themselves.

Shorris saw intellectual muggings as part of the forces of the surround. These muggings left the poor (and slaves) in a place where imperatives ruled, where there was no time for reflection, no alternatives.[56] Some intellectuals rob the poor *and slaves* by defining their experience in such a way as to blame the historical victims, or even better, shift blame from the oppressors onto the oppressed. In this way, as Shorris noted and Antonio Gramsci

54. Raymond of Peñafort had earlier suggested that baptism did not justify freedom, and Sant' Antonino mentions a Raymond as an authority on this matter. See André Vauchez, "Note sur l'esclavage et le changement de religion en Terre Sainte en XIIIe siècle," in *Figures de l'esclave au Moyen-Age et dans le monde moderne*, ed. Henri Bresc (Paris, 1996), pp. 91–96, here p. 94. This article is also good on the context of the papal letters discussed above.

55. Sant' Antonino, *Summa Theologica*, cols. 201: "Infirmatis ipsis curam procurare, non ad hospitale mittere, quia nec Centurio ethnicus circa puerum suum, idest servum, hoc egit, sed in domo paralyticum gubernari fecit & pro sanatione ejus ad Christum accessit, Matth. 8. Nec benefacientes eos impediant, sed sollicitent, cum de eis Domnio habeant reddere rationem." His puer = servus is interesting and certainly accurate in this context.

56. E. Shorris, *New American Blues*, pp. 188–89.

might have agreed, the poor and slaves (at least some of them) came to see their own experiences through the eyes and with the values of the dominant social and economic groups. To be intellectually mugged is to be stripped bare of one's moral claims, and this happened to people who had already lost so much. Plainly, if the poor and slaves come to believe that morality, religion, and the markets are not on their side, or that they deserve their fate, the more powerful social groups can elicit, by words alone, a kind of self-policing. The poor and slaves themselves will strengthen the forces around them.

Here, our interest is on those intellectual muggings that occur in the marketplace. A place to begin is regret, defined by Janet Landman as "a more or less painful judgment and state of feeling sorry for misfortune, limitations, losses, shortcomings, transgressions, or mistakes."[57] Regret is a very historical emotion, and there is a rational part of it as well because regret rests on a considered evaluation of the past (and sometimes the future). As Landman also notes, "regret, properly understood, is the past alive in the present."[58] Personal remorse is a narrower feeling about one's own failure to act, or about one's own guilt. Explaining the difference between remorse and regret in the context of slavery requires us to see personal remorse as the feeling a slave owner might have about owning or mistreating a particular slave. Regret too looks back on the past, but it goes beyond remorse about personal conduct to include a wider judgment about the context of morally dubious situations. Collective, social regret does not exist because groups of people seldom experience a common response of feeling sorry in the same way for what they did. (This is why group or national apologies seem so meaningless, unless there is agreement on the collective response or penance, like on a payment.) The individual sense of participation in big issues is ordinarily too small to sustain real regret. Hence modern Italians (or Americans) are not likely to feel any personal remorse or even regret about past slavery, except perhaps in those American families where the memory and even the benefits of owning slaves remain alive in the present day.[59] For Italians, the historical experience of slavery is too remote and impersonal, excepting of course the kind of slavery Primo Levi and others endured during the Holocaust. What regret their masters felt is another story.

57. Janet Landman, *Regret: The Persistence of the Possible* (New York, 1993), p. 4.
58. Ibid., p. 263.
59. Hence only an American could have written the remarkable book by Edward Ball, *Slaves in the Family* (New York, 1998), his account of his family's past and his own efforts to reach out to the descendants of the slaves his ancestors owned. There is a nice understanding of the issues of regret in this book.

To consider regret in our context, we must go back into the past and find some contemporaries expressing or evading it.

Regret in an economic context can arise when a person feels that he or she has made an unfortunate or unwise contract. These small regrets or second thoughts never provided sufficient grounds for breaking any contract for buying a slave. Especially for slaves, an item of commerce hard to know well in advance, the market made no room for regrets. Manumissions offer more fertile ground for regrets because this act might seem a way to balance accounts, to offset any regrets about slavery by a spontaneous act of kindness. Even the emancipation by the Sienese knight Bartolomeo di Tuccio, which stated that before God there was no possession of people, and which freed his own child by a slave, did not express any regrets about slavery.[60] The impersonal verb construction *paenitet*, the Latin for "regret" that eventually supplied Church Latin with the word *paenitentia* "penance," did not appear in any documents concerning slavery. Nor did the Italian noun *pentimento*, which always carried a meaning heavier in repentance than regret. These manumissions, usually dripping with claims that the owner freed the slave for the good of his or her soul, never conceived of freeing a slave as an act of penance for owning one. The complete absence of any sign of regret about slavery again highlights just how successful society and the marketplace were in treating slavery as a normal, unexceptional economic activity.

Without regret as a price of slavery, was then hypocrisy the key to explaining the apparent normalcy of Italian slavery? Fully aware of Jesus' many pointed comments about hypocrites, members of this society were not eager to join their ranks. A good working definition of hypocrisy is that it signifies "the pretense of virtue, idealism, or sympathetic concern used to further selfish ends."[61] Every word used to justify and continue practicing slavery as an acceptable part of the economy constitutes in our eyes an act of hypocrisy. But to the Italians under review here pretense was not an issue. They sincerely believed slavery to be part of the world as it was. Far more important than the ahistorical assigning of hypocrisy to past peoples is the necessary task of exploring their admitted or blatant hypocrisies *by their own standards*. The words of hypocrites contributed to the forces surrounding the poor and slaves.

Hypocrisy exists in economic relationships because pretense is part of the normal give and take in bargaining. In this sense "hypocrisy," a word

60. G. Prunai, "Notizie," pp. 273–75.
61. Ruth W. Grant, *Hypocrisy and Integrity: Machiavelli, Rousseau, and the Ethics of Politics* (Chicago, 1997), p. 1.

(like slavery) with no positive meanings, can become an acceptable means to good ends, a tool with redeeming traits.[62] Everyone's selfish aim in a market is to obtain the best terms in transactions. The problem, as Adam Smith explained so well, is: "How is it possible to ascertain by rules the exact point at which, in every case, a delicate sense of justice begins to run into a frivolous and weak scrupulosity of conscience? When it is that secrecy and reserve begin to grow into dissimulation?"[63] The same question engaged Pope Innocent IV five centuries previously, when he concluded that bargaining crossed the line into sin when the intent of negotiating was to deceive. For the pope, bargaining that deceived the poor was clearly unjust, so long as it fell outside the normal range of the just price.[64] For Smith, this would be meaningless casuistry, and he preferred to decide the questions on the basis of the human sympathies of the bargainers, on a case-by-case basis.[65] Smith's "dissimulation," drawing on classical Latin, is our hypocrisy, and to him to dissimulate was the same as to lie, which was too far beyond the pale for an acceptable tool in bargaining.

At issue here is where to draw the line to define moral bargaining—from the later position of the Quakers (a fixed price with no haggling) right up to the flexible boundary between negotiating and fraud. Slaves, like all other commodities, raised these moral quandaries. What in particular about buying and selling slaves raised special concerns about hypocrisy in bargaining? First, the motives of buyers could be morally complex. In the de Gogi case discussed in Chapter 2, we saw an owner, with a dead female slave on his hands, attempting to recover the purchase price. The lawyer Bartolomeo de Bosco succeeded in changing the issue to the owner's purchasing of the slave for sex, his own impotence, and a case of skin mites incompetently treated as reasons to deny the claim.[66] Base motives might sully the purchase of land or a mule, but nothing about these sales seems as personal as buying a slave mainly for sex and then trying to get one's money back for ostensibly correct reasons. Hypocrisy arises in exploiting the commodity, which was undoubtedly the buyer's prerogative, but was clearly a different matter in the case of a young girl. Ordinary human sympathy for the girl's

62. Ibid., p. 18, but Grant's interest is in hypocrisy as a political tool.

63. A. Smith, *The Theory of Moral Sentiments*, p. 339.

64. A point discussed in detail and with references, in my "The Theory and Practice of the Just Wage," p. 63.

65. A moral theory based on human sympathy would not likely appear in a slaveholding society. This is another reason why sin provided so attractive a moral explanation for slavery.

66. See above, p. 83.

plight, which Bosco seems to have felt, and something that even in an un-sentimental age a few would feel even for a mistreated mule, complicated and introduced hypocrisy into the bargaining over her. The small percent-age of people in Italian societies who owned slaves were probably the least sympathetic to them. Those owners choosing to free a slave were perhaps motivated by a gradually increasing sympathy resulting from daily contacts with the slave over the years. Ways in which legal regulations lumped to-gether slaves and the poor suggest that masters may have feared solidarity, nothing more than mutual sympathy, between the two downtrodden groups. The other way in which the parties to a sale engaged in dissimula-tion was to pretend that the slave could not speak for itself or proclaim its own defects or virtues. Instead, the slave, like other wares, remained silent in the bargaining, deprived of language, because in civil law the slave was a dead object.

Shorris's last category, ethnic antagonisms, leads us into the final subject of this book, the complex relationship between price and skin color as a proxy for ethnicity. Before exploring this issue, let us summarize briefly the forces of the surround thus far discussed. Whether these forces cost or saved money or relied on words alone to accomplish their purposes, the point is that the social fate of the poor *and slaves* became bound together in late medieval Italy. The economic consequences of slavery shaped the ways in which society sanctioned the use of coercion on other disfavored social groups. As the market became more depersonalized, parts of it, especially the labor sector, became increasingly impervious to moral claims for justice. Instead, people began to soothe their consciences with the self-serving be-lief that "market decisions" themselves defined justice and spontaneously created a morally responsible marketplace. Accepting people as commodi-ties, even in limited contexts, embedded in the economy a certain habitual conduct that affected all people. And when these slaves became, over the course of the later Middle Ages, increasingly identifiable as members of other ethnic groups, the participants in the market also began to complicate existing ethnic antagonisms by literally putting a price on them.

THE LANGUAGE OF PRICE

Markets use price to signal value. The number attached to a slave—so many lire, florins, ducats, ounces of gold—quantifies a value the buyer and seller saw in a slave at the moment of sale. The problem with price as a sig-nifier is that it bundles up all the factors affecting price in a way that makes it nearly impossible to separate them. For example, standard insurance contracts on slaves in midfifteenth-century Genoa most often valued the life, or value, of a slave at L150—sometimes L140 or L160, but usually the rounded figure, giving us an estimate of their sense of a slave's standard price.[67] An insurance contract presumably noted the color or race of the insured as a way to identify the property, but the rounded sums do not suggest that these factors greatly influenced the slave's *insured value*, an abstraction. It is as if L150 represented a base price, from which the parties might bargain down—when the slave was male, older, darker, lame, blind in one eye, malarial, from a less desirable ethnic group—or bargain up—when the slave was female, in the prime of life, fairer, healthy, and of good stock. The contracts provide only a few variables—price, name, age, ethnicity, and sometimes color or some other striking characteristic—and leave out important factors like beauty, personality, and demeanor, to name just a few. Bargainers of course varied in skill, and occasionally the price tells us more about the quality of the haggling than about the merchandise. Enough evidence survives to show where slaves came from and that Italian slavery became increasingly female, especially in the north, in the later Middle Ages. Also, slaves were cheaper as children or when elderly, and more costly in their prime.

To be more specific about the factors affecting price is more difficult. For example, on 28 March 1349, right after the catastrophic plague year 1348, three partners in Genoa scrupulously divided up the 317 florins received from the sale of seventeen slaves to a Catalan, presumably for reexport to Barcelona.[68] This remarkable lot sale, the largest known to me, presumably involved Tartar slaves, at about nineteen florins a head, but we know nothing about the actual sex, age, condition, and value of the individual slaves. The fact that merchants were still risking capital on a commodity as perishable as slaves in a time of plague is itself an amazing testimony to the resilience of the slave trade. But the average price of these slaves tells us almost nothing.

The more copious sources available after 1300 make it possible to collect enough information, notably in Genoa and Palermo, to answer some deeper questions on the language of prices. The central issue, involving the entire scope of this book, concerns how ethnicity or color affected the slave's price. This is a fundamental question about Italian slavery because this early evidence can help to explain the subsequent Italian understanding of race, centuries before the conventional beginning of the subject. Also,

67. Domenico Gioffrè, *Il mercato degli schiavi a Genova nel secolo XV* (Genoa, 1971), unpaginated final tables as for example of insurance contracts for 1441.
68. ASG, CN, Cart. N. 287, 87v–88r, Benvenuto de Bracelli notary.

given the role some Italians played in the first phase of exploring and exploiting the New World, and the fact that the Spanish ruled an increasing share of Italy in the fifteenth and sixteenth centuries, these Italian practices concerning ethnicity and color had significance outside Italy. A few issues need to be discussed at the start of this analysis. First, as the Florentine data in Chapter 3 clearly revealed about the ethnic label "Tartar," these categories sometimes masked considerable variety, especially by color. The labels "Moor" and "Saracen" raise the same problem, as these people came in black, white and every shade between. These labels also meant other things to contemporaries, since they carried information about religion, language, "national" or "racial" characteristics, and other factors. Other types of slaves, like Hungarians, Bosnians, Serbs, Abkhazians, Circassians, Mingrels, Canary Islanders, and Guineans were more homogeneous, at least to Italian eyes. Second, in order to make progress on color, ethnicity, and price, we will have to hold other factors constant. In practice, this will mean focusing on women slaves between the ages of fifteen and thirty, their prime years on the market. (These years reveal what preoccupied the mostly male buyers—sex and endurance.) The numbers of male slaves are usually so low as to preclude this type of analysis, and of course this fact is revealing and cries out for explanation. So, where age and sex can be isolated, we have the best chance of understanding the value attributed to ethnicity and color.

A survey of the earliest evidence, from Genoa between 1186 and 1226, indicates that at this phase of slavery Saracens, presumably mostly from Spain, were by far the most numerous category of slaves, and that male and female slaves, roughly equal in number, cost about the same amount, 4 lire.[69] The small numbers will not sustain any sweeping conclusions about color and price. Michel Balard, who studied Genoese slavery in the second half of the thirteenth century, found that Saracens comprised about 70 percent of the slave population in the years 1239–74, but that during 1275–1300 slaves from the Black Sea began to predominate.[70] For the complete sample (418 slaves) Balard found these percentages by color: white, 29 percent; brown, 8 percent; olive, 15 percent; black, 10 percent; not given, 38 percent.[71] Balard looked carefully at the influence of ethnicity and color on price, and he concluded that, when age and sex were taken into account,

69. Giovanna Balbi, "La schiavitù a Genova tra i secoli XII e XIII," *Mélanges offerts à René Crozet*, ed. P. Gallais and Y.-J. Riou (Poitiers, 1966), pp. 1025–29, here p. 1029.

70. Michel Balard, "Remarques sur les esclaves à Gênes dans la seconde moitié du XIIIe siècle," *Mélanges d'archéologie et d'histoire* 70 (1968): 627–80, here p. 643.

71. Ibid., p. 647.

Saracen and "Eastern" female slaves did not differ appreciably in price.[72] The effect of color was hard to fathom in this small sample, but Balard found that among all women slaves, white ones commanded somewhat higher prices. He did not find the same trend among male slaves, where color had little or no influence on price.

For reasons having to do with the quantity of the surviving notarial sources, it is hard to find enough information on slavery in Genoa in the early trecento to draw any conclusions. After 1350, the numbers significantly improve, and by then the new slaves in Genoa are mainly young Tartar women. A study of slavery in the late trecento found that color had a negligible role in determining price, but this is not surprising in a sample of almost exclusively Tartar slaves, themselves a complex and diverse group. [73] I collected a sample of twenty-three Tartar women, all sold in Genoa before the same notary between 1358 and 1384, and from ten to twenty-five years old.[74] This notary did not note skin color for any of these women, but since nearly all the slaves who passed under his eyes were Tartars, he may have thought it was enough to write that fact alone. The prices in this sample range from 34 lire to 60 lire, with a slight increase in prices in the 1380s. Hence females cost on average about 50 lire in this period, but in 1376 two Tartar women, both twenty years old, sold for L30 and L45, a 50 percent difference that might be explained by color, or temperament, or any number of factors. A similar study of slaves in Venice from 1388 to 1398 found that of the 292 slaves in one notary's records, fully 80 percent were women, 78 percent of these were Tartars, and 62 percent of all women were between eleven and twenty years old.[75] There was a strong Tartar component to both Venetian and Genoese slavery at the end of the trecento.

Before looking more closely at the issues of ethnicity, gender, and price, we should turn to the situation in Palermo to explore slavery in another context. A somewhat different view of slavery emerges from Sicily in the

72. Ibid., pp. 656–57, for this and what follows. Males comprised about one-third of his sample and women two-thirds, a slight shift in favor of women.

73. Robert Delort, "Quelques précisions sur le commerce des esclaves à Gênes vers la fin du XIVe siècle," *Mélanges d'archéologie et d'histoire* 77 (1966): 215–50, here p. 239.

74. ASG, CN, Cart. N. 289, 290, 293, 294, 295, all by Benvenuto Bracelli notary.

75. Bariša Krekič, "Contributo allo studio degli schiavi levantini e balcanici a Venezia (1388–1398)," *Studi in memoria di Federigo Melis*, (Naples, 1978), 2:379–94, here p. 380.

trecento and quattrocento. Henri Bresc has studied Sicilian slavery, mainly for Palermo, where he estimated that in the period 1290–1460 slaves comprised less than 12 percent of the population.[76] Whatever the numbers, slaves were probably a higher percentage of the population in Palermo than in any other Italian city. Around 1300 slavery in Sicily was still predominantly "Saracen"; slaves were Muslims from North Africa largely supplied by the Catalans. What little remained of the indigenous Muslim population after 1300 was under pressure to convert or emigrate, so being a Saracen or Muslim increasingly meant being a slave. Some sub-Saharan blacks, converted to Islam in their passage to slavery, also appeared in Sicily. Frederick III's law code of 1310 required all slave owners to ensure that the children of their Christian or Saracen slaves were baptized, under penalty of instant freedom for these infant slaves.[77] This rule, probably in force elsewhere in Italy, guaranteed that a Muslim mother could not pass her religion on to her child.

Women comprised about two-thirds of the Sicilian slave population, again suggesting a luxury trade in domestic servants. It may be, however, that we need to know more about the sources of supply in order to understand the gendered style of Italian slavery. Demand for male slaves in the Muslim world was high, and men were more likely to be killed in wars or slave raiding, so at least part of the reason for the smaller proportion of male slaves may have been the lack of such slaves on the market. Still, from the demand side, the pull remained for high-priced female slaves. The arrival of increasing numbers of Greek slaves in Sicily after 1307/9 highlights the "global" aspects of Mediterranean slavery, in which Italians played an active role as traders but a lesser role as consumers. These Greek slaves, victims partly of anarchy and partly of gradual Ottoman advances, enjoyed higher status and more lenient conditions that Saracens.[78] They were, after all, Christians, and they were virtually certain to be emancipated eventually.

After the plague, and the continued rise in slave prices, Bresc found 1360–99 to be a period when an ethnically diverse group of Tartar slaves, supplied by the Genoese, began to dominate in Sicilian markets. As in Genoa and Venice, these Tartars were mostly female and expensive, making emancipations less likely. Palermo was the main entrepôt and supplied slaves to the other parts of the island. In common with the rest of Italy, the

76. Henri Bresc, *Un monde méditerranéen: Economie et société en Sicile 1300–1450*, vol. 1 (Rome, 1986), 1:439; pp. 439–63 for what follows.

77. *Capitula Regni Siciliae*, ed. by Francesco Testa (Palermo, 1741), p. 78.

78. H. Bresc, *Un monde mediterranéen*, p. 443.

average price of a female Tartar in Palermo was high—7.16 ounces of gold—which made such slaves a more risky investment after the plague.[79] However, the rise in wages and labor shortages, as well as higher per capita wealth, especially among the rich, made buying a slave a good risk. For 1400 to 1439 Bresc found a period of equilibrium in Sicilian slavery; as Catalans began to replace the Genoese as main suppliers of slaves, blacks and Saracens again became more common on the island, and slaves from the Black Sea and eastern Mediterranean less so. With these changes the numbers of male and female slaves became roughly equal.[80] After 1440, more and more sub-Saharan African slaves, usually called Ethiopians, came onto the market. There was a slight gender division of labor within slavery, as men were destined for agricultural work and women more likely to be in domestic service in the cities.

By the 1460s, Greeks had largely disappeared from the Sicilian slave markets and Tartars were also in decline as the Turks gradually closed Italian access to the Black Sea. The Genoese no longer supplied many slaves; the Catalans and Aragonese replaced them. What evidence we have from outside Palermo, mainly from Corleone and Trapani, confirms these patterns. It is natural to think of Sicily, just before the voyages of Columbus, as a potential archetype for a plantation-style slave economy. The problem for Sicily was not moral reluctance but the climate—the low level of rainfall. Although sugarcane and cotton were grown on the island in small quantities, neither crop was going to thrive in this dry place. Wheat, Sicily's durable export, had a low and seasonal demand for labor that could not efficiently use high-priced slaves. The Atlantic islands, Madeira and the Canaries, were better suited as models for what would later occur in the Caribbean, though Italian merchants and investors brought their knowledge of slavery to these places, as Columbus himself did to Hispaniola. The arrival of black African slaves in Sicily would continue, however, and garden farming for urban markets could absorb a good number of them. These Africans made slaves more easily identifiable as black, so we need to consider racism's growing role in this slavery. "Racism" here, in a premodern context, simply means the valuing or devaluing of people primarily on the basis of their *razza*, ethnicity, which was strongly linked to color and other traits.

The problem is how to measure and evaluate the racial component of slavery. Bresc believed that black slaves had a harder time being freed, but that once they were manumitted, racism did not prevent their integration

79. Ibid., p. 444.
80. Ibid., p. 447.

into society.[81] Yet his own price data for the years 1440–60 reveal a 40–50 percent higher price for white women (Circassians 14.15 ounces of gold, Abkhazians 15.12 ounces) than for black women (10.6 ounces).[82] Saracens at 11.16 ounces and Tartars at 12.22 ounces confirm the pattern that color significantly affected price. Bresc's information about age suggests that it was not the factor causing these disparities in prices—the ages of the slaves sold were roughly equal. Black African females were the most numerous type of slave in the market (sixty-eight), but the fifty Russian women at 14.11 ounces again suggest that white slaves were more expensive because Sicilians preferred them. Color could not determine the price of a slave in terms of the work expected. Some residual factor was causing the big differences in price and consumer preference, and what else could it be but racism?.

We can return to fifteenth-century Genoa for an answer to this question. Table 2 presents information on women slaves between the ages of fifteen and thirty by ethnic group. The year 1453, when Constantinople fell to the Ottoman Turks, marks a useful dividing line in the century because afterward the types of slaves available in Genoa changed significantly. For example, Tartar slaves became very hard to buy, and none were apparently sold after 1464. Before 1453, Eastern slaves predominated; there is not one Moorish woman in the sample before that date. All the Eastern slaves, except possibly some of the Bulgarians, came to the city originally via the Black Sea trading routes. The closeness of the average ages, all within a few months of twenty-one and a half years, indicates that we are looking at basically the same kind of woman across ethnic groups in this century. In the first half of the century slaves from the four white groups (Abkhazians, Russians, Circassians, and Bulgarians) on average cost more than those from the one mixed group—the Tartars. The difference is large between the Russians and Abkhazians on the one hand and the Tartars on the other. It is even greater when we recall that an unknown but sizeable percentage of Tartars were in fact white. "No ethnicity" is included in this table because these slaves were likely to be whites born in Genoa. Their average age is in line, and their high price appears to validate the assumption about their ethnicity.

After 1453 and the curtailing of supplies from the East, slaves became more expensive in Genoa, as the table shows. Only one Russian slave was sold after 1456 when slaves were reaching their highest prices, and this accounts for why the average Russian price was not even higher. To compete

81. Ibid., p. 449.
82. Ibid., table on p. 450.

Table 2. Women Slaves in Genoa by Ethnicity and Price, 15–30 Years Old

	1400–1453			1453–1500	
	Average Price (L)	Average Age		Average Price (L)	Average Age
			Moors[a] (46)	148.5	22.5
			All Moors (51)	152.2	22.6
Tartars (69)	105.6	21.9	Tartars (8)	120.0	26.5
Bulgarians (16)	111.1	21.2	Bulgarians (13)	176.9	20.8
Circassians (50)	117.1	21.2	Circassians (61)	188.1	23.3
Russians (92)	124.4	21.5	Russians (40)	176.9	23.0
Abkhazians (31)	133.2	21.3	Abkhazians (31)	184.1	23.7
			Bosnians and Serbs (33)	229.6	21.1
No Ethnicity (11)	142.7	21.6	No Ethnicity (7)	191.4	27.4

Source: D. Gioffrè, Il mercato degli schiavi a Genova nel secolo XV (Genoa, 1971), register in appendix.
[a] Excluding those named as whites.

with the tighter supplies and higher prices of Eastern slaves, Moors, this time mainly from North Africa, were again imported into the city. This category included women of various colors, so I have excluded the five explicitly called white (and there were doubtless whites whose color was not specified) to show just how strongly color was affecting the prices of these slaves. The average ages were still roughly similar, except for the significantly higher ages of the few Tartars, now in short supply, and the slightly younger Bulgarians, an anomaly. The other Eastern slaves appear just a bit older—perhaps a sign that the top of the market was going elsewhere. Price differences are of course striking. Another new type of slave in Genoa, the Bosnian and Serbian women caught up in enslavements accompanying the Ottoman advances in the Balkans, was highly prized and costly, as this type also was in Venice, which was closer to the sources of supply. These women cost about 50 percent more than the Moorish women *of the same age*, a significant premium that must have had a reason behind it. (Tartar slaves appear cheaper because they disappeared before the big price increases later in the century.) Demand for slaves was still able to pull Circassian, Russian, and Abkhazian slaves to Genoa through trade routes now dominated by others, but by century's end some of these slaves fetched more than 300 lire, a huge sum. Black African slaves were still quite rare in Genoa in the fifteenth century (only eight on record), and this fact suggests that racism was playing an even stronger role in the north of Italy in the decision to buy a slave.

This is the world Columbus grew up in and where he learned his trades. When he sailed around Hispaniola in 1498 and estimated that the island could export four thousand slaves a year, he drew on centuries of collective experience about the economics of slavery.[83] When he wrote that they would die at first, as the blacks did, he revealed special knowledge of the lethal conditions aboard slave ships. He may have even believed that they could be sold in Genoa, perhaps for around the price of a Tartar. All the conditions for a language of a Great Economy were already in place, but the irony was that it may have rejected slavery in Italy not because of moral qualms about having slaves, but simply because of the color and type of slaves the market was capable of supplying. And of course there were a great many local poor people available anyway—as white as any Bosnian, and cheap enough into the bargain.

83. For details on Columbus and slavery, see Epstein, *Genoa and the Genoese*, pp. 310–11.

CONCLUSION

A vision experienced by a French priest celebrating his first Mass in Paris on 28 January 1193 was transformed by Italian artisans into the remarkable mosaic still gracing the facade of San Tommaso in Formis in Rome (see color plate). The priest, Jean de Matha, probably a Provençal, raised his eyes toward heaven and beheld a majestical Jesus holding in his hands two men, one black and deformed, the other thin and pale.[1] The priest, aware of how Christian prisoners languished in Muslim hands—a subject especially vexing to Christian Europe since the defeat of the Crusader states at Hattin in 1187—found his life's work in rescuing these captives. Jean quickly received strong support from Pope Innocent III, and he went on to establish the Trinitarian Order of the Church, whose special missions were to care for the poor and sick in Europe, and to ransom people from the Muslims. Jean went to Rome, and the pope granted the new order property and the church of San Tommaso, where the founder was buried in 1213. The mosaic, portraying the guiding inspiration for Jean's mission, was completed around 1210, so he lived to see the words describing his vision become real in the work of the Trinitarians as well as in the mosaic. Jean's accomplishments contributed two enduring themes to the language of Italian slavery: an order of the Church, and a mosaic that has helped generations of Romans and other Italians to think about black and white, slave and free, down to the present day.

The Trinitarian Order's international activities focused on the religious frontiers in Spain and the Holy Land, and apart from Rome, its earliest

---

1. I. Marchionni, *Note sulla storia delle origini dell'ordine della SS. Trinità* (Rome, 1973), pp. 321–23, for the anonymous record of this occurrence; the relevant passage here is: "Qui vero, cum oculos in celum erigeret, vidit majestatem Dei et Deum tenentem in manibus suis duos viros habentes cathenas in tibiis, quorum unus niger et deformis apparuit, alter macer et pallidus." This book is good on the early history of the order and has an edition of all the early documents. I am grateful to the Trinitarian Order for permission to reproduce the mosaic.

Mosaic, San Tommaso in Formis Rome.
Courtesy of the Trinitarian Order.

convents in Italy were not established until the late sixteenth century—Naples in 1560, Genoa in 1569, and Palermo in 1581, among others.[2] In the centuries before these foundations the Italian cities, states, and churches had been securing the release of captives by treaty, payment, or exchange. The Ottoman victories in the sixteenth century certainly gave the Trinitarians more reasons to be active in Italy itself, and also prompted, as we have seen, Genoa and other states to take a more bureaucratic approach to the problem of captives. The continuing work of the Trinitarians, and of other orders, relates in two ways to our understanding of slavery in its broadest context. First, the order divided its income into thirds, using one part for its convents, the second part for helping the poor, and the third part for rescuing captives. That the order itself equated the poor at home and captives abroad as equally charitable causes sustains the view in Chapter 4 that the poor and slaves need to be studied together, provided we can make a connection between captivity and servitude.

Of course language in context provides the key. Captivity results from an act of violence that takes a person out of an orderly world and thrusts him or her into a state of disorder.[3] This perspective on captivity is from the point of view of the home society; in the Muslim world the process of capturing people for ransom or slavery was an orderly, purposeful activity, as was the slave trade in Italy. Slavery, however, was a state of order, once one overlooked the violence behind it, because the purpose of slavery was to create a permanent condition of subordination, subject only to the master's whims. Hence in Italy slavery was normal, though maintained by force, and the slaves were not thought of as captives to be ransomed, but as chattels to remain enslaved until death unless their owners manumitted them. An Italian captive languishing in the East or North Africa, in contrast, was a victim of violence who should be rescued. In Giulio Cipollone's neat formulation—a captive is in the hands of an enemy and can be ransomed, a slave is in the hands of a master and can be sold or freed. Cipollone's sense of the orderliness of slavery results from passing over the forces of the surround needed to begin and maintain the system, but oblivion accurately reflects the mindset that establishes the "Other" with special rules (slaves in Italy) while seeing the brethren (Italian captives/slaves abroad) in quite a different light.

2. Ibid., pp. 237–38. For a valuable study of a medieval order devoted to the same activities, see James William Brodman, *Rescuing Captives in Crusader Spain: The Order of Merced on the Christian Islamic Frontier* (Philadelphia, 1986).

3. See Giulio Cipollone, *Cristianità-Islam: Cattività e liberazione in nome di Dio* (Rome, 1996), pp. 157–58 for what follows, but I have changed some of the terms and emphasis.

The fates of these Italians held abroad from the twelfth through the eighteenth century ranged from captivity while awaiting ransom to permanent slavery. The Trinitarians could not rescue everyone, nor could other charitable enterprises. People understood this, and constructed a discourse on captivity and slavery that permitted keeping enslaved Christians, not to mention Muslims and Jews, at home, while seeing Muslims doing the same thing to Christians in their states as something needing to be set right. Hence the mosaic at San Tommaso also makes vivid the kind of cognitive dissonance needed to sustain slavery in some contexts and fight it in others.

Jean's vision was not Italian in origin, but it became local when the mosaic masters made it possible for everyone in Rome to see it. The mosaic is centered on Jesus (133.5 centimeters); on his left stands the black captive/slave (74.5 centimeters), and on his right is the white captive, just a bit taller at 76 centimeters.[4] Jesus' right hand holds the white man by his right forearm, and the captive carries a cross in his left hand. The white person, exactly the same color as Jesus and dressed simply in drawers, has a set of chains or manacles on his feet that have been loosened, and the end of the chain goes to Jesus' feet—showing the ultimate source of the white captive's freedom.[5] The black prisoner is a puzzling presence in Jean's vision and this mosaic. The white captive has a detailed face; the black one has a featureless face except for a dot as an eye and a small slit of a mouth. As in Jean's vision, the white captive is thin and the black one burly in the upper body and somewhat deformed in appearance. Jesus holds in his left hand, the dirty one of insult, the black prisoner's left forearm. The black captive holds in his right hand a long object that Cipollone sensibly identifies as a whip.[6] Chains still bind the black's feet. He is not freed, but what is he doing in this mosaic?

The Trinitarians were not mainly in the business of exchanging prisoners, and it would be a mistake to see Jesus presiding over an exchange. God, through the order's work, breaks the chains on the white and frees him. The black, still manacled to sin or an infidel creed, holds the whip and must be

4. Giulio Cipollone, *Il mosaico di S. Tommaso in Formis a Roma (ca. 1210)* (Rome, 1984), p. 97 for dimensions.

5. Giulio Cipollone, "Il dopo guerra santa: Cattività e liberazione," in *Verso Gerusalemme*, ed. Franco Cardini et al. (Lecce, 1999), pp. 245–71, here p. 267—where Cipollone still stresses that the chains of the white captive are loosened and stretch toward the feet of his Redeemer.

6. Ibid. Cipollone has consistently identified the object in the black's hand as a whip, and it is difficult to see what else it might be.

the captor whom Jesus now holds or commands. There is no way that Jesus is setting the black free. The captive is deep black, a type seldom seen in Paris or Rome around 1210. He represents the evil from which the white captive deserves to be liberated. The black also represents the legitimately enslaved. In the early thirteenth century most slaves in northern and southern Italy were Moors from Spain or North Africa, or indigenous Sicilian Muslims. They were all perhaps darker than most Italians, but only a few were quite dark, and none actually as black as our captive on the front of San Tommaso in Formis. And yet the black captive stands as a harbinger of slavery's future in the wider world, though not so much in Italy, where we have seen some sub-Saharan blacks in sixteenth century Sicily, but also white slaves—Hungarians, Circassians, and others, all present down to the end of slavery.

The Trinitarians also apparently used some of their resources to purchase pagan captives to exchange for Christian ones. Hence another possible explanation is plausible and the mosaic may reflect this very act: liberating a white for a black still chained, who is perhaps to be freed by his own people, though this is not the order's concern. Whatever the black captive is holding in his right hand, especially if it is a whip, and his deformed appearance, remain serious problems for this interpretation. Jean de Matha never explained what he saw, at least in the surviving records, so we are left with the ambiguities of captive and slave, of rescue and enslavement, the grey zone on the boundaries of the language of slavery. Black and white seem clear enough in the mosaic, if not in language.

The Tuscan version of Marco Polo's book on his travels, written down in the trecento, describes an unusual custom on the Coromandel coast of India. Indian boys and girls were born black, and people oiled themselves to become even blacker "because in that country the one who is more black is more esteemed."[7] These Indians also painted their gods black and their demons white as snow. The tone of the passage suggests that only in a topsy-turvy place might this be so.

In exploring the power of scientific and racial ideas to shape the fate of Italy's Jews and its scientific community, Giorgio Israel and Pietro Nastasi worried, as have others, that the sentiments of religious or racial hatred remain the same across history, and what changes is merely the language used

7. Marco Polo, *Milione*, ed. Valeria Bertolucci Pizzorusso (Milan, 1994) p. 266: "ché in quella contrada quello ch'è più nero è più pregiato." For present purposes, the reliability of Polo's account does not matter—the issue is language about color.

to express these views.[8] Perhaps the commonplace distinction between the religious-inspired prejudices of the Middle Ages and the scientific, racist sociology and anthropology of the modern era is simply an issue of how hate and oppression are packaged in words. These are complex questions upon which reasonable people differ, but this book is based on the premise that changes in language, the power to use and shape words, are the fundamentals of history. Sentiments, however destructive, must be expressed in language to have their effect. Even race hatred, or slavery, requires the meaningful function of language in order not only to move from the thought to the deed, but of course even to form the thought in the first place. The people under study in this book used language to shape the rules regarding slavery. Being or owning a slave were behaviors learned through the use of words in contexts ranging from contracts to defenses of slavery. Markets were places where people used language to merchandise people, among other things. Whether as consumers, jurists, theologians, or so-called bystanders, the Italian people used the language of slavery for many centuries, and in turn this language informs us about the context that gave birth and continued life to one style of slavery.

It is also important to be clear that this book has explored the language of slavery in Italy in a world where the Italian contribution to slavery has been in global terms rather insignificant. Far from being a reason to neglect to study slavery and its language in Italy, this very marginality has enabled us to see some wider issues from a fresh perspective of a people not prominent in modern colonialism, but with some role, via Cesare Lombroso and others, in propagating modern racism. No white American is entitled to pass blame off to the Italians in these two matters, and it has not been my intention in any case to be an arbiter of morality. Instead, I have written about a major issue in world history, slavery, from a different perspective, Italy. I conclude by offering in general terms what the broader Western experience has to offer other cultures struggling with their roles in the history of slavery.

Long ago people took prisoners and thought that sparing these unfortunates justified enslaving them on the grounds that they had forfeited liberty and could cheat death only through the generosity of their captors. Roman law embodies the spirit of such a culture. Aristotle thought that some people were slaves by their own natures, that they were born to be enslaved, but the ancient consensus held that slavery resulted from bad luck and did not

8. Giorgio Israel and Pietro Nastasi, *Scienza e razza nell'Italia fascista* (Bologna, 1998), p. 60 (relying on the work of Léon Poliakov).

necessarily reflect badly on the slave's character. After all, anyone might become a slave through honorable defeat or capture, and no one chose to be born a slave. The ancient Hebrews generally shared the pagan attitudes on slavery except for the Essenes who rejected the practice altogether. Yet the Hebrews, who enslaved their own coreligionists for debt, believed that their brethren should be regularly released from bondage and treated with exceptional mildness while in it. Early Christian writers like Saint Paul did not obligate masters to free their Christian slaves, but they too argued for leniency in this life and salvation for all, slave and free, in the next. Saint Augustine was one of the thinkers who began to explain slavery for some as the result of human sinfulness. The idea that slaves deserved their fates because of sin, either their own or their share of humanity's collective guilt, had a long and terrible sequel in Western history. But this belief was a choice not dictated by scriptural authority or the words of Jesus, as was Augustine's view that slaves had to wait until the end of all injustice for their own claims for justice to merit redress. Saint Thomas Aquinas rejected the idea of natural slaves and chose to stress force rather than sin as the power behind slavery. For Aquinas, slavery resulted from its usefulness under the law of nations, and existed by human agreement, not by natural law. Yet by the end of the Middle Ages, at least one prominent thinker, Sant' Antonino of Florence, had concluded that divine law itself sanctioned the practice of slavery, and he was prepared to use both Hebrew scripture and the New Testament to support the legitimacy of slavery in the fifteenth century.

And so there is a kind of declension, from bad luck to sin to force as evolving, overlapping, even mutually confirming explanations for slavery. After all one could easily believe that it was bad fortune for a particular sinner in a world of sin to be coerced into slavery by other sinners. Ethnicity or color came to be a proxy for bad luck. It was bad luck to be a Moor captured in Spain or a Tartar sold to the Genoese in Caffa. In more complex ways color also became a proxy for sin itself, as people came to believe that belonging to certain ethnic groups, or even being a particular color, justified enslavement. So, from bad luck to sin to force to color—the history and language of slavery in a nutshell.

SELECTED BIBLIOGRAPHY

The bibliography on slavery is enormous, and most of this vast literature treats Italian slavery only in passing. What follows is a list of the main works used here, which are in turn a comprehensive guide to the wider literature.

MANUSCRIPTS
Genoa
  Biblioteca Universitaria di Genova
    Avvisi di Genova, no. 27, 19 July 1797
    Gazzetta nazionale genovese, no. 5, 15 July 1797
    Giornale degli amici del popolo no. 15, 17 July 1797
  Archivio di Stato di Genova
    Cartolari Notarili
    Cart. N. 4, Lanfranco et al.
    Cart. N. 8, Parentino de Quinto
    Cart. N. 18, pt. 2, Giannino de Predono
    Cart. N. 24, pt. 1, Bonovassallo de Cassino
    Cart. N. 26, pt. 2, Bartolomeo de Fornari
    Cart. N. 27, Bartolomeo de Fornari
    Cart. N. 31, pt. 1, Matteo de Predono
    Cart. N. 55, pt. 2, Azone de Clavica
    Cart. N. 138, Conrado de Castello de Rapallo
    Cart. N. 167, Lanfranco de Nazario
    Cart. N. 168, Lanfranco de Nazario
    Cart. N. 169, Lanfranco de Nazario
    Cart. N. 242, Predono de Pignolo
    Cart, N. 253, Zinetto de Porta
    Cart. N. 287, Benvenuto de Bracelli
    Cart. N. 288, Benvenuto de Bracelli
    Cart. N. 289, Benvenuto de Bracelli
    Cart. N. 290, Benvenuto de Bracelli
    Cart. N. 293, Benvenuto de Bracelli
    Cart. N. 294, Benvenuto de Bracelli
    Cart. N. 295, Benvenuto de Bracelli

Magistrato delle arti, Busta 178
Società ligure di Storia Patria, Palazzo Ducale
  Pamphlet collection
  Carte Staglieno 331
Munich
Bayerische Staatsbibliotek, Nr. 14056. Huguccio of Pisa, *Derivationes*.
Vatican City
Archivio Segreto Vaticano, Segreteria di Stato
  Anno 1903, Rubrica 204
  Anno 1907, Rubrica 204
  Anno 1921, Rubrica 12

PUBLISHED PRIMARY SOURCES

Acta Curie Felicis Urbis Panormi. Vol. 5, *Registri di lettere ed atti (1328–1333)*. Edited by Pietro Corrao. Palermo, 1986.

Alfieri, Vittorio. *Vita*. Edited by Giampaolo Dossena. Turin, 1967.

Antonino, archbishop of Florence, Saint. *Summa Theologica*. Vol. 3. Verona, 1740; facsimile ed., Graz, 1959.

Aristotle. *Politics Books 1–2*. Translated by Trevor J. Saunders. Oxford, 1995.

Atti del quarto congresso nazionale della Società Antischiavista d'Italia (Decembre 1926). Rome, 1927.

Augustine of Hippo, Saint. *The City of God*. Translated by Henry Bettenson. Harmondsworth, 1972.

——*De civitate dei*. 2 vols. Turnholt, 1955.

Azo. *Summa Aurea*. Lyon, 1557; facsimile ed., Frankfurt, 1968.

Balbi, Giovanna. *L'epistolario di Iacopo Bracelli*. Genoa, 1969.

Balbus, Johannes (Balbi, Giovanni). *Catholicon*. Mainz, 1460.

Bandello, Matteo. *Tutte le opere di Matteo di Bandello*. Edited by Francesco Flora. Verona, 1943.

Basile, Giambattista. *Il pentamerone*. Edited and translated by Benedetto Croce. Bari, 1957.

Beccaria, Cesare. *Dei delitti e delle pene*. Edited by Franco Venturi. Turin, 1965.

Belgrano, Luigi T. "Cartario genovese ed illustrazione del registro arcivescovile." *Atti della Società Ligure di Storia Patria* 2 pt 1 (1870).

Bernardo de Rodulfis: Notaio in Venezia (1392–1399). Edited by Giorgio Tamba. Venice, 1974.

Boccaccio, Giovanni. *Decameron*. Edited by Vittorio Branca. 3d ed. Milan, 1996.

Bonaini, Francesco. *Statuti inediti della città di Pisa dal XII al XV secolo*. 3 vols. Florence, 1854–70.

Bosco, Bartolomeo de. *Consilia egregii domini Bartolomei de Bosco Famosissimi iuris consulti genuensis*. Edited by Gian Francesco Senarega. Loano, 1620.

Bugarella, Pietro. *Le imbreviature del notaio Adamo de Citella a Palermo (1 registro 1286–1287)*. Rome, 1981.

Capitula Regni Siciliae. Edited by Francesco Testa. Palermo, 1741.

Carletti, Giuseppe. *Vita di S. Benedetto da S. Filadelfo*. Rome, 1805.

Carletti, Tommaso. *I problemi del Benadir*. Viterbo, 1912.

Cavazzi, G. A. *Istorica descrizione de' tre regni Congo, Matamba, et Angola*. Bologna, 1687.

Chiaudano, Mario. *Oberto Scriba de Mercato 1186*. Turin, 1940.

Chiaudano, Mario, and R. M. della Rocca. *Oberto Scriba de Mercato 1190*. Turin, 1938.

Chiaudano, Mario, and Mattia Moresco. *Il cartolare di Giovanni Scriba*. 2 vols. Rome, 1935.

Codex Theodosianus. Edited by Theodor Mommsen. Dublin, 1970.

Codice diplomatico barese, Le Pergamene di S. Nicola di Bari. Vols 4 and 5. Edited by Francesco Nitti di Vito. Bari, 1900, 1902.

Corpus Iuris Civilis. Vol. 1, *Digesta*. Edited by P. Krueger and T. Mommsen. Dublin, 1973.

Cristóbal Colon: Textos y documentos completos. Edited by Consuela Varela and Juan Gil. Madrid, 1992.

Dante Alighieri. *La Divina Commedia*, Edited by C. H. Grandgent and Charles Singleton. Cambridge, Mass., 1972.

D'Aranda, Emanuel. *The History of Algiers and it's Slavery with Many Remarkable Particularities of Africk*. Translated by John Davies. London, 1666.

Della Porta, Giovan Battista. *Dell'fisionomia dell'uomo*. Edited by Mario Cicognani. Parma, 1988.

Egidi, Pietro. *Codice diplomatico dei saraceni di Lucera*. Naples, 1917.

Fonte Ricciane. Edited by Pasquale D'Elia. Rome, 1942.

Gramsci, Antonio. *Quaderni del carcere*. Turin, 1975.

Gulotta, Pietro. *Le imbreviature del notaio Adamo de Citella a Palermo (2 registro 1298–1299)*. Rome, 1982.

Hall, Margaret, Hilmar C. Krueger, and Robert L. Reynolds. *Guglielmo Cassinese*. Turin, 1938

Leges Genuenses: Historiae Patriae Monumenta. Edited by Cornelio Desimoni and Luigi T. Belgrano. Vol 18. Turin, 1901.

Leges Langobardorum. Monumenta Germaniae Historica, Leges, vol. 4. Edited by G. H. Pertz. Hanover, 1868.

Leopardi, Giacomo. *Tutte le opere di Giacomo Leopardi*. Vol. 1, *Zibaldone di pensieri*. Edited by Francesco Flora. Milano, 1953.

Liagre-De Sturler, Léone. *Les relations commerciales entre Gênes, La Belgique et L'Outremont*. 2 vols. Brussels, 1969.

Limor, Ora. *Die Disputationen zu Ceuta (1179) und Mallorca (1286)*. MGH, Quellen zur Geistesgeschichte des Mittelalters, vol. 15. Munich, 1994.

Manetta, Filippo. *La razza nera nel suo stato selvaggio in Africa e nella sua duplice con-dizione di emancipata e di schiava in America*. Turin, 1864.

Manzoni, Alessandro. *I promessi sposi*. Translated by Bruce Penman. Harmonds-worth, 1972.

Mazzini, Giuseppe. *Scritti editi e inediti di Giuseppe Mazzini.* Vols. 29, 30. Imola, 1919.

McKee, Sally. *Wills from Late Medieval Venetian Crete 1312–1420.* 3 vols. Washington, D.C., 1998.

Montaigne, Michel de. *Travel Journal.* Translated by Donald Frame. San Francisco, 1983.

Morelli, Giovanni di Pagolo. *Ricordi.* Edited by Vittore Branca. Florence, 1969.

Papias Vocabulista. *Elementarium doctrine rudimentum.* Venice, 1496.

Petrarca, Francesco. *Le Familiari.* Edited by Vittorio Rossi. 4 vols. Florence, 1933–42.

Petrarch, Francis. *Letters of Old Age: Rerum senilium libri I–XVIII.* Translated by Aldo S. Bernardo, Saul Levin, and Reta A. Bernardo. 2 vols. Baltimore, 1992.

Powell, James M. *Liber Augustalis.* Syracuse, N.Y., 1971.

Polo, Marco. *Milione.* Edited by Valeria Bertolucci Pizzorusso. Milan, 1994.

Prochiron legum. Edited by F. Brandileone and V. Puntoni. Fonti per la storia d'Italia, vol. 30. Rome, 1895.

Promis, Vincenzo. "Statuti della colonia genovese di Pera." *Miscellanea di storia d'Italia* 11 (1871): 513–780.

Prunai, Giulio. "Notizie e documenti sulla servitù domestica nel territorio senese (secc. VIII–XVI)." *Bulletino senese di storia patria* 7 (1936): 133–82, 245–98, 398–438.

Robecchi-Brichetti, Luigi. *Dal Benadir: Lettere illustrate alla Società Antischiavista d'Italia.* Milano, 1904.

Sacchetti, Franco. *La battaglia delle belle donne, le lettere, le sposizioni di vangeli.* Edited by Alberto Chiari. Bari, 1938.

———. *I sermoni evangelici, le lettere ed altri scritti inediti o rari.* Edited by Ottavio Gigli. Florence, 1857.

Scritti politici dell'Ottocento. Vol. 1. Edited by Franco della Peruta. Milan, 1969.

Sorrentino, Giorgio. *Ricordi di Benadir.* Naples, 1912.

Spathaphora, Bartolomeo. *Quatro orationi.* Venice, 1554.

Statuta et decreta communis Genuae. Edited by Antonio Maria Visdomini. Bologna, 1498.

Statuto dei padri del comune della repubblica genovese. Edited by Cornelio Desimoni, Genoa, 1885.

Strozzi, Alessandra Macinghi. *Lettere di una gentildonna fiorentina del secolo XV ai figliuoli esuli.* Florence, 1877.

Thomas Aquinas, Saint. *Summa Theologica.* 4 vols. Rome, 1923.

Tria, Luigi. "La schiavitù in Liguria." *Atti della Società Ligure di Storia Patria* 70 (1947).

Varagine, Jacopo de. *Iacopo da Varagine: Cronaca della città di Genova dalle origini al 1297.* Edited by Stefania Bertini Guidetti. Genoa, 1995,

Voragine, Jacopo de. *The Golden Legend: Readings on the Saints.* Translated by William Granger Ryan. 2 vols. Princeton, N.J., 1993.

Vidulich, Paola Ratti. *Duca di Candia: Quaternus Consiliorum (1340–1350).* Venice, 1976.

Vigna, Amedeo. "Codice diplomatico delle colonie tauro-ligure." *Atti della Società Ligure di Storia Patria* 7, pt. 2 (1879).

SECONDARY WORKS

Abulafia, David. *Frederick II: A Medieval Emperor*. Oxford, 1988.

——. *A Mediterranean Emporium: The Catalan kingdom of Majorca*. Cambridge, 1994.

Angiolini, Franco. "Schiave." In *Storie delle donne in Italia: Il lavoro delle donne*, edited by Angela Groppi, pp. 92–115. Bari, 1996.

Aymard, Maurice. "De la traite aux chiourmes: La fin de l'esclavage dans la Sicilie moderne." *Bulletin de L'Institut historique belge de Rome* 44 (1974): 1–21.

Backman, Clifford. *The Decline and Fall of Medieval Sicily*. Cambridge, 1995.

Balard, Michel. "Remarques sur les esclaves à Gênes dans la seconde moitié du XIIIe siècle." *Mélanges d'archeologie et d'histoire* 70 (1968): 627–80.

Balbi, Giovanna. "La schiavitù a Genova tra i secoli XII e XIII." In *Mélanges offerts à René Crozet*, edited by P. Gallais and Y.-J. Riou, pp. 1025–29. Poitiers, 1966.

Ball, Edward. *Slaves in the Family*. New York, 1998.

Belgrano, Luigi T. *Della vita privata dei genovesi*. Genoa, 1875.

Bellomo, Manlio. *The Common Legal Past of Europe 1000–1800*. Translated by Lydia Cochrane. Washington, D.C., 1995.

Berry, Wendell. *What Are People For?* New York, 1990.

——. *Home Economics*. New York, 1984.

Blackburn, Robert. *The Making of New World Slavery*. London, 1997.

Bonaffini, Giuseppe. *La Sicilia e i Barbareschi: Incursioni corsare e riscatto degli schiavi (1570–1606)*. Palermo, 1983.

Bongi, Salvatore. "Le schiave orientali in Italia." *Nuova antologia di scienze, lettere ed arti* 2 (1866): 215–46.

Boswell, John. *The Kindness of Strangers*. New York, 1988.

Bradley, Keith. *Slavery and Society at Rome*. Cambridge, 1994.

Bresc, Henri. "Esclaves auliques et main-d'oeuvre servile agricole dans la Sicile des XIIe et XIIIe siècles." In *Figures de l'esclave au Moyen-Age et dans le monde moderne*, edited by Henri Bresc, pp. 97–114. Paris, 1996.

——. *Un monde méditerranéen: Economie et société en Sicile 1300–1450*. 2 vols. Rome, 1986.

Brodman, James William. *Ransoming Captives in Crusader Spain: The Order of Merced on the Christian-Islamic Frontier*. Philadelphia, 1986.

Brown, Peter. *The Body and Society: Men, Women, and Sexual Renunciation in Early Christianity*. New York, 1988.

Brundage, James A. *Medieval Canon Law*. London, 1996.

Burkert, Walter. *Creation of the Sacred: Tracks of Biology in Early Religions*. Cambridge, Mass., 1996.

Bush, M. L., ed. *Slavery & Serfdom: Studies in Legal Bondage*. London, 1996.

Campe, Rüdiger, and Manfred Schneider. *Geschichten der Physiognomik*. Freiburg im Breisgau, 1996.

Chirichigno, Gregory. *Debt-Slavery in Israel and the Ancient Near East*. Sheffield, 1993.

Cipollone, Giulio. "Il dopo guerra santa: cattività e liberazione (1099/492H–1187/583H)." In *Verso Gerusalemme; II Convegno Internazionale nel IX Centenario della I Crociata (1099–1999)*, edited by Franco Cardini, M. Belloli, and B. Vetere, pp. 245–71. Lecce, 1999.

———. *Cristianità-Islam: Cattività e liberazione in nome di Dio*. Rome, 1996.

———. *Mosaico di S. Tommaso in Formis a Roma (ca. 1210)*. Rome, 1984.

Combs, I. A. H. *The Metaphor of Slavery in the Writings of the Early Church*. Sheffield, 1998.

Constable, Giles. *Three Studies in Medieval Religious and Social Thought*. Cambridge, 1995.

Constable, Olivia Remie. "Muslim Spain and Mediterranean Slavery: The Medieval Slave Trade as an Aspect of Muslim-Christian Relations." In *Christendom and its discontents*, edited by Scott Waugh and Peter D. Diehl, pp. 264–84. Cambridge, 1996.

D'Amia, Amerigo. *Schiavitù romana e servitù medievale*. Milan, 1931.

Davis, David Brion. *Slavery and Human Progress*. New York, 1984.

Delort, Robert. "Quelques précisions sur le commerce des esclaves à Gênes vers la fin du XIVe siecle." *Mélanges d'archéologie et d'histoire* 77 (1966): 215–50.

Dennis, T. J. "The Relationship Between Gregory of Nyssa's Attack on Slavery in His Fourth Homily on Ecclesiastes and His Treatise *De Hominis Opificio*." *Studia Patristica* 17 (1982): 1065–72.

Egidi, Pietro. *La colonia saracena di Lucera e la sua distruzione*. Naples, 1912.

Epstein, Steven A. *Genoa and the Genoese 958–1528*. Chapel Hill, N.C., 1996.

———. "A Late Medieval Lawyer Confronts Slavery: The Cases of Bartolomeo de Bosco." *Slavery and Abolition* 20 (1999): 49–68.

———. "The Medieval Family: A Place of Refuge and Sorrow." In *Portraits of Medieval and Renaissance Living: Essays in Memory of David Herlihy*, edited by Samuel K. Cohn, Jr., and Steven A. Epstein. pp. 149–71. Ann Arbor, Mich., 1996.

———. *Wage Labor and Guilds in Medieval Europe*. Chapel Hill, N.C., 1991.

———. "The Theory and Practice of the Just Wage." *Journal of Medieval History* 17 (1991): 53–69.

Evans, Daniel. "Slave Coast of Europe." *Slavery and Liberation* 6 (1985): 41–58.

Fabbrini, Fabrizio. *La Manumissio in Ecclesia*. Milan, 1965.

Ferrara, Mario. "Linguaggio di schiave del quattrocento." *Studi di filologia italiana* 8 (1950): 320–28.

Fogel, Robert William. *Without Consent or Contract: The Rise and Fall of American Slavery*. New York, 1989.

Freedman, Paul. *Images of the Medieval Peasant*. Stanford, Calif., 1999.

Friedman, Ellen G. *Spanish Captives in North Africa in the Early Modern Age*. Madison, Wis., 1983.

Garnsey, Peter. *Ideas of Slavery from Aristotle to Augustine*. Cambridge, 1996.

Gaudioso, Matteo. *La schiavitù domestica in Sicilia dopo i normanni*. Catania, 1926.

Gavitt, Philip. *Charity and Children in Renaissance Florence: The Ospedale degli Innocenti, 1410–1536*. Ann Arbor, Mich., 1990.

Genovese, Eugene D. *Roll, Jordan, Roll: The World the Slaves Made*. New York, 1976.

Gioffrè, Domenico. *Il mercato degli schiavi a Genova nel secolo XV*. Genoa, 1971.

Goglia, Luigi. "Note sul razzismo coloniale fascista." *Storia Contemporanea* 19 (1988): 1223–66.

Goglia, Luigi, and Fabio Grassi. *Il colonialismo italiano da Adua all'impero*. 2d ed. Rome, 1993.

Gould, Stephen J. *The Mismeasure of Man*. New York, 1981.

Grant, Ruth W. *Hypocrisy and Integrity: Machiavelli, Rousseau, and the Ethics of Politics*. Chicago, 1997.

Greenidge, C. W. W. *Slavery*. London, 1958.

Grendi, Edoardo. *La repubblica aristocratica dei genovesi*. Bologna, 1987.

Guardacci, Piero, and Valeria Ottanelli. *I servatori domestici della casa borghese toscana nel basso medioevo*. Florence, 1982.

Hall, Kim F. *Things of Darkness: Economies of Race and Gender in Early Modern England*. Ithaca, 1995.

Harding, Vincent. *There Is a River: The Black Struggle for Freedom in America*. New York, 1981.

Heers, Jacques. *Esclaves et domestiques au Moyen Age dans le monde mediterranée*. Paris, 1981.

———. *Gênes au XVe siècle*. Paris, 1961.

Herlihy, David. *Pisa in the Early Renaissance*. New Haven, Conn., 1958.

———. "Tuscan Names 1200–1530." *Renaissance Quarterly* 41 (1988): 561–82.

Herlihy, David and Christiane Klapisch-Zuber. *Les Toscans et leurs familles*. Paris, 1978.

Hess, Robert L. *Italian Colonialism in Somalia*. Chicago, 1966.

Israel, Giorgio, and Pietro Nastasi. *Scienza e razza nell'Italia fascista*. Bologna, 1998.

Jensen, Lionel. *Manufacturing Confucianism: Chinese Traditions and Universal Civilization*. Durham, N.C., 1997.

Jordan, Winthrop. *The White Man's Burden*. Oxford, 1974.

Kahane, Henry, and Renée Kahane. "Notes on the Linguistic History of *Sclavus*." in *Studi in onore di Ettore Lo Gatto e Giovanni Maver*, pp. 345–60. Florence, 1962.

Kedar, Benjamin Z. *Crusade and Mission: European Attitudes toward the Muslims*. Princeton, N.J., 1984.

———. *Merchants in Crisis: Genoese and Venetian Men of Affairs and the Fourteenth-Century Depression*. New Haven, Conn., 1976.

———. "On the Origins of the Earliest Laws of Frankish Jerusalem: The Canons of the Council of Nablus, 1120." *Speculum* 74 (1999): 310–35.

Kelly, J. N. D. *Golden Mouth: The Story of John Chrysostom*. Ithaca, 1995.

Kertzer, David I. *The Kidnapping of Edgardo Mortara*. New York, 1997.

Krekič, Bariša. "Contributo allo studio degli schiavi levantini e balcanici a Venice (1388–1398)." *Studi in memoria de Federigo Melis*, 2:379–94. Naples, 1978.

Landman, Janet. *Regret: The Persistence of the Possible*. New York, 1993.

Langholm, Odd. *The Legacy of Scholasticism in Economic Thought*. Cambridge, 1998.

Le Goff, Jacques. *Your Money or Your Life: Economy and Religion in the Middle Ages*. Translated by Patricia Ranum. New York, 1990.

Lenci, Mario. *Lucca, il mare e i corsari barbareschi nel XVI secolo*. Lucca, 1987.

——. *Lucchesi nel Maghreb: Storie di schiavi, mercanti e missionari*. Lucca, 1994.

Levi, Primo. *Opere I*. Turin, 1987.

Levi Della Vida, Giorgio. "La corrispondenza di Berta di Toscana col Califfo Muktafi." *Rivista storica italiana* 66 (1954): 21–38.

Lewis, Bernard. *Race and Slavery in the Middle East*. Oxford, 1990.

Livi, Ridolfo. *La schiavitù domestica nei tempi di mezzo e nei tempi moderni*. Padua, 1928.

——. "La schiavitù medioevale e la sua influenza sui caratteri antropologici degli italiani." *Rivista italiana di sociologia* 11 (1907): 557–81.

Lombroso, Cesare. *L'uomo delinquente*. Rome, 1971.

——. *L'uomo bianco e l'uomo di colore*. Padua, 1871.

Lucchini, Enrica. *La merce umana: Schiavitù e riscatto dei liguri nel Seicento*. Rome, 1990.

Marchionni, I. *Note sulla storia delle origini dell'ordine della SS. Trinità*. Rome, 1973.

Marrone, Giovanni. *La schiavitù nella società siciliana dell'età moderna*. Caltanissetta, 1972.

Martin, Jean-Marie. *La Pouille du VIe au XIIe siècle*. Rome, 1993.

Meillasseaux, Claude. *The Anthropology of Slavery: The Womb of Iron and Gold*. Translated by A. Dasnois. Chicago, 1991.

Mey, Jacob L. *Pragmatics: An Introduction*. Oxford, 1993.

Molà, Luca. *La comunità dei lucchesi a Venezia: Immigrazione e industria della seta nel tardo medioevo*. Venice, 1994.

Morabito, Leo. *Il giornalismo giacobino genovese 1797–1799*. Turin, 1973.

Morazzoni, Giuseppe. *Mostra de le antiche stoffe genovesi dal secolo XV al secolo XIX*. Genova, 1941.

Morris, Thomas D. *Southern Slavery and the Law 1619–1860*. Chapel Hill, N.C., 1996.

Muir, Edward. *Civic Ritual in Renaissance Venice*. Princeton, N.J., 1981.

Müller, Wolfgang. *Huguccio: The Life, Works, and Thought of a Twelfth-Century Jurist*. Washington, D.C., 1994.

Musso, Gian Giacomo. *Navigazione e commercio genovese con il Levante nei documenti dell'Archivio di stato di Genova (secc. XIV–XV)*. Rome, 1975.

Niceforo, Alfredo. *La fisionomia nell'arte e nella scienza*. Florence, 1952.

——. *Forza e richezza: Studi della vita fisica ed economica delle classi sociali*. Turin, 1906.

Nirenberg, David. *Communities of Violence: Persecution of Minorities in the Middle Ages*. Princeton, N.J., 1996.

Ong, Walter J. *The Presence of the Word*. Minneapolis, 1981.

Origo, Iris. "The Domestic Enemy: The Eastern Slaves in Tuscany in the Four-teenth and Fifteenth Centuries." *Speculum* 30 (1955): 321–66.

Patterson, Orlando. *Slavery and Social Death*. Cambridge, Mass., 1982.

———. *The Sociology of Slavery*. Rutherford, N.J., 1969.

Peverada, Enrico. *Schiavi a Ferrara nel Quattrocento*. Ferrara, 1981.

Phillips, William D., Jr. *Slavery from Roman Times to the Early Transatlantic Trade*. Minneapolis, 1985.

Powelson, John P. *Centuries of Economic Endeavor*. Ann Arbor, Mich., 1994.

———. *The Moral Economy*. Ann Arbor, Mich., 1998.

Riddle, John M. *Contraception and Abortion from the Ancient World to the Renaissance*. Cambridge, Mass., 1992.

Ridolfi, Maria A. Ceppari, et al. *Schiave ribaldi e signori*. Siena, 1994.

Roccatagliata, Ausilia. "Notai genovesi in Oltremare: Atti rogati a Pera 1453." *Atti della Società Ligure di Storia Patria* 39 (1999): 101–60.

Romano, Dennis. *Housecraft and Statecraft: Domestic Service in Renaissance Venice 1400–1600*. Baltimore, 1996.

Ronco, Antonio. *Storia della Repubblica Ligure 1797–1799*. Genoa, 1988.

Ste Croix, G. E. M. de. *The Class Struggle in the Ancient Greek World from the Archaic Age to the Arab Conquests*. Ithaca, 1981.

Sen, Amartya. *Inequality Reexamined*. Cambridge, Mass., 1992.

Shorris, Earl. *New American Blues: A Journey Through Poverty to Democracy*. New York, 1997.

Smith, Adam. *The Theory of Moral Sentiments*. Indianapolis, 1984.

Smith, Dennis Mack. *Mazzini*. New Haven, Conn., 1994.

Steiner, George. *After Babel*. 2d ed. Oxford, 1992.

———. *Errata*. New York, 1997.

Stortoni, Laura Anna. *Women Poets of the Italian Renaissance: Courtly Ladies and Courtesans*. New York, 1997.

Tenenti, Alberto. "Gli schiavi di Venezia alla fine del Cinquecento." *Rivista storica italiana* 67 (1955): 52–69.

Thiriet, Freddy. *La Romanie vénitienne au moyen âge*. Paris, 1975.

Thornton, John K. *The Kongolese Saint Anthony: Dona Beatriz Kimpa Vita and the Antonian Movement, 1684–1706*. Cambridge, 1998.

Tollison, Robert, and Roger Congleton. *The Economic Analysis of Rent Seeking*. Aldershot, 1995.

Trexler, Richard C. *The Journey of the Magi: Meanings in History of a Christian Story*. Princeton, N.J., 1997.

Tullock, Gordon. *The Economy of Special Privilege and Rent Seeking*. Boston, 1989.

Vauchez, André. "Note sur l'esclavage et le changement de religion en Terre Sainte au XIIIe siècle." In *Figures de l'esclave au Moyen-Age et dans le monde moderne*, edited by Henri Bresc, pp. 91–6. Paris, 1996.

Veblen, Thorstein. *The Theory of the Leisure Class*. New York, 1967.

Verga, Ettore. "Per la storia degli schiavi orientali in Milano." *Archivio storico lombardo* 32 (1905): 188–95.

Verlinden, Charles. *L'esclavage dans L'Europe médiévale.* Vol 2. Ghent, 1977.

———. "L'origine de *sclavus = esclave.*" *Bulletin Du Cange* 17 (1943): 97–128.

Verschueren, Jef. *Understanding Pragmatics.* London, 1999

Watson, Alan. *Roman Slave Law.* Baltimore, 1987.

Williams, Bernard. *Shame and Necessity.* Berkeley, Calif., 1993.

Yule, Henry. *The Book of Ser Marco Polo.* 3 vols. London, 1929.

Zamboni, Filippo. *Gli Ezzelini, Dante e gli schiavi.* Rome, 1906.

Zazzu, Guido Nathan. *Sepharad addio: 1492: I profughi ebrei dalla Spagna al "ghetto" di Genova.* Genoa, 1991.

ACKNOWLEDGMENTS

I am grateful to the Rockefeller Foundation, which provided a residency in 1997 at Bellagio, where I began to write this book. I benefited there from good advice offered by my colleagues Jef Verschueren and Ed Muir. A faculty fellowship from the University of Colorado made this stay possible. Thanks to a Guggenheim Fellowship in 1998–99, I was able to complete a first draft of the book. During that year I received from the Bogliasco Foundation a residency at the Liguria Study Center for the Arts and Humanities. The wonderful atmosphere at Bogliasco made this stay near Genoa especially productive and rewarding. At Bogliasco, Peter Davison advised me on the first chapter and suggested the book's title.

I have been most fortunate to have received help and suggestions from astute readers. Paul Freedman, James B. Given, Gary Holthaus, Benjamin Z. Kedar, and Barbara Rosenwein greatly improved this book. I am especially grateful to Barbara, and to John Ackerman at Cornell University Press, for bringing my manuscript to publication. Gavin Lewis and Nancy Winemiller superbly edited the manuscript and improved this book. My colleagues at the University of Colorado, Ann Carlos, Robert Ferry, and John Stevenson, have sustained me in many ways.

I dedicate this book to my wife Jean, and remember well her grandmother Amanda Brown, the daughter of slaves, who helped me to see more clearly what I might some day write.

Steven A. Epstein

Louisville, Colorado

INDEX